# HAMLIN GARLAND'S DIARIES

EDITED BY DONALD PIZER

THE HUNTINGTON LIBRARY

SAN MARINO, CALIFORNIA

1968

PRINTED IN THE UNITED STATES OF AMERICA BY THE CASTLE PRESS, PASADENA, CALIFORNIA

FOR CAROL

# CONTENTS

# INTRODUCTION AND EDITORIAL NOTE

AT VARIOUS times during his early career, Hamlin Garland kept dated journals in which he commented on his reading and traveling, but it was not until January 1, 1898 (at the age of thirty-seven), that he began to keep a day-by-day record. He maintained such a diary until his death in March 1940. Its forty-three volumes, now in the Huntington Library, are a valuable addition to American literary history.

Garland's diaries are neither intimate nor philosophical. He does not "tell all," and he does not discuss abstract ideas. Rather, he records his activities—whom he was seeing, what he was doing— with occasional longer entries on a job or a journey completed or a personality encountered. But he also takes up—as one might in conversation with a close friend—such concerns as the general condition of his health and spirits, his family hopes and worries, and his financial and literary plans and problems. The importance of Garland's diaries is not that they startle us with a portrait of a "new" Garland. Their interest lies in the range of his activities as an American man of letters and in the depth of his response to the conditions of his life.

Acquainted with an extraordinary number of literary and political figures, and active in many social and literary organizations, Garland could scarcely avoid making his diaries a review of a major segment of American cultural history. But Garland was also a tragic figure, not in the sense of his having experienced a major personal disaster but in the sense that most private lives have their intense disappointments and disillusionments. Garland's descriptions of his personal life suggest an integrity and depth to his character not always acknowledged by recent literary history. In

recording both aspects of his work—the public and the private—
Garland is almost always the professional writer, expressing himself cogently and often vividly. Garland's best diary entries are not
only significant personal and literary history but good writing as
well.

Since Garland published seven autobiographical books in his lifetime, it is necessary to clarify the relationship between these and
his diaries. (He also published many autobiographical articles, almost all of which he later incorporated into the seven autobiographical volumes.) His first three autobiographies—*A Son of the
Middle Border* (1917), *A Daughter of the Middle Border* (1921), and
*Back-Trailers from the Middle Border* (1928)— are primarily personal and family autobiography from 1860 to 1928. Garland then
published four volumes—*Roadside Meetings* (1930), *Companions
on the Trail* (1931), *My Friendly Contemporaries* (1932), and *Afternoon Neighbors* (1934)—which emphasized his literary affairs and
friendships. These works cover the years from 1884 to 1930. In the
first series of autobiographies, Garland used his diaries principally
to verify chronology and general impressions. In *Back-Trailers*,
however, he began to draw upon them for more specific detail, particularly on those sections which dealt with his European tours of
1922 to 1926. Garland's second autobiographical series relies heavily on his diaries. *Roadside Meetings* is an exception to this practice,
since most of its events antedate 1898. But in the later volumes
Garland increasingly depended on his diaries. *Afternoon Neighbors*
thus consists almost entirely of transcribed (though edited) diary
entries with some continuity supplied by Garland.

The diary entries included in *Hamlin Garland's Diaries* do not
appear in any of Garland's autobiographical volumes. This material
was not published for a number of reasons. First, Garland's published autobiographies end their account at 1930. The ten years of
diary from 1931 to 1940 contain excellent entries on such figures as
Robert Frost and Herbert Hoover as well as some of Garland's most

pointed reflections on old age and on the decline of American morality. Second, the diaries before 1930 include important entries which Garland declined to publish because of his later antagonism toward the figure (Theodore Dreiser), or because the material was semiscandalous (Frank Lloyd Wright), or because he had already published a full account of the figure (W. D. Howells and Theodore Roosevelt). Third, the diaries contain much depiction of social and political events (such as the coming of the automobile or the Progressive revolt of 1912) which Garland felt inappropriate to autobiography. Finally, Garland did not publish much of the commentary on his own life which was depressed or bitter in tone.

There are readily available chronological accounts of Garland's life, and his diary entries fall into distinct and useful thematic groupings. Both of these facts have led me to organize this volume of selections thematically rather than chronologically, though I have usually kept a chronological progression within subject divisions. In this way I have sought both to crystallize a particular aspect of Garland's thought and to reveal the change (or lack of change) within that aspect.

*       *       *

Since diaries are not written for publication, they entail special editorial problems. Perhaps the only useful rule for editing material of this kind is that editorial practice should emerge out of the material itself. I have therefore adopted two editorial principles appropriate to the diary as a literary form and to Garland as an author. The first is that a Garland diary entry does not require the editorial scrupulousness that one would bring to a manuscript of a poem by Keats, in which every canceled line, every misspelled word, and every faulty punctuation might prove valuable for the understanding of Keats's creative imagination. Second, as a professional writer, Garland himself was aware of the difference between an early draft and later revisions by himself or an editor in which many errors of haste and carelessness would be corrected. He would consider it a disservice to have errors and inconsistencies reproduced merely because he wrote them at one stage in his composition.

These principles have led me to adopt the editorial practice of presenting a "clean" version of a Garland entry. To be more particular, I have silently corrected Garland's misspelling of names and titles as well as all other obviously unintentional misspellings. I have spelled out most of his abbreviations, have punctuated titles and numbers uniformly, and have occasionally changed comma and dash usage for clarity. I have not, however, corrected Garland's few grammatical lapses. In no instance has my emendation resulted in the alteration of the meaning of Garland's text.

When Garland in the late 1920's prepared his diaries for use in his second autobiographical series, he revised many of the entries on the diary page, adding or dropping a sentence here, changing a word there—in short, undertaking a stylistic revision of a first draft. I have published this revision, since my study of the diaries has revealed that virtually none of Garland's omissions and revisions are significant enough to warrant the editorial apparatus necessary to reproduce his original as well as his final text. My intent, in short, has been to publish an accurate, readable version of Garland's diary entries rather than an exact reproduction of the diary page.

Several other editorial practices require explanation or comment. A typical entry often contains two or three topics or events, only one of which is of interest. In such instances, I have omitted the irrelevant material without indicating the omission, since this material almost always occurs either before or after the published portion. On the few occasions in which I do omit passages within an entry, I of course indicate such omissions by ellipses. Garland often added titles to his entries, principally to remind him of their contents as he prepared his autobiographies. I have omitted these but have added, in brackets after the entry date, the place in which the entry was written. Finally, I have attempted in the introductions and headnotes to supply the information necessary to understand the entries. With some exceptions, my practice has been to identify figures the first time they appear, and to identify only those figures who are significant and whose full name and background are not readily known today or are not apparent from the text. The curious reader can use the index to determine the full name of all persons (when known) and to locate the initial appearance of any figure.

In addition to Garland's diaries, the Huntington Library owns a number of miscellaneous Garland letters, notebooks, and memorabilia. Among these is a notebook titled by Garland, "Meetings with Authors. Lecture Notes," which he prepared during the early 1920's for his lectures on literary personalities. In it he summarized his recollections and impressions of many of his literary acquaintances in order to refresh his memory about these figures before lecturing. I have included a small number of these accounts in this volume, always indicating their source as Garland's lecture notebook.

## ACKNOWLEDGMENTS

I WISH to thank John E. Pomfret, former Director of the Huntington Library and Art Gallery, for inviting me to examine the Garland diaries and for his unfailing courtesy and aid during the early stages of this project. At a crucial stage Allan Nevins contributed some excellent suggestions about the organization of the volume. Carol Hart Pizer helped decipher some of the more intractable puzzles presented by Garland's handwriting. Mrs. Mildred Gillespie, Mrs. Kay Talton, and Mrs. Martha Talton aided in the preparation and typing of the text, as did the Tulane University Council on Research with a grant-in-aid. In the later stages of preparing the volume for the press I have profited from the corrections and suggestions of Lloyd Arvidson, Mrs. Nancy C. Moll, and Mrs. Anne Kimber.

PART ONE

HAMLIN GARLAND

---

SOCIAL AND LITERARY EXPERIENCES

HAMLIN GARLAND was born on a farm near West Salem, Wisconsin, on September 14, 1860. West Salem is in the coulee region of western Wisconsin, an area of wide, farmable ravines about ten miles from La Crosse and the Mississippi. After a move to Minnesota in 1868, the Garland family settled the following year near Osage, Iowa. There Garland grew to young manhood, his year divided between work on the farm and "free time" at the Burr Oak country school. In 1876 he entered the Cedar Valley Seminary at Osage, graduating in June 1881. ("Seminary" was a midwestern term for any educational institution beyond the high school.) By this time Richard Garland was again restless, and the Garland family migrated to the newly opened Dakota lands. Young Hamlin Garland, however, had vague hopes of becoming a teacher and orator. After several years of wandering and indecision, he settled in Boston in 1884 in order to continue his education. By 1887 Garland had begun his dual career as writer and lecturer, and in the same year he also began that incessant journeying from one end of the country to the other which was to characterize his life until the 1930's.

In 1893 Garland moved to Chicago. He wanted to be close to his parents, who had retired in West Salem, and he also wished to contribute to the cultural awakening of Chicago and the Midwest. There he met Zulime Taft, sister of the sculptor Lorado Taft and herself a painter. They were married in 1899. Mary Isabel Garland was born in 1903, Constance Garland in 1908. Throughout his Chicago years Garland spent much of each summer in West Salem, though he also undertook long trips to the Rocky Mountains in pursuit of literary material. During the winter he often spent several months in New York seeing a book through the press and renewing literary acquaintances.

Garland was increasingly drawn to New York because of its literary and cultural density. In 1916 he gave up both his West Salem and Chicago homes (his mother had died in 1899, his father in 1914) and moved to Manhattan. Summers were now spent in the Catskill resort of Onteora and in England. In 1931 Garland made his last move, to Los Angeles, drawn by the mild climate and by the presence of his married daughters and his grandchildren. He died on March 5, 1940, some two years before the death of Zulime Garland.

Garland's literary career divides into three phases. His early work, from 1887 to 1895, dealt principally with the bleak side of midwest farm and village life and often contained single tax and feminist reform ideas. From 1896 to 1916 he devoted himself to popular Rocky Mountain romances, though these frequently had a mild conservationist theme. The last phase of Garland's literary career, from 1917 to his death, was that of autobiography. Throughout his career Garland was an indefatigable joiner and organizer of movements, clubs, and associations. At first these groups were devoted primarily to political and artistic reform, but gradually they became more social in character. During the 1920's he was intensely absorbed in the American Academy of Arts and Letters.

\*     \*     \*

## PRAIRIE MEMORIES

### JUNE 1-5, 1903 [OSAGE, IOWA]

FATHER and I took the 10:30 train for Spring Valley. From there we went down to Osage. Our farm seemed so level (seen from the train) that I could hardly place it. The badgers used to build on these ridges, and I recalled the suck-holes. We found a fine hotel at the end of our journey and soon Mitchell Morrison came to meet us. As we went up the street we held an informal reception the whole length of the block. The word was passed along the street and many old friends whom we had supposed to be still on their farms came clustering about us. The Hills, Frazers, Burtches, Connells and others I had almost forgotten. Some of them seemed uncouth, others were still admirable.

\*　　\*　　\*

My classmate John Cutler came round and took me to see the town. We called on a number of old friends and then at 3 we went to the old seminary where I met a goodly number of alumni at the "Banquet."

At night we sat in the Opera House and listened to an "oration" by a lad who looked as I must have looked at twenty-one. Then Frank Seaman read a poem and I gave a talk which was intended to be humorous but which didn't seem to affect my audience in that way.

The whole day a revelation of the intense seriousness and habit of piety of these people. The stillness was painful as I rose to speak. My auditors seemed to think they were in church. No one ventured a smile, much less a laugh.

\*　　\*　　\*

Hiring a team I drove father up to the old farm at Dry Run and over to Burr Oak School House. I have not trod these ways for sixteen years and it marks a period in my life. It divides me from the old. All this commonplaceness, this definition, cuts me off from the past—or rather it separates me from these people and scenes.

I do not intend to return. It is all too painful, too depressing. I am ready to go back to New York. My old-time world, the world that appealed to my imagination, is gone. This flat, stale and unprofitable world inhabited by melancholy ghosts of the past was a sad surprise to both father and myself. I see it with the eyes of the city man, he with the eyes of age.

\*　　\*　　\*

Fonda called and took us for a ride around over the Brushes' mill road. Osman Button, our old neighbor, rode with us and enjoyed it keenly. He talked of old times quite like himself.

In the afternoon I met the members of my class and at night read my "Joys of the Trail" to an audience in the Opera House. Again they sat as still as a congregation but cheered heartily at the close.

This closes the chapter of Iowa life so far as I am concerned. I shall do nothing more for the seminary. I see no future for it. It was well enough as a pioneer school of the Middle Border but in these days of many Iowa universities it is merely a denominational attempt to hold a certain claim.

*    *    *

After addressing the pupils of the high school I went over to visit the Buttons and so it came out that we took the last hour of our stay in Osage for a visit to the neighbor whom we first met in 1870. Button is an unusual man in many ways, and I enjoyed talking with him. He clung to us, would hardly let us go.

We left on the noon train and had a tedious ride, although the day's sun was glorious and the country beautiful.

This is the last visit I shall ever make to the home of my boyhood. It saddened me. So many were dead—so many missing. The "girls" were old and gray, some of the "boys" old and shiftless. It was a magic world once; it is a dismal region now.

SEPTEMBER 6, 1912 [WEST SALEM]

OUR neighbor was threshing grain and I took the children over to study it. It was a dirty job and I wonder if we of the pioneer time were as filthy as these poor fellows appeared today. Their shirts were caked with dried sweat and dust. They will very likely sleep in these shirts. They go home to houses without bathrooms and it is probable that they will wear these shirts till Sunday. They were mostly bent, thin, discouraged-looking, presenting nothing of the old-time elation which we used to feel. The children enjoyed every sight and sound and I could hardly get them away from the place. To them the stack was a towering peak, and the falling dust a storm—as it was once with me.

AUGUST 4, 1913 [WEST SALEM]

*[Garland was visiting Green's Coulee, where he had spent his first eight years.]*

WE all went down to Onalaska and round to the old coulee. The children were deeply interested in it all. We found the old Roach cottage and the windowless ruin of the room in which I spent my first term of school. I could dimly recall just how the door led into the room. We found an old *New York Tribune* on the walls, and brought it home. Its date was June, 1862. The trees were larger at the Green place and the house was improved but remained in the same general condition. The children asked many questions and seemed to understand the significance of the visit.

JANUARY 30, 1919 [NEW YORK]

*[Angus is Angus Shannon, Garland's brother-in-law. Walter Ehrich was the son of Garland's old Colorado friend, Louis Ehrich.]*

ANGUS turned up at 11 a.m., just after Zulime had gone out. We went down to the club together and later met at the theater where we joined the Wrays to see a Dunsany play, *The Laughter of the Gods*. I liked the play. It had many fine lines and a sardonic humor which pleased me. Wray was bored, he said.

We hurried home expecting to meet Angus but he phoned to have us come down and bring the children to dinner. This we did. The dinner was at "Pierre's," one of the most costly and popular places in the city, and the dinner was a very carefully planned list of dishes. The children looked very pretty and were deeply excited by the character of the party. Mr. Loeb's son was one of the party, also Mr. and Mrs. Ehrich. I liked Loeb who is one of these enlightened Jews who can joke about Jews. He is a very able citizen and is a man of ideals. Mrs. Ehrich is in charity and very earnest.

The crowded café, the rich folk dining, the wine, the rare dishes —caviar pancakes, fish and grape sauce, baked ice cream—nothing much further from the entertainment which I shared with my father and mother could be imagined than this dinner which probably cost five dollars for each of us. It made me think—by contrast —of riding away on a still, cold night to Burr Oak to a "Grange Supper" or a "Church Sociable." Nights so cold we would be obliged to get out and run beside the sleigh to keep warm. Nights when a bowl of oyster soup was the most delicious treat in our world. We expected to be cold. Riding in the back of the sleigh was a test of endurance. Mother shivered in the front seat. We all came to the school house numb with cold, and how delightful the hot air seemed, and with what appetite we ate our soup and crackers. The laughter, the smiling faces, the songs and speeches were wonderfully sweet.

SEPTEMBER 14, 1923 [NEW YORK]

*[Garland's nicknames for Mary Isabel included Mebs, Mebsie, and Mebbie. Irving is Irving Bacheller.]*

ZULIME went away to Westport leaving Mary Isabel and me at home alone. Our family has never had just this division and I felt my responsibility, for Mebs went out to the theater with John Davis and did not return till after one o'clock. As I was reading Irving's book *The Scudders* I felt some of the helplessness he depicts in the case of modern fathers and mothers of girls.

I find Mebs has an entirely different notion of life to that which I had at her age. I wanted to "get somewhere." She wants a good time. I don't recall that I had any definite notion of seeking pleasure. I seized every chance for play but I was brought up to believe in work as a normal business of man, and before I was twenty I had decided to succeed somehow in something. It was very vague but I knew that pleasure seeking was not my job. I sought work and through work I hoped for fame.

AUGUST 31, 1930 [ONTEORA]

IN writing a little article for the *Saturday Review*, I have been peering back into my childhood home and the homes of my companions on the prairie, trying to recall the books in them. I can discover very little other than the Bible and certain newspapers. We took the *Toledo Blade* for some reason (I think because Nasby wrote for it) and the county paper. One or two of our neighbors took the *New York Weekly Tribune*, but books were scarce in our township. So far as I know there were no libraries. I believe we began to get books through the Grange in '74 or '75. I cannot recall any books in the home of Osman Button, one of our most intelligent men, nor in the home of John Gammons, although there must have been something. We had Franklin, Barnum, Milton—my first book, a present from Mother—and *Nurse and Spy*, a book on the Civil War. It seems incredible that such a condition existed within my memory. We have come centuries from that time and place.

SEPTEMBER 17, 1930 [YAMA FARM]

[*The Garlands frequently visited Yama Farm, a semiprivate inn near Ellenville, New York. Mrs. Frances Trollope's book is* Domestic Manners of the Americans *(1832).*]

AMONG other diversions today I read Mrs. Trollope's notorious book on America and Americans of one hundred years ago. I read at it when a youth in Boston, but did not consider it carefully. I now reread it with amused acceptance. That it was true of that day I know, for I have myself seen many of its barbarities which still survive in nooks and corners of the West and South. The spitting, the profanity, the gobbling of food, the frightful religious revivals are all familiar to me. I have met the "insolence" of the hired girls, and the use of "lady" in speaking of cooks and washerwomen. Mrs. Trollope did not philosophize over these manners as inescapable products of a new and democratic country. She condemned them as evils which could not exist under a monarchy. Her book is of great value as a picture of our frontier.

### NOVEMBER 30, 1935 [LOS ANGELES]

*[Garland's son-in-law was Joseph W. Harper, a grandson of the founder of Harper and Brothers.]*

CONNIE and Joe flew down to Palm Springs leaving the children in our care. We lunched with them in some state and they deported themselves with dignity. What a contrast between my conditions and theirs! I was living in a small farmhouse in Green's Coulee in a climate which was white winter at the middle of November. No one used a napkin or a four-tined fork and children were wedged in wherever they could find a place. Not one touch of beauty was in our pioneer home, and comfort was only by way of contrast with outside wind and snow. And yet we were happy. We valued what little we had and by that appreciation raised it to luxury. It is incredible. I have lived centuries since that time. I rode in an open lumber wagon. My daughters ride in aeroplanes. A horse is a wonder to my grandchildren. Their toys are motor cars and flying machines.

## MEMORIES OF BOSTON

### SEPTEMBER 22, 1899 [CHICAGO]

*[Garland had been very active in the single tax movement dur-
ing his Boston years, writing on the subject for Henry George's*
Standard *and frequently speaking at meetings of the Boston
Single Tax Club.]*

A DAY of rain. I worked some six or seven hours at the *Boy Life*,
which is soon to go to the printer. Went to the studio at five p.m.
The Heckmans and Miss Taft came in at 6 and we all dined at the
Pullman. Afterward I went to the studio for an hour and came
home early. On the way home I stopped into the single tax club
for a few moments. It stirred something in me—something not altogether pleasant. I still regard the system as the best yet devised
and it is vital in a sense, but it no longer seems so vital as some other
things. I do not now expect it to do more than modify thought.
Once I thought it might change our way of living. So it will, but
long hence probably. There was pathos in the faces I saw, rugged,
serious, devoted.

### JANUARY 10, 1900 [BOSTON]

*[Garland had met James Whitcomb Riley at the Parker House
in 1888.]*

WE left New York at 9 a.m. for Worcester and I delivered my lecture
on Grant at 3 p.m. to a large audience of women in Association
Hall. The address was long, too long, but they seemed to enjoy it.
All listened most attentively and at the end applauded softly. We
took train at six for Boston and put up at the Parker House, very
tired by the day's work but feeling very content. I had a special
pleasure in going to the Parker House, for it was at one time my

highest notion of luxury, of quiet grandeur. There I visited Riley
when he came on his conquering visit to town and there Mark
Twain and other grand travellers lodged. It was in fact a small and
very quiet hotel, and our room was modest.

### JANUARY 11, 1900 [BOSTON]

[*Bella Pratt, Cyrus Dallin, and John Enneking were Boston
artists. Garland had been particularly close to Enneking, whose
impressionist landscapes he admired. Garland and Herne had
worked together for single tax and theater reform during Garland's Boston years. Charles Hurd was literary editor of the
*Transcript *and Edward Clement its managing editor. B. O.
Flower was editor of the *Arena, *a Boston reform journal which
had published much of Garland's early work.*]

WE spent today in seeing Boston. Examined and criticized the
Public Library. It seems dark and less spacious than the Congres-
sional Library. We called on Bella Pratt and Dallin and also upon
John Enneking. The old man had grown a little gray, but was as
vigorous as ever. He showed us a great many pictures which he has
lately done. We felt his big, blundering, genial, manly personality.
A really great painter of landscapes.

At night we went to see James A. Herne in *Sag Harbor,* a delightful little play in the vein of *Shore Acres.* Old friends called at our
hotel, Chas. E. Hurd among others. I on B. O. Flower and Clement
of the *Transcript.* I found them all to be comparatively unchanged,
a little grayer, a little sadder, that was all. The city changes more
rapidly than the people. It is not attractive to me now. The nice
weather ended suddenly in sleet.

### OCTOBER 4, 1900 [WEST SALEM]

A LETTER from B. O. Flower told of his reinstatement as editor of
the *Arena.* He was a good friend to me at a time when I needed

friends and it is a deep gratification to know he has gone back to the magazine his own personal genius built up. He is one of the most unselfish men I ever knew. "Organized altruism," I have sometimes called him. He is a crank of course and a faddist but a brave and generous and high-minded eccentric after all is said. I wrote to say I was glad and would help him with an article.

### FEBRUARY 23, 1903 [NEW YORK]

WE had a number of callers during the afternoon and at 8:30 I went up to 79th street to do honor to a little woman from Boston who has been very loyal to the cause of Henry George, Mrs. Tarbell. I met there Mrs. George and Harry [Henry George, Jr.], Miss Colbron, and a number of others interested. The whole thing very suggestive. I have moved on, leaving these stock phrases behind. They still retain the usual arguments. They carried me back into my own striving past. It was at once humorous and pathetic to me.

### FEBRUARY 18, 1924 [WINTER PARK, FLORIDA]

HIRAM POWERS came to take me for a ride and on the way we picked up William Sloane Kennedy, of Boston, whom I have not seen for more than thirty years. We were two of the earliest "Whitmanites" in New England. He was one of the proofreaders on the *Transcript* and lived in Belmont near Howells at that time. He is now an old man—like myself—and a bit run-down but mentally vigorous and almost as cocksure of his judgments as when I knew him. He gave me the proof of his book on Burroughs and I read it at night. I found it vigorous and on the whole sound.

### AUGUST 23, 1932 [LOS ANGELES]

DRIVING down to Palos Verdes we left Zulime there and came home in time for me to meet a young girl who is writing a thesis on "Realism in American Literature." Her name is Perry and she comes from a farm in central Illinois. She was a pretty, little, round-faced girl who confessed that she had to milk cows when at home. She will go far if she does not lose her health. She displayed detailed knowledge of her subject and a keen grasp of the problems involved. She has been living here with her grandparents but must now go home. She didn't want to go but she felt it her duty to go. She is working for a master's degree and is writing her thesis to that end. She is almost precisely in my attitude in Boston when I felt that I must go back to the farm in Dakota. I spoke of going back to "shingling." She speaks of going back to cow milking. I did my best to cheer her up and to furnish her with the information she wanted concerning Kirkland, Eggleston, Howe, and other early realists.

## CHICAGO YEARS

### APRIL 13, 1898 [CHICAGO]

*[Garland was helping organize the literary congress held in conjunction with the Omaha Trans-Mississippi Exposition.]*

GOT off a lot of letters to literary people whom it is desirable to have at the Omaha congress. I have great doubts of the success. Omaha is pretty far west for a convention of this kind, but if the railroads can offer free transportation to these literary folk some of them may be willing to come and see the West. The wording of this call is not the best possible and may expose me to ridicule, but the East is coming to respect us out here. And each year will see a still greater change of sentiment.

### NOVEMBER 3, 1898 [CHICAGO]

*[Israel Zangwill, the English author, was visiting Chicago. The Little Room was an informal club which met in one of the studios in the Fine Arts Building each Friday afternoon. Its name was derived from a short story by Madeleine Yale*

*Wynne about a disappearing room. Its members were princi-
pally Chicago writers, artists, and musicians. Charles Francis
Browne, Lorado Taft, and Henry Blake Fuller were Garland's
closest Chicago friends. Browne was an artist, Taft a sculptor,
and Fuller a novelist. Anna Morgan was a drama coach.*]

MORE of Zangwill. His talk on the drama was profound and witty.
He came to The Little Room at 6 p.m. and met our people in a
pleasant manner and was whirled away. I was unable to go to see
Modjeska with him and so we said good-bye.

I took dinner with Browne. Taft, Fuller, and myself caravanseried
into the dining room giving a complete surprise to Mrs. Browne
who bore up under it most nobly. We had a lively session. Miss
Taft, Lorado's sister, very interesting. She is just back from four
years in Paris and is full of the latest theories of art. She was dressed
in a red gown and looked very handsome. We went to Miss Morgan's studio afterwards and discussed Tolstoy's new book on *What
Is Art?* This was a free fight. It ended inconclusively and I got home
at night worn to a fringe.

### NOVEMBER 25, 1898 [CHICAGO]

A BAD day for me. I made little headway in the story and as Von
Saltza did not come, I went out to lunch alone. After lunch I went
down to Browne's and to The Little Room. Hall Caine, the Manx
novelist, was at The Little Room today. I did not meet him. John
Fox, the young Kentuckian story writer, came in and stayed a few
minutes. As for me I was there and made my usual number of
enemies by blurting out my real mind instead of being gallant and
lying. I called on Miss Dorsey in the evening and managed to make
her feel miserable by telling her I pitied her among the "elite" yesterday. So it goes. I manage to make enemies right and left and
before and behind.

The night was beautiful with snow. It filled me with memories of the plains.

### MARCH 10, 1899 [CHICAGO]

[*Myra Reynolds and Elizabeth Wallace were teachers at the University of Chicago. Garland's* Rose of Dutcher's Coolly *(1895) contains a section on the experiences of a young girl at the University of Wisconsin.*]

DINED with Miss Reynolds, Miss Wallace and Fuller at Foster Hall, Chicago University. It was very charming, the neat little dinner table in the little library, the bright and cheerful women, Fuller witty and tactful as ever. After the dinner we attended the comic opera given by the students in the "gym." It was a fine experience, the wide hall crowded with eager, beautiful, youthful forms, the girls in cap-and-gown, the smiling faculty, the primitive stage, the boyish wit of the play, the singularly clever assumption of girl parts by the young fellows. Fuller laughed immoderately and so did I. It was all a sort of rereading of what I had put into *Rose*—or tried to: purity, ecstasy of living, boundless hope, carefree outlook on life, and serious intent even in their fun. The girls all seemed so young, mere children. The boys were smooth-faced as the girls and as infantile. O wonderful, unresting, satisfying world of youth!

### DECEMBER 29, 1900 [CHICAGO]

[*Garland occasionally spelled Zulime as the name was pronounced. He also frequently abbreviated the name to Z. Fuller's story was part of his collection* Under the Skylights *(1901). Taft, Browne, and Garland had organized the Central Art Association in 1894 in order to encourage the creation and appreciation of a native Western art. Taft was an instructor in the Art Institute of Chicago and later became its president. Garland was more fully satirized in another story in Fuller's collection, "The Downfall of Abner Joyce."*]

ZULIEMA painted and I wrote till noon. We then walked downtown, a miserably cold, windy, dirty walk. I was ready to leave Chicago forever by the time we had reached Kohlsaats and had eaten our lunch in the nerve-shattering clatter of the place. We went on and loafed around the studios till six. Lorado asked us to dinner and afterward read Henry Fuller's "Dr. Gowdy and the Squash" while we shouted over it. It is capital satire; just the right tone, and hit off art conditions here most happily. It had a little of me, a good deal of the Central Art Association, the Institute and also a good deal of himself and his controversy with colonels of militia and wholesale grocers on art matters. He is doing a most diverting history of the art colony. This story is only a part of it.

### JANUARY 7, 1905 [CHICAGO]

[*Jane Addams of Hull House and Rollin D. Salisbury of the University of Chicago were both members of The Little Room.*]

AT night we joined the studio to supper, a jolly party, some fine personalities. Jane Addams was there looking very worn. She was as intense as ever and quite admirable. Professor Salisbury was on hand as a caterer, producing coffee and sandwiches. Fuller was uncommonly gay. It was amusing to see Salisbury, a big man and one of our best known geologists, fussing about over the coffeepot, with Fuller looking on and making suggestions.

### APRIL 6, 1906 [CHICAGO]

[*Robert Herrick, the novelist, and Robert Morss Lovett, the literary historian, were both at the University of Chicago. George Vincent was influential in the Chautauqua movement; Percy MacKaye was a dramatist. Colonel Edwin Emerson was a war correspondent who had covered the Russo-Japanese War.*]

I LUNCHED with Robert Herrick, Morss Lovett, George Vincent and young MacKaye. There was much talk and pretty good talk largely concerning the condition of our stage, etc.

In the afternoon I went to The Little Room meeting the usual "gang." Fuller came home with us and we all dined with Lorado and went to hear Colonel Emerson talk of his visit to Port Arthur. It was all very interesting but not very important. It left nothing in my mind.

### DECEMBER 26, 1906 [CHICAGO]

[*Sigmund Zeisler, a lawyer, and Mrs. Zeisler, a pianist, were members of The Little Room. The "camp" was The Eagle's Nest, a summer art colony on Rock River, a hundred miles west of Chicago. Garland had proposed to Zulime there in the summer of 1899.*]

At night Mrs. Browne and I went over to the Zeislers' to their "at home." Some rather interesting people there—some musical Hebrews—and the usual "camp crowd": Ponds, Heckmans, et cetera. Mrs. Zeisler played with great fire and enjoyment. It was a part of the best side of Chicago life but I was rather out of sorts and did not enjoy it very much. It possessed, however, a more cosmopolitan character than most of the Chicago parties I share.

### NOVEMBER 6, 1908 [CHICAGO]

I WENT down to The Little Room today. It is now about fifteen years since we started this organization and Mrs. Wynne, the author of the story, is still with us but grayer and less sparkling than at that time. Madame Zeisler, Pond, Lorado, Clarkson, *all* show the passage of the years as do I. Some of these men and women have not lived up to their promise; others—a few—have gone beyond it.

### JANUARY 3, 1910 [CHICAGO]

[*The club is the Cliff-Dwellers, a name borrowed from the title*

of Henry B. Fuller's Chicago novel. Garland had organized it
in 1907 and served as its first president. He had hoped that it
would be a center of Chicago cultural life, but it soon was
dominated by businessmen who used it principally as a luncheon club.]

I WENT down to the club where I found Lovett and Herrick lunching together and we had a little talk. They are both at work on new
books and will stay in town for the winter. They are at present
about the only representatives of the literary side of the university.
It is discouraging to find this great institution so lacking in scholarship for scholarship's sake. The spirit of literature is without a nook
in these buildings.

### APRIL 30, 1910 [CHICAGO]

[*Waterloo and Read were novelists as well as newspapermen.
Roche was the son of a former mayor of Chicago.*]

AT eight the press club gave a memorial meeting to Mark Twain.
The old guard were in evidence, Stanley Waterloo heavily laden
with "grog," Opie Read purple-visaged walking sedately and talking
a lot of "guff," John Roche's bringing forward into the Chicago of
the present the methods of the Chicago of the past. It was not in-
spiriting; it was rather tragic. They had not made good.

### FEBRUARY 8, 1911 [CHICAGO]

AT the club as usual. I am as persistent as the manager of a hotel,
and nearly as busy. The place is full of life these days. I am on hand
as regularly as though I were a salaried superintendent. So long as
I will do everything, every member will let me do it.

### MARCH 31, 1911 [CHICAGO]

THE club fills up each day but there are few men of any bigness or seriousness of purpose to be met there. I wonder when this town will begin to retain and honor its really creative men? The performance at the club tonight was very slight and disappointing to me. An art student's "stunt," not a work of art. At such times I feel discouraged over the whole question of club entertainment. Chicago is only a big country town even now with its two millions of people. Our men in art are all feeling timidly or reflecting dimly. The personalities around me appear admirable but small and lacking in power. The making of a living is about all any of us can compass. We have a narrow margin for experiment.

APRIL 13, 1912 [CHICAGO]

*[Garland had helped organize the Chicago Theatre Society, an independent theater group led by Donald Robertson. The failure of the Society and the decline of the Cliff-Dwellers contributed to Garland's growing disaffection with Chicago life.]*

THIS day winds up our season with the Drama players and a big weight will roll off our shoulders. It has become very depressing these last weeks.

Later comment. This entire venture was a failure. We all gave time and money and vast enthusiasm to the attempt to found an independent literary theater but the public would not come, not even our literary public. I got into it almost without knowing it and acted as executive secretary of it, giving time and energy to it when I should have been attending to my own book.

MARCH 24, 1913 [CHICAGO]

*[The famous Armory Show had transferred from New York to Chicago. Garland had admired impressionistic painting.]*

WE inspected the cubist exhibition and found it uninspiring. It does not seem to me important even as a joke.

MARCH 20, 1914 [CHICAGO]

[*Zona Gale, the novelist, and her friend Laura Sherry were both from Wisconsin. Harriet Monroe had founded* Poetry *in 1912. The* Little Review, *founded by Margaret Anderson in Chicago, published its first number in March 1914.*]

ZONA GALE and Miss Sherry came into The Little Room and afterward we all went to the club to dinner. Zona sat on one side of me and Harriet Monroe on the other but didn't seem to realize that I had other guests to look after. A curious, self-centered creature, Harriet is getting "difficult." The artists all dislike her, partly on account of her austere judgments, partly because of her superior manner when she meets them.

At The Little Room the talk was all of the new review and its flock of unknown "great" young writers. "They aim to push us from our stools" was the jest we passed among us. Margaret Anderson is its editor.

DECEMBER 29, 1914 [CHICAGO]

[*Charles L. Hutchinson and Frank Logan were bankers and members of the Cliff-Dwellers.*]

AT Mr. Hutchinson's request I went downtown and at the bank talked over the club muddle. He urged me to stand for reelection to the board and upon his representation that he would be left in a dubious position if I did not, I consented. He said that Logan would run again and that this was the only way in which the situation could be cleared up. As I was beginning to be cleared of the worry, in some degree I resented being dragged back into it. I'm just tired of the club—and of Chicago. I am going away to get into a less depressing atmosphere.

DECEMBER 16, 1915 [CHICAGO]

WITH a card to the University Club I went down to take luncheon but I felt so strange and out of place that I came away without luncheon. I begin to feel alien to Chicago and all its interests. I begin to see that I made the best of a bad bargain all these years. It is a cold, bleak, dismal place to me now.

### MARCH 2, 1916 [CHICAGO]

I AM doing and thinking of nothing outside my home and children. I have lost the power to work in Chicago. I have shifted ground. I have now a sense of impermanency, a desire to get back to New York where my real home now is. As soon as we can sell the house we shall move.

### NOVEMBER 8-9, 1920 [CHICAGO]

MY visit here has brought me in touch with former friends but has not created in me a desire to return. On the contrary I go away with a sense of relief. Something in the place deadens me. To settle down here now would be a surrender to decay. This may be a kind of weakness in me but that is my feeling. It is a place for young, vigorous, enthusiastic business men—builders, not men of meditation.

*     *     *

I left Chicago with relief. It is not easy to say why the city makes such an unpleasant stir in my brain. It has no joyous associations. Its people for the most part seem only halfway to anywhere. It is ugly in its outward aspect and uninspired at its heart, I fear.

### NOVEMBER 12, 1923 [CHICAGO]

CHICAGO now produces in me not a fierce resentment such as I once felt when the daughters were young and tender but a kind of weariness. It is all so appallingly bleak and drab that I want to get away from it. I feel its intellectual halfway-house atmosphere. Its judgments are by men who have only advanced from Omaha or Sioux City or at best from some college and who are so sure of their opinions. I sense also the rude, crude taste of the people who support such judgments and who buy such newspapers. The Sandburgs, Masterses, and Hechts do not interest me. The physical aspect of the city is worse than ever in some regards or else my senses are sharpened to it. By contrast with New York it is "flimsy," "impermanent," "ugly." These are the words to use in describing most of our cities, but they apply with special force to Buffalo, Chicago, and Detroit, which have hardly one permanent and beautiful building.

## FIRST VISIT TO ENGLAND AND PARIS

### APRIL 27, 1899 [LONDON]

BANG! I find myself plump in the middle of London. After a swift ride through green England under a misty white sky I shot suddenly under a yellow pall which overhung the great English-speaking maelstrom. It was not unlike the change which comes in sweeping into Chicago from the West. I found the city distracting with its ugly omnibuses, its rush of cabs, and its maze of streets, but less noisy, less imposing in bulk than I had imagined it would be. It seemed dingy, dark, multitudinous but not toweringly impressive. I stayed at a little hotel called the Edwards House near the Euston Station. A very primitive place. Indeed, everything I saw was primitive.

### MAY 7, 1899 [HINDHEAD]

[*Hindhead is forty miles south of London. Grant Allen, a novelist, died later in 1899.*]

EARLY after breakfast while Shaw was at work I went out for a walk on the heath among the flowers and the larks, a ground lark not unlike our horned lark. All about was a wide desolate country, blackened as if by fire.

Afterward I called on Conan Doyle and after a visit and looking about stayed to lunch. Played a game of tennis. Doyle very fine and hearty. I liked him immensely. Thereafter with Shaw I called on Grant Allen and his wife, both extemely nice and cordial. He thin, active, more like an American than an Englishman. She hearty and cheerful and unaffected, like a fine New England matron. Doyle came in and we had a very cheerful and jolly time. The whole life of Hindhead is not unlike the summer cottage life of a New England seashore.

Shaw grew more and more human and humane as well as humorous during the evening and urged me to stay all night.

The day was unusually bright and clear and the life of these people very attractive. Shaw and I became each moment better acquainted and the serious side of his nature came uppermost.

### MAY 8, 1899 [LONDON]

ON the way home about 12 p.m. I saw hundreds of nightwalking women on the Strand. They prowled like hyenas, lying in wait like cats. Some sang to advertise their trade, others called "Hello darling!" A few sauntered insolently, all were haggard and painted. Poor thin, angular, undersized creatures for the most part, bent and hatchet-faced. Some were like walking sepulchers, all white without, disease within. An appalling army!

### MAY 9, 1899 [LONDON]

*[Harland, under the name of Sidney Luska, had published stories of New York East Side life. He had then immigrated to London, where he edited the* Yellow Book.]

WITH Zangwill I attended the private view of the International Art Exhibition. Found a throng of English, French and Americans of high type swarming through the rooms. We met many people that we (Zangwill) knew. Benj. Swift Patterson, a tall rather foppish young Scot; Henry Harland, expatriated American Jew; H. Dingman, a painter from New York, looking spic and span; young Harrison Rhodes of Stone and Co.; Albert Kinross and several others. Zangwill wore the worst hat in London but mine was a close second. Harland (Sidney Luska) invited me to dinner and introduced me to his wife. Zangwill introduced me to two very lovely Jewesses. Really if I had known what I was going to meet I would have donned a long-tailed coat. It was not unlike a similiar affair in New York. The women were not so pretty and the men were better dressed.

### MAY 25, 1899 [LONDON]

[*William Heinemann published many American authors during the 1890's. Elizabeth Robins was an American actress whom Garland had met in Boston some years earlier. She was very successful in England and spent most of her life there.*]

I LUNCHED with Heinemann and his partner. His wife remained only a few moments, an alert little woman, intense and very outspoken. Afterward I called on Miss Robins, meeting Elihu Wolf and a Mr. Sidney Law. Out of the talk which followed I plucked a huge disgust with the "American Colony" whose members pursue utterly selfish ends in abandoning their native country.

I feel enough of the disease for social advancement to understand the motive which is, at bottom, heartless and egoistic to a most destructive degree. I said as much very plainly to Miss Robins, and came away bitter and disgusted with the whole raft of socially ambitious Americans who drift from West to East crazy for social recognition, for a wide fame, greater consideration because they imagine themselves better than their fellow citizens.

It is useless to argue against it but nevertheless I am hot with anger against them—and myself.

[*Antoine's Théâtre Libre (1887-1894) had been one of Garland's models in his attempt to found an independent theater in Boston in 1891. In 1897 Antoine inaugurated his own Théâtre Antoine.* Les Gaités de l'escadron *is a military farce by Georges Courteline.*]

A FEW hours in the Louvre, a stupendous collection but of little value to me. I came away tired, weary of art and all the chatter about it. The most of these paintings and figures have no interest to me. They are only of value as showing the darkness out of which men are emerging. The medieval artist was not aware of sunlight, nor the sanity of nature. His outlook on life was colored by the windows of his church or by the work of his masters.

The most vivid impression I carry away from this walk is the richness and dignity of the Assyrian decorations. Next the wealth of vases and the like in the Etruscan and Greek. The Rubenses are an avenue of horrors. The famous Greek statues were tame, the great mass of the paintings forced and unnatural.

In the evening I went to see Antoine in his own theater, a fine little auditorium. The plays were by no means important but they were exceedingly well done. Antoine himself an exceedingly natural actor. The soldiers were all very good in *Les Gaités de l'escadron,* several of the comedians being exceedingly funny.

## SECOND VISIT TO EUROPE

### MAY 27, 1906 [EN ROUTE TO LIVERPOOL]

As I got up we were rounding the Cape of Race and there was a gentle swell and fall to the boat. The day was very beautiful and the sea calm. I felt rather queasy but ate breakfast. No more land now till we reach the other side. I stopped going to meals and took my soup and stuff in my berth. The boat rose and fell through pretty wide arches fore and aft and I was taking things on the safe side. What damnable business. There isn't one person on shipboard who interests me, not one. They are not musical or artistic or even literary. If they were Germans they would sing. If they were American they would joke. If they were Frenchmen they would chatter. Being Canadian English they walk about with grave stodgy faces defending themselves from each other.

### JUNE 4, 1906 [LONDON]

THIS being "Bank Holiday" I determined on a trip to Windsor Castle. The trip was rather tiresome and while I got a great many impressions they were not of literary value. It was a gorge of quaintness, especially as regards Eton. The Castle was entirely English, plain, substantial as beef. Coming home early I went out to 'Ampstead 'Eath to see the costermongers and a sad sight it proved. Such swarms of runty girls and degenerate boys, such gray hags, such rat-like sharpers. They could not sing, only howled. It was all a kind of melancholy Coney Island, a day of desperate gaiety.

I soon wearied of the haggard faces and stunted bodies and came away sadly.

### JULY 3, 1906 [SOUTHERN FRANCE]

TOULOUSE was a very dirty town, an ill-smelling town, and did not interest me. Neither did its people. I hurried on to Carcassonne as soon as I could. Carcassonne was a worse disappointment. It too was ill-smelling and its narrow streets disgustingly dirty. The great fortified city on the hill turned out to be as squalid as an Indian pueblo and I soon tired of the human vermin which infested it and befouled it.

The fortress is but a shell within which the "poor quarter" exists. The women, loud-voiced, vulgar and savage, got on my nerves. A wedding was going on in the church and all the old beldames of the gutter were out of doors making the streets resound with their *blagues*. The place stank. I hurried away to Cette where I took a plunge in the sea to cleanse myself.

I find Nîmes a very bright gay place tonight. The band is playing and the plaza swarming with good-looking young people promenading.

### JULY 7, 1906 [GENOA]

I AM delighted with Genoa. It is marvellously paintable, it seems to me—colorful, varied in line! I wonder artists do not abound here. I wandered all day about the town climbing to the tops of the hills and plunging low into the old town along the port. It was all extremely interesting and put into my head a thousand water-color paintings, aquarelles and the like. It is the most colorful and the most picturesque town I have ever seen, as interesting as Avignon with a wilder environment and more vivid colors. I ended by a walk up to the first commanding plateau to study the town in the gloaming. It was a lovely view and a most impressive hour.

### JULY 23, 1906 [VERONA]

VERONA interested me so much I determined to stay another day. I wandered about the streets till the last minute. First of all by good luck I blundered into the cattle market and got an enfilading shot at a crowd of several hundred farmers. I stood about watching them barter. They looked not unlike Kansans of the "hard times" of 1890—lean, brown as leather, and poorly clothed—but when they began to trade they were of a different world! They yelled, they pushed, they pulled. They became fierce of face and ego. A trade was a battle. It was all deeply diverting to me.

## NEW YORK LIFE

### DECEMBER 19, 1898 [NEW YORK]

I AM settled in a neat room at 58 East 25th and now sit writing therein waiting for my trunks to arrive. Already I feel the superciliousness of this old town, not toward me but toward my people. The feeling that nothing worthwhile exists in the West, that things are so much superior here. This conception runs through every conversation. It annoys and embitters me.

### NOVEMBER 4, 1900 [NEW YORK]

*[Garland had met Ida Tarbell, the biographer and social historian, when they both wrote for McClure's. Brander Matthews, one of Garland's closest New York friends, was professor of Dramatic Literature at Columbia. William Trent was a literary historian. In the election of 1900 between McKinley and Bryan, Herne, Garland, and Traubel (Whitman's friend) supported Bryan.]*

Miss Tarbell called at 5. We were on our way to visit the Hernes. After our call there we took the car for 93rd St. to call on Brander Matthews. Trent, the historian, came in and we had a pleasant call. We then went to the Irving Theatre to hear Herne speak on the issues of the campaign. Horace Traubel and his wife were there. After the meeting we all went to Pabst Cafe. The Hernes were full of the heat of the campaign and Z. was overwhelmed by the tempest of words. The passion of these "cranks." Traubel interested her very much and I enjoyed as always his curt, meaningful phrases. On reaching home found Mr. Howells' card, the third time he has left one [with] us without seeing us. I had taken the book and some flowers to his house meantimes.

### JANUARY 18, 1903 [NEW YORK]

AT Zulime's instigation we went to the Cathedral to hear mass at 11 a.m. The building surprised me by its vastness and its beauty of a certain well-established order. The service appealed to me as being only an aggrandizement and enrichment of the Hopi snake dance. There was the same elaborate respect for the altar and the sacred things upon it. The candles were the prayer sticks, the singing like the song of the priests of the snake. It was a fine piece of drama.

### FEBRUARY 4, 1903 [NEW YORK]

[*Colonel George Harvey had become the head of Harper's, Garland's publisher, after its failure and its rescue by J. P. Morgan. He was well known for his lavish entertaining of literary celebrities.*]

THIS was a red-letter day for Zulime. First of all we found a necklace which she liked and bought it. Then Colonel Harvey took us to see *Faust*, a great performance, for Edouard de Reszke was as great as ever and as Marguerite, Suzanne Adams was very sweet and girlish.

After the opera Harvey took us to Delmonico's for midnight supper. It was a delicious supper but bad for literary persons. We did not leave the room till after one o'clock and the sinister liqueur which was served to us at the end of the meal made sleep impossible. Such doings are not to my liking. Perhaps twenty years ago I would have regarded them differently. I lost a day's work by reason of this feast.

### NOVEMBER 17, 1905 [NEW YORK]

[*Richard Watson Gilder, editor of the* Century, *was also a poet. William Vaughn Moody, playwright and poet, had taught at the University of Chicago. Madison Cawein, Charles De Kay, and Edward A. Valentine were minor poets. Douglas Robinson, a banker, was the husband of Corinne Roosevelt Robinson, who wrote poetry. Clara Clemens was Mark Twain's daughter.]*

AT Gilder's I met Mr. and Mrs. Cawein of Louisville. Also Vaughn Moody, John Burroughs, Adele Aus der Ohe, Douglas Robinson, a Mr. Valentine, Clara Clemens and Charles De Kay. "Quite a gathering of the poets," Gilder called it. Aus de Ohe played very finely and Mrs. Cawein sang. It was all very pleasant and the poets behaved very well. A Miss Roosevelt, very pretty, like Mary Isabel only older. Clara Clemens, dark Spanish, fragile of body but most interesting.

Moody smelled of beer and tobacco as a true collegian should, and had almost nothing to say.

### DECEMBER 31, 1906 [NEW YORK]

*[Frederick Duneka was one of the principal editors at Harper's. Garland had joined the Players' Club in the 1890's and remained a member until he joined the Century Club in 1918. Stewart Edward White, one of Garland's close friends during the 1930's, was a novelist of the Far West.]*

THE rain continued all day, a slashing warm rain, but I got out and went down to the office to see Duneka. I met Stewart White at the Players' and went to his room to plan a trip into the Sierras. He is distinctly older but a fine, clean, bright, masculine young fellow full of the out-of-doors spirit.

I saw Langdon Mitchell's play in the evening and watched the old year out at the club. I didn't much care for the exercises and the drink and smoke of the place.

The city crowds seemed very alien, very European and very wild to me. A mad throng filled Broadway and the faces in the cars were all foreign—few familiar types. It made Chicago seem small and quite homogeneous by contrast, also very dirty and dingy.

## JANUARY 26, 1914 [NEW YORK]

A CLUBMAN, well known, elegantly dressed, staggered up the stair-way and took a seat on a sofa muttering to himself. It was plain that he was "stewed" but as the moments went on he got worse and finally fell asleep. A fellow member came up and said, "ticket please." The drunken man woke up but saw no humor in the re-mark. Shortly after he rose and tried to walk. He pitched headlong to the floor and tried helplessly to rise. We called a boy who helped him rise. He got down the stairs and into a cab and went away home! Think of the wife.

## OCTOBER 5, 1915 [NEW YORK]

IF there were no escape from this club life I might grow to the point of hating it. The habitués are of course bachelors, old and fussy, and for the most part uninteresting. We are as familiar one to the other as the paper on the wall. We greet each other with cold and formal word as we pass. We discuss the war, always with a sure knowledge of the other man's opinion. It is the occasional visitor who is of interest.

## DECEMBER 18, 1916 [NEW YORK]

[*Charles P. Brainerd had just become head of Harper's. After more than fifteen years with that firm, Garland in 1917 trans-ferred to Macmillan's, which remained his publisher until his death.*]

A VISIT to the old shop at Franklin Square brought out the sad changes which have set in there. Brainerd, big, commonplace, slip-shod in utterance, spent fifteen minutes telling me of a dogfight in Cripple Creek. Then invited me to come into his office, the famous old office. It needed but a glance to discover the decay. It is in ruins. The blackened chimney, the andirons staggering across the hearth, the bookshelves in disarray, the confusion of papers, the slovenly, ratty decayed air of the whole place was melancholy—and there, in the seat of great publishers, was this advertising man. And yet he may be the spirit of the hour. He has no illusions. "It is all a matter of advertising," he said. "I am low-brow and I am selling books to low-brows."

### JULY 16, 1917 [NEW YORK]

[*George P. Brett was head of Macmillan's for many years. Edward C. Marsh edited a number of Garland's books. Henry Mills Alden had edited* Harper's Monthly *from 1869. He died in 1919.*]

JUST to give Mary Isabel a glimpse of the old-time publishing house, I took her down to Franklin Square. First we went to Macmillan's where she met Mr. Brett and Mr. Marsh. Then down to City Hall Square. From the Square we walked down the narrow street which leads to Franklin Square. She was greatly interested in the old part of the city and somewhat appalled by the smells. At Harper's we poked about a little. I showed her the little cubby hole in which Alden has edited *Harper's* for over sixty years, one of the most venerable of all the offices in America. Alden was not there, although it is said he comes down almost every day. He is pretty feeble and very remote these days. Some day he will vanish entirely. Mebs saw none of these things, of course; it was all a picture to her.

### MAY 15, 1918 [NEW YORK]

[*The figures named are Richard Burton, author and professor of English at the University of Minnesota; Augustus Thomas, playwright; Arnold W. Brunner, architect; Arthur Whiting, musician; and Cass Gilbert and William R. Mead, architects— all members of the National Institute of Arts and Letters, as was Garland.*]

LUNCHING with Irving [Bacheller] at the Century I met Dick Burton and Gus Thomas, Brunner, Whiting, Cass Gilbert and Mead—all members of the Institute—and I was made to realize that I now belong here rather than at the Players'. I fear the Players' is in for a decline unless someone takes hold to build it up. It is a sad admission to make but the war and other causes have cut down the number of its distinctive characters and that one sees there only the commonplace editors and illustrators, men of not much distinction for the most part. A few come in now and again but on some days there are no specially interesting men, and no guests at all. No one entertains any more. This seems also true of the Century. This is not a time for entertaining.

## OCTOBER 14, 1919 [NEW YORK]

*[Edwin Booth, the founder of the Players', was one of Garland's heroes during his Boston days. Albert Bigelow Paine was the friend and biographer of Mark Twain.]*

THE time has come when I am to break with The Players'. They are to raise the dues to $120 per year and I can not afford this. For over twenty-two years it has been my home while in New York and it is a painful wrench to resign but I do not feel able to continue at that expense, especially as I am about to go into the Century Club.

The world to which I belong and which used to seem so stable is breaking up. Few of the men at the club care anything about Edwin Booth's memory. They are mostly young men of rather prosaic, not to say commonplace, minds. Many are assistant editors or managers of departments in book publishing offices. My friends, men like Thomas, Paine, Matthews, seldom are seen there now. I shall miss it, but [not] as much as I would have done five years ago.

## NOVEMBER 12, 1919 [NEW YORK]

REACHING home at two I found the children insistent that I should go to the Book Show as "Nathaniel Hawthorne" and this I did.

With darkened mustache, high collar stock and the rest, my resemblance to Hawthorne caused a sensation—so Zulime said—and many were kind enough to say that I suggested the character. The party was a successful one. Albert Paine spoke marvellously well, amazing those who knew that he had stammered all his life. His humor, his delightful English made him a joy and he was roundly applauded. Rupert Hughes made a special plea for erotic literature, a speech which was coldly received. It was essentially base, "tawdry," Fuller would have called it. It left a bad taste in my mouth, for I have always thought well of Hughes, although I don't like his books. Lewis Tracy spoke very well for journalistic fiction. On the whole the evening was as we had planned it. Many lovely costumes made a pleasant show.

### OCTOBER 1, 1920 [NEW YORK]

[*The National Institute failed to award a medal for poetry in 1920.*]

WILLIAM BROWNELL and I at the club fell into mild discussion as to who among all our poets was worthy of the Institute Medal this year. "So far as I can judge from a limited reading," I said, "Amy Lowell appears to be the dominant figure of the present mode." He was inclined to vote for Olive Tilford Dargan whose work I confessed I knew only in bits. He spoke of her poetic drama in high praise. Brownell is a quaint, lifeless figure at the club, one that few speak to or about, scholarly in a parasitic way, a bookworm, a student not an artist.

### FEBRUARY 7, 1921 [NEW YORK]

[*Of these novels by Zona Gale, Edith Wharton, and Sinclair Lewis, Mrs. Wharton's* The Age of Innocence *won the prize.*]

IN pursuance of my duties as Chairman of the Pulitzer Prize Committee on novels I read *Lulu Bett* and *The Age of Innocence*—both

good books. The one fresh, original, condensed, humorous; the
other careful, meticulously exact in its social history but arid in
some regards and treating an old theme. There was in it no savor of
novelty. It was the usual "triangle"—European at that—and yet it
was well done and moved me at the close. Up to the present *Main
Street* and *Lulu Bett* have most distinction.

### JANUARY 25, 1922 [NEW YORK]

*[Poets not fully identified are Anna Hempstead Branch, Witter
Bynner (president of the Poetry Society), Arthur Davison Ficke,
Edmund Garnett, and John Van Alstyne Weaver.]*

THIS was a day of life among the poets, and I am not greatly heart-
ened by it. At Mrs. Sandford's, Max Bodenheim, Arthur Guiterman,
Edwin Markham, Amy Lowell, and Margaret Widdemer and I
helped entertain a small audience.

Bodenheim was an apparition. A "red" Jew who entered the
drawing room with his pipe in his hand, a belligerent Greenwich
Villager, grotesque, badly dressed, raw and self-assertive. He repelled his hostess and disgusted me. Amy Lowell, who bustled in at
the last moment, was authoritative and bluntly critical of those
who had read too long. Miss Branch was an especial offender.

At night a big dinner with more important little poets. Bynner,
President, talked too much in introducing the speakers, and Amy
Lowell again told us what's what. The hit of the evening was Dr.
Chang, a visiting Chinese scholar who spoke with depth, beauty,
and power. He made all those who followed him seem the raw
newspaper humorists which they are. Ficke was very good and so
was Garnett but the general effect was of a lot of small verse writers
taking themselves too seriously both personally and as a movement. Dr. Chang's mellow culture, distinction of phrase and beauty
of tone made the cheap, egotistic appeal of the others detestable.
Amy Lowell, for all her claims to subtlety in poetry, was boldly

prosaic—a kind of New England schoolmistress speaking her mind.

The program was too long. We came away before Sandburg came but as he wore a blue shirt with his dinner coat he resembled a back-country drug clerk. He, too, takes himself so seriously that people laugh at him. No doubt he and Bodenheim and Weaver are indications but they are not much more than that. The Poetry Society has undoubtedly built up a vast "claque" for the encouraging of verse writers.

NOVEMBER 7, 1924 [NEW YORK]

*[Robert E. Ely was the founder of Town Hall.]*

AT a luncheon with Ely I consented to act as Chairman of the Town Hall Membership Committee. The club is now nearing completion and promises to be a very real meeting place for the Arts and Letters. It is central, cheap, and democratic. It can be made a notable institution by going about it in the right way. I agreed to serve if I could invite the men and women who are to serve on the committee with me. This Ely was glad to grant. It is, as usual with me, a piece of folly perhaps, but I shall try to help the plan through its initial stages.

APRIL 7, 1926 [NEW YORK]

*[The university was Columbia.]*

THIS meeting with the Graduate Students' English Club proved to be rather successful in that it brought out a roomful of young men and women who are especially interested in literature. Some of them are working for degrees and are hard at certain theses, and others are expecting to write or are writing fiction or verse but mainly, I imagine, they are teachers. My talk was most informal and rambling but perhaps it served a purpose. I met a number of them afterward, fine earnest souls from the hinterlands. One young man spoke of the vastness of the university, of its impersonal character, of the impossibility of ever knowing the faculty. "Everything goes by number, ticket, printed form," he said.

As I rode down Fifth Avenue today musing on the swift changes which have come to it in my day—even in the last ten years—I came to the chilling conclusion that as it is now so it will be when my curfew bell sounds. Great as these walls are, permanent as they seem to others, they are but a flimsy adaptation to present needs. They will give place to later and finer forms but these forms I shall not see. I once had vague dreams of a superbly beautiful city, a great city. Now I know that it will become more populous in the few years which remain to me but it will not be different in quality from that which it is today. It will be swifter, more tumultuous and more extended but it will not have gained greatness or beauty in the sense in which I dreamed it might attain. Its population will grow even more repellent to me and its press more sensational, more democratic, in its appeal.

APRIL 29, 1928 [NEW YORK]

*[Dr. and Mrs. Edward Jones were close friends of the Garlands in New York and at Onteora.]*

THE cold continues and proves very depressing to me. It does not seem like spring at all. We dined at one with Dr. and Mrs. Jones in their lovely apartment in the Apthorp and walked home through the blowing dirt, forlorn pedestrians and flimsy ugliness of Broadway—ten miles of street with not one beautiful or permanent object on which to rest our eyes. Comfortable, abounding in food, clothing, furniture, New York is disgusting[ly] dirty, appallingly ugly, and cheaply transient. Only here and there is the observer repaid for his walk. Filthy scraps of newspaper, clouds of dirt made our walk a test of patriotism. No one else cared. It is safe to say that not one in ten thousand of these strollers noticed the dirt and ugliness.

At night we got the other side of life in New York. In the quiet, beautiful, great lounge of the Town Hall Club we sat to hear a highly civilized talk by the President, Francis H. Sisson.

[*The American Council of Learned Societies was the sponsor of the* Dictionary of American Biography. *John Finley was associate editor of the* Times. *Mark Sullivan, who had resigned from* Collier's *to become a Washington correspondent, was a close adviser of Hoover's. Arthur Hobson Quinn was professor of English at the University of Pennsylvania, and Abbott and Henry Seidel Canby were editors and biographers.*]

THE dinner of the Learned Societies was not as large or as important as I had imagined it would be. A large number of the men were in street clothing and there were few women. Finley was toastmaster and the speakers were professors of history or biography. Mark Sullivan was there and made a short and rather humorous speech. He told me that he was to be a guest with Hoover on his South American trip. I saw only a few that I knew. Professor Quinn sat beside me and I met Lawrence Abbott and H. S. Canby. Altogether it was a very quiet and uninspiring affair but the work they are doing is important. Adolph Ochs, owner of the *Times*, was guest of honor, for he had given half a million dollars to make the researches necessary for the twenty-volume dictionary—a fine thing to do. I left before the end of the speaking and so missed his talk. Finley was graceful, as ever, as chairman.

[*Curtis Hidden Page, professor of English at Dartmouth, was the current president of the Poetry Society. Edward J. Wheeler had been president during 1910-1920. William Griffith, Coningsby Dawson, and Mrs. Edwin Markham were early members of the Society.*]

NOTWITHSTANDING my lame ankle I ventured down to Roosevelt house to speak to the Poetry Society. I couldn't have done it without Professor Page's aid. He came for us in his big car and sent us home in a taxi. Some hundred and more poets and friends gathered to hear my talk which was entirely reminiscent of Whitman, Joaquin Miller, Crane, and Moody. Page was pleased with it and they all treated me as a veteran, which I now feel myself to be. We met in the lovely hall of the Roosevelt memorial and many familiar faces were looking up at me as I rose to speak. It was less brilliant, less impressive than it used to seem in Edward Wheeler's days, however. I felt less pugnacity, less egotistic faith in a personal revelation. Some had begun to grow gray. Amy Lowell and her group of militants, Corinne Robinson and her associates were absent. I saw few poets that I knew. Guiterman, Griffith, Dawson were there and Mrs. Markham, Mrs. Sprague and other old-time auditors and doers, but the general effect was colorless and amateurish.

### NOVEMBER 15, 1930 [NEW YORK]

AFTER a hurried, worried two hours we left our little flat in the hands of the janitor and rode down to the station in a dark drizzle which lessened in some degree our regret at leaving the city whose winter life had begun to appeal to us. It seems a quixotic action on my part—this giving up the city and all it holds for me just at the beginning of the season, but there is logic in it. Zulime needs her children and her children need her. A new grandchild is coming and a grandmother's care is demanded. Our share in the great city's life is illusory. We are too old to actively share it. We sit in our small apartment and read about or hear about it on the radio. Nevertheless, I acknowledge a pang as I leave it behind. It is not grand but it is the best we have. Its journalism is not the best in the world but it is the best in the West. It is a vast and sultry metropolis and as long as I keep my health I shall want to share its life.

NOVEMBER 8, 1931 [NEW YORK]

As the time for leaving the city draws near, I begin to feel the pangs incident to cutting loose. The city was at its best today. The air was cool, the trees of the park still in leaf and as I rode up along the familiar route, it all appealed to me with such power that a feeling of sadness quite took away something of my joy in the thought of returning to my children. For forty years I have been coming here. I have seen many of the city's changes and I have cursed all its dirt and noise, and suffered its dull humanity, and yet it is our great center.

Now that I am about to leave it, perhaps not to return to it, its power and beauty appeal to me with such poignancy that I am saddened by the thought. As it is now it will be during my lifetime. It will not greatly change in the few years I have to live and so I have a wish to enjoy all of the best of it. My chief consolation is that I am seeing the best of it and that winter is coming to make it harshly ugly and dangerous to age.

NOVEMBER 2, 1938 [NEW YORK]

AFTER a talk with Mr. Barbour and Mr. Dale at the bank, I went up to the Academy and worked for three hours sorting and arranging my MSS. It was a hard job. At seven I dined with the Book Show people and made a short unimportant talk. It was not a brilliant group. I was so tired that I came away at 9:30 and went to bed. My shoes hurt my feet and I find it hard to get about. The city now seems not only familiar but commonplace. Its people are less foreign in appearance but as a matter of fact, it is less American than it was in 1930. It has an Italian mayor and a Jewish Commissioner of Parks.

It is hard for me, at times, to remember my age and the probability that I shall never see the city again but as I limped back to my club last night, I realized all my years and longed for my home.

There is no value in a big city when a man's death nears. I do not really want anything in this big town.

## CALIFORNIA

### APRIL 14, 1923 [LOS ANGELES]

*[Garland's brother Franklin had settled in Los Angeles. "Unearned increment" is a single tax term.]*

GLENN, a friend of my brother Franklin, called in his car and took me for a long ride down to Long Beach—thence to "Venice" and Santa Monica and back to Hollywood. It was a lovely day and Glenn was steadily amusing with his perfectly frank talk of making dollars.

Everywhere we went we saw "new territory"—little new bungalows, new homes, new oil derricks and all the talk was "boom," "dollars," "boom," "greatest in the world," "sure to double in price," etc., etc. It was contagious. If I were a young man I should undoubtedly be lured into this business but now it wearies and depresses me. The whole coast wearies me with its incessant and self-conscious advertising, its eternal boom, its monotonous note of optimism. It is all based on the hope of unearned increment. If that could be stripped away from it, it would be a paradise. Everyone hopes for this increment.

### APRIL 19, 1923 [LOS ANGELES]

A MR. ALLEN, Madame Alberti's brother, took me in his car and gave me a ride all about Hollywood, passing in ranks hundreds of the gay little stucco bungalows in the Spanish-Mexican, Italian-Swiss, and many other styles, a conglomeration that cannot be equalled anywhere else on earth I am quite sure. Someone has laid awake nights to think up these queer facades, porches, roofs, and towers.

Some were cheery but many were merely curious or petty. Some elaborate places were English or partly Italian with formal gardens and stately trees.

I have never seen so many buildings going up all at one time. There are thousands in process in every direction I looked.

We rode back into the hills where they put their cars into their attics—literally—and have their stump of house on the edges of the cliffs. Some of it was quite like Italy. A mad era of house building is on. How long it will continue is a question but I see no reason why it should not continue. The whole Middle West wants to come here. It is the only alternative to New York.

FEBRUARY 15, 1928 [LOS ANGELES]

WE both felt rather relaxed today and hence did very little beyond necessary correspondence. We have had a rather strenuous week of travel and talk, and welcome this chance to settle down. Constance took me for a ride to Beverly Hills and Santa Monica where some very picturesque and costly estates are being built among the hills. It is an astounding development. There is, however, a disturbing effect of unreality in it. It is like a stage setting, something built in a hurry, in a flurry of enthusiasm, of sudden wealth. It suggests the eagerness of those newly rich. Twenty-five years from now this region will look settled but it will still lack the settled quality which I love in old New England. If I were young I might, possibly, find it to my liking because to my interest. I have no future. My task is to record the past.

JANUARY 5, 1929 [LOS ANGELES]

THE days go by very quietly, very much as they do in Onteora. I work each morning and in the afternoon we walk or drive. The weather is quite perfect—warm and sunny during the day and cool after the sun goes down. We have only one mail delivery at about nine so my mornings are quite free. Zulime and I went into the city

on a bus and were greatly interested in the floods of Middle West-
erners filling the streets. The throngs of women shopping, and the
crowds of men in the park, were all American, of familiar form and
coloring. The shopkeepers were of the same sort. These people have
mostly acquired a small fortune in Iowa, Illinois, Minnesota or
Kansas and have fled the long cold winters. They are here to spend
their declining years in comfort. They are not intellectuals but they
are intelligent and self-respecting. The city gives the effect of a
great, sprawling western town in holiday trim and holiday spirit—
clean, bright, jocose in architecture, and a kind of costuming for
a part.

DECEMBER 27, 1930 [LOS ANGELES]

THE Iowa Society dinner turned out to be a very plain affair with
poor food, poor speaking and no smoking! Some six hundred wind-
scarred men and women, mostly elderly, came in simplest attire,
only a few of the men in dinner jackets and none of the women in
evening gowns. Each man was seated beside his own wife and a
place was set beside me for my wife. They were all nonliterary,
nonaesthetic and utterly outside the dinner coat zone. They made
me understand the contemptuous remarks of the San Franciscans.
They were in truth incredibly unaesthetic and yet they were worthy,
fine serious folk who do not believe in drinking, smoking, or phi-
landering. They were elderly fugitives from the cold and snow of
farm and village winter life in the central West. They were able
politicians and lawyers. Many judges were among them. Six or
eight judges were presented to me. Some of them liked my poems
and some were rather dazed by them. They expected a speech.

JANUARY 27, 1931 [LOS ANGELES]

[*Ernest C. Moore was provost of the University of California at
Los Angeles, which had recently moved to its new campus in
Westwood.*]

WE lunched today with Dr. Ernest Moore and his wife in their new official home at the University and afterward he took us through the beautiful buildings. The library, which is entirely Sienese or Bolognan, is an amazingly colorful and intricate scheme of carving in brick and marble. It was quite amazing. So was the entrance and the ceiling of the auditorium. The Union Hall was Tudor-Gothic and almost equally superb. Moore deepened the pleasant concept we had of him. Under his harsh exterior he is an enthusiast and a man of kindly spirit.

This group of buildings to my way of thinking is alien to the Southern California scene. It was thrust upon Westwood Hills by the regents who live in and about San Francisco. It should have been in the Spanish style rather than the Italian. Beautiful as these designs are, they seem bare, misplaced, and exotic.

### MARCH 11, 1931 [LOS ANGELES]

AT the invitation of Lee Shippey of the *Times,* I lunched at the Writers' Club of Hollywood, a small club at the corner of Las Palmas and Sunset. W. R. Burnett and Homer Croy, novelists of a sort, and Richard Barry were the other men at the table. A lively young Jew, Al Cohen, sat with us for a time. They all treated me with respect as a veteran and an Academician but I felt out of key with them. They all represented the journalistic side of writing, and the club itself—as they admitted—is essentially a screen writers' organization. There was something cheap and evanescent about the place. Scholarship, careful workmanship do not count here. I felt myself to be on the fringes of the moving picture set. It was easy to imagine the bustle, the hustle, the scurry taking place amid the scenario offices. These men reflected it in some degree, although they are all successful writers of one sort or another.

AUGUST 1, 1932 [LOS ANGELES]

I SAW the Olympic Games for the first time this afternoon and found them highly interesting. First of all the crowd was Nordic and largely midwestern in type. The stadium is on level land and surrounded by pleasant lawns and wide streets, so that the crowd was cared for easily. Over fifty thousand people assembled without confusion or ill temper. It was a handsome, well-dressed throng, mainly young and blond except for the hazelnut brown of their tanned faces and arms. They all had the California tan—so large is the proportion of the outdoor life. The sky was clear, the sea wind cool and fresh—an ideal day. The spectators sat in the two middle sections, spread like a rich rug from the ringside to the rim. The games proceeded leisurely but on time. Several running heats on the part of girls showed speed and endurance of a sort which Atalanta of Calydon could not have surpassed. The men were breaking records in almost every trial and the crowds cheered them with decorum. Here is a new America.

MARCH 10, 1933 [LOS ANGELES]

As we were listening to the radio at 5:55 this afternoon, the machine suddenly ceased and a moment later the house began to sway under our feet. We all rushed out-of-doors and stood expectantly, not greatly alarmed, wondering what would come next. It seemed a slight shock such as an exploding dynamite "shot" might make. Soon reports came in over the radio telling of disaster at Long Beach and other coast towns. These disasters thickened as the evening wore on and then, as usual, the reporters began to dramatize the catastrophe. Voices became excited. Exaggerated reports of tidal waves and fires were broadcast, and the night became one of joyous excitement. Being bored we all welcomed the change and so did the newspapers. We had something other than the depression to talk about. Small shocks kept coming, each weaker than the other. I went to sleep with these quivers shaking my bed.

JUNE 30, 1933 [LOS ANGELES]

*[Garland was attempting to find backing for a Los Angeles art museum which would be directed by Lorado Taft.]*

"Now that my home is definitely in California, I am faced with the problem of how to use my leisure to the best advantage of myself and the community." In some such way as this I began a letter to Harry Chandler of the *Times* who is so keenly interested in Lorado Taft's museum concept. I ended by saying, "I am inclined to think that the establishment of such a museum would be a noble finish to Taft's career." There are ways, no doubt, I can be of service to the community in these my declining years and Chandler is one who can suggest a use for my tongue and pen. I am offering to advance the organization of psychic research and I hope to see the factions united at a future meeting. I cannot quite content myself with a daily routine here on this small lot with my grass and trees. There is still some power for good in me. I have moments of content with our comfort and security but at other times I confront the immediate future with [the] question, "Can I go on living without doing?"

SEPTEMBER 14, 1933 [LOS ANGELES]

*[The occasion was a dinner honoring Garland's seventy-third birthday. Gaylord Beaman, a Los Angeles businessman, was one of Garland's principal friends during the 1930's. Robert A. Millikan, whom Garland had known in Chicago, was president of the California Institute of Technology. Paul Jordan Smith was literary editor of the* Los Angeles Times *for many years. John Erskine was a novelist and professor of English at Columbia, and Harry Leon Wilson was a popular novelist. Pinchot was a conservationist, and Young a diplomat.]*

THE dinner at the University Club was counted a great success and I think it was. The great dining room was filled with a handsomely

dressed entirely urban throng and the speaking was interesting and
not too long. Gaylord Beaman, who was responsible for the whole
celebration, read nearly fifty messages from my old friends and
colleagues in the East, and Robert A. Millikan presided at the early
part of the program. Dr. Martin of the Cooper Institute, Paul Jordan
Smith, and Will Rogers made the principal addresses and kept the
audience smiling. There was nothing funereal about the dinner,
nothing even sad except a feeling of regret that Zulime could not
have been there. I asked Mary Isabel to read a few pages from *A
Daughter of the Middle Border* describing the meeting of Zulime
with my mother and this was counted a fitting end to the program.
Rogers was especially delighted with her voice and manner. In a
sense it was a welcoming dinner to a newly arrived citizen, for not
many knew that I had built a home here. Some of the messages and
letters spoke of regret of my leaving the East and I felt a pang of the
same regret, but, after all, what would a few more years in New
York avail? I had done my active work, my committee work, and I
am in better situation to write here than there, and my chances for
an added year or two are stronger. I was surprised by some of the
messages from men whom I had counted unsympathetic, men like
John Erskine and Harry Leon Wilson. It was a surprise also to have
warm commendations from Gifford Pinchot, Owen D. Young, ex-
president Hoover and other public men. Altogether it indicated
that my Middle Border books and *Main-Travelled Roads* had taken
place in the minds of my friends as history and that they had a fair
chance of surviving all changes in literary styles. But (as Rogers
shrewdly remarked) I suspect that the speakers had not read my
other books. However, I cannot complain of any neglect.

NOVEMBER 23, 1935 [LOS ANGELES]

[*Rufus von KleinSmid was president of the University of
Southern California. Others receiving honorary degrees were*

*Senator Elbert D. Thomas, Professor Carl E. Seashore of the State University of Iowa, and Dr. George F. Zook.*]

AT eight this morning, Constance and I motored over to Dr. von KleinSmid's house for an academic breakfast. From here I went to the president's office where I donned cap and gown and marched into the Bovard Auditorium where along with Senator Thomas, Dean Seashore, Dr. Zook and one other I received the honorary degree of Doctor of Literature. We then went to the Women's Building for luncheon where I met many of the faculty, who warmly congratulated me on my honor. It was all very pleasant to an old fellow who is tending toward a solitary life and sad reflection. Zulime did not go to the breakfast or lunch but was able to sit in the auditorium and hear and see the exercises. I was tired when I got home but in retrospect it seemed worthwhile. These collegiate folk seem friendly and their ways congenial to mine, not as congenial as that of creative writers, but worthy.

### AUGUST 20, 1936 [LOS ANGELES]

[*Garland Greever, professor of English at the University of Southern California, was a close friend.*]

SOME seven professors were brought to me by Dr. Greever today and I served coffee for them on the patio. One man was from Stanford University, one from the University here, and the others were all from Pasadena where they are doing research work in the Huntington Library. They all sat and stared while I talked. They came for this and probably welcomed my loquacity but I felt afterwards that I had overdone this part of the entertainment. As I did not know a single one of them, I could not ask them questions concerning their work, and if I had, the others would have been bored. Perhaps they were bored with me but then they came to see what I was like and went away with knowledge if not with liking.

# REFLECTIONS ON LIFE AND CAREER

GARLAND's public roles during his later career were those of a successful author and a powerful member of the literary establishment. The Garland revealed in his diaries, however, was far from self-satisfied complacency. No doubt one cause of the gloom which pervades many of Garland's reflective entries is the tendency of diaries to serve as the repository for a man's darker thoughts. But there were also a number of more specific causes. Garland, like Theodore Dreiser, had absorbed from his early hardships a lifelong fear of poverty despite his relatively comfortable circumstances after the late 1890's. Moreover, his friends were increasingly men of wealth whose lives accentuated his own economic worries and deficiencies. Most of all, Garland was haunted throughout his later life by advancing age with its accompanying loss of earning power, of reputation, and of physical well-being and strength. He was a man whose essential nature called him to be up and doing but whose later years confirmed the ephemeralness of much that he had done and the impossibility of doing more. His diary entries of the 1930's thus possess the poignancy and depth of the man of insight squarely facing the central human dilemma of transience and of age and decay.

*   *   *

APRIL 28, 1898 [ASHCROFT, BRITISH COLUMBIA]

[In Literature for April 9, 1898, Henry James had stated that "saturation" in the life of an area was one of the most valuable qualities for an author. He had then characterized Garland as "a case of saturation so precious as to have almost the value of genius." Garland, he concluded, was "the soaked sponge of Wisconsin."]

48

DOUBLEDAY, my publisher, has just sent to me a copy of *Literature* containing a London letter from Henry James wherein he rejoices at my Americanism and hopes I will not soon set sail for Europe. If he could see me now, here in Ashcroft in the midst of miners and teamsters and indistinguishable therefrom, he would think my quality native to my bones.

### OCTOBER 8, 1898 [MADISON, WISCONSIN]

I AM surrounded with gay young life. Hundreds of feet go by in the walks. Jests, quips, catcalls and other outcries of youth come to me from below. Tomorrow I shall be among them, but to them I will be a middle-aged man of renown. Some of them will envy me my achievements, others will be content with their youth.

They all seem so boyish and girlish to me, which is to say I am growing old.

### DECEMBER 21, 1898 [NEW YORK]

GRAY days! From my little anchorite cell, No. 58 East 25th, I look out on the dull skies which roof New York, and I am not very happy. My editor friends are all full of plans concerning my future and still I am not happy. Everybody I meet seems interested in me and my work and still I am not happy, nor secure. So much I set down for the benefit of posterity.

### APRIL 9, 1899 [CHICAGO]

I DON'T feel that the last five years has brought me very much. There is no feeling of having widened my reputation or made any considerable impression on the art and literature of my country. Perhaps I have done more than I think. Just now it all seems very little worth while.

### JUNE 9, 1900 [WEST SALEM]

[*Garland had spoken at an old settlers' meeting in La Crosse.*]

THE papers made a great deal of my talk to the old settlers and represented me as criticizing them when in fact all I said was that they had no reason for suffering hunger in those days with all the wealth of nature at their hand. They should have made use of it as the redman did. It only shows first of all that I must be more and more careful of my words and second that I am all out of key with certain of my fellow citizens. I do not worship the same gods. My political, religious, literary and sociologic heresies make me a disturbance when I speak naturally. For all these considerations I shall speak no more except to people who will at least grant me the right of being myself. The *Chicago Tribune* wired, and the *Milwaukee Journal* wrote for a denial but I declined.

### SEPTEMBER 16, 1900 [WEST SALEM]

[*There was some confusion in the Garland family as to whether Hamlin was born on the fourteenth or sixteenth of September.*]

THIS is said to be my fortieth birthday and the thought of it is not cheerful. It is the youth of old age to me as well as the old age of youth. I am at my high point so far as creative power goes. I imagine, though, I may do a larger work yet than any I have thus far finished. Taking thought to it, I realize that I am a middle-aged man. Otherwise I seem to be still a young man and to be counted among "the younger school" of writers. It is not healthful to take close thought of one's future, or past, for that matter. Life will not bear close investigation. It yields depressing results at its best. At its worst it is not a road to be retravelled.

### JUNE 16, 1903 [WEST SALEM]

[*Turbie is Zulime's sister, Turbie Taft Shannon. Edward Bok edited the* Ladies' Home Journal.]

Two characteristic dreams last night. Z. dreamed that Turbie was washing the little baby and let it grow cold, to its mother's agony.

I dreamed of making a big address before some national convention—a kind of "people's message" to the President. It was very inclusive with many heads and I could see the proof slips from which I was [to] read. Of course these slips got mixed and the speech was too long but I came off victor.

My dreams are often literary in this way. I meet Howells or Roosevelt and talk important matters, or I sketch out a story to Duneka or Bok. These dreams are not only very real but logical, just as I might act in actual life.

Zulime just as logically dreamed of nursing a baby.

### JUNE 2, 1909 [CHICAGO]

THE Pen Club of the University of Chicago having asked me to read for them, I hurried over in the midst of a pouring rain (they did not think of sending a carriage for me) and gave a program of Song and Verse.

I could not help thinking how casual it all was. Perhaps the occasions when Lowell did things for Harvard were accepted in this casual way but I fear not. The literary man of today gets more money but less honor. He is more in the nature of an entertainer of the public, and in this case I got no pay and very little honor. I shall refuse hereafter to do anything in this way.

### AUGUST 9, 1909 [WEST SALEM]

I ORDERED the barber to shave my beard but it did not produce as much sensation in my family as it should have done. Mebbie rather liked it. Constance didn't seem to notice the change and Zulime was noncommittal. I had some photos taken of myself and the babies.

I think this ends my "Van Dyke." It has been getting smaller and grayer year by year and now it is gone. I don't want the children to see me with a gray beard. Beards are "out" anyway.

### FEBRUARY 12, 1910 [NEW YORK]

WHILE with Howells today young Martin Johnson came in fresh from Chicago on the way to the old world. He was tremulous with wonder and excitement. He is of those beginning a career while Howells is ending one. I stand between.

I feel the passage of time these days—surely, surely. I begin to feel the uselessness of half the pursuing I do. I shall wait now and let things come to me. Perhaps at fifty, one may expect things to come one's way. All my life I have striven and restlessly sought. As I look back upon it my activity is appalling.

### JANUARY 1, 1911 [CHICAGO]

WE dined at the Tafts' this day beginning our New Year in good health, for which we are grateful. 1910 was the best year in point of income I have ever had, and I not only paid up some debts but made some further investments. The children are developing rapidly and pleasingly. They sing and dance prettily and Mebbie is beginning to read very well. She has a vocabulary of nearly two hundred words—printed words. She has many more that she uses in speech. Connie is alert and picking up much learning from hearing Mebbie's lessons.

My work at the club continues and takes up much of my time and thought. I don't see how I could live in Chicago without it now. I continue to lecture and travel about the land.

### DECEMBER 31, 1912 [CHICAGO]

THE year is closing in depression. I have not felt so helpless and unproductive in many years. No doubt this is the beginning of my supersedence by the younger men. Next year it will be more marked. It is my comfort that I have laid aside part of my earnings against these dull times.

## AUGUST 10, 1913 [WEST SALEM]

I'VE been rereading Hawthorne's *Mosses [from] an Old Manse* and contrasting his life with mine. How little I have to work with as compared to his Concord—at least so far as the historical is concerned. The only moss I have is on the woodshed. The only family portraits enlarged photographs. The history of my house is but fifty years long and quite commonplace. It was but a pioneer shack originally. It is only an enlarged shack today. It has very little perspective and no grace. It sticks close to the concrete walk of the village street and is open to every passing dog or cow.

## SEPTEMBER 24, 1914 [WEST SALEM]

As I look around my poor little study and think of the spacious rooms filled with costly books, the sumptuous desks and easy chairs of the older literary men I have a feeling of being only a camper. To make this my permanent study would be to fix myself at a distance from the city and from all that embellishes a literary man's life. If it were not for my old father I should go to New York each winter and so have some part in the literary "atmosphere." Soon for the sake of the children we must get out of our rut. It will not be fair to them if they do not reach a wider circle of friends.

## SEPTEMBER 23, 1915 [NEW YORK]

WE lunched at the club together and [Mark] Sullivan came along to say goodby before going west, and the youngsters came along to say something about "The Hope of American Literature." We two old gray heads are getting almost venerable! As we left the room I noticed a couple of young fellows pointing us out. We have become picturesque, as Mark Twain and Stedman used to be. Well, there's no help for it so far as I can see. I only hope I shall not get lonely like old Joe Holland who hobbles in and eats alone at a side table—a pathetic figure.

DECEMBER 21, 1918 [NEW YORK]

*[Irving Bacheller, Ernest Thompson Seton, and Albert Bigelow Paine were successful popular authors.]*

ZULIME, fresh from her ten-day stay at a hotel which cost at least nine dollars per day, bent to the task of cleaning house with all the energy of a farming wife, and seeing her so employed I sensed once again the humiliating realization that my "success" is a very weak and helpless honor. So long as my wife must scrub floors and my children wear threadbare garments, I am a failure. Measured by the rewards my fellows enjoy, my condition is disgraceful. Measured by my Iowa playmates, I am a marvel. The vexing fact is I am not comparing myself to them but to Bacheller and Seton and Paine. The worst of it is that at fifty-eight one does not make any great changes in one's fortunes. It is a process of saving and planning hereafter. My hope is in the children, who are very happy in their school and developing swiftly toward self-reliant womanhood.

MARCH 23, 1919 [NEW YORK]

EACH day makes me realize more clearly than before the fact that life is now a battle—a battle which is sure to go against me. The ebb of vitality which set in at fifty is now increasingly swift. It takes so little to lay me low!

MAY 20, 1919 [NEW YORK]

WITH Zulime drudging as a housekeeper and the shabby little flat getting shabbier every day I do not feel in the least like a success. As a member of the Academy, as one of those who are counted among the older established authors, I here set down the fact that my income does not suffice to relieve my wife of household toil nor enable my children to dress as they should. It is hard for any man to maintain any high opinion of himself when his best efforts count for so little. At times all that I have gained seems illusory. Other men have houses, cars, offices as evidences of their ability. I have nothing tangible. At its best it is but a poor showing.

AUGUST 18, 1919 [NEW YORK]

AT eleven I read at the Library a short paper on the modern magazine and started a discussion which became quite hot. I assumed the attitude of the "old fogey" who believes the magazines of the past were better than those of the present, and this aroused some of the defenders of the present.

It was counted a successful meeting but it left an unpleasant taste in my mouth, as always happens when I give out too much of myself. I pretend to like controversy but as a matter of fact I don't. The older I grow the more I feel like letting controversial subjects alone. It isn't worth the disruption of friendships which comes of hot debate. No doubt some of my hearers took my position as a sign of age. Well, why not? I see no reason why I should struggle to be young. The normal thing is to grow old. The abnormally sprightly person is an offense. I don't intend to ossify but I shall not pretend to youth.

AUGUST 29, 1923 [NEW YORK]

FULLER, who has been here all summer and is remaining on with us, sleeps in the little room off the kitchen (the one which Lorado occupies when he comes) and seems to be happy in his idleness. He is doing very little work and does not feel inclined to seek actively for more, but I urge him to it. As the day was warm we both put on our Palm Beach suits, to the effect that while riding up the Riverside

Drive, the bus conductor called to us, "You boys will have to change here."

We told this at dinner and provoked shrieks of laughter from Zulime and the girls. I wonder why they laughed.

It is not easy for me to realize that I am an "old codger." Sometimes I feel it but most of the time I don't. Only by reference to certain portraits of Howells and Clemens at the age of sixty do I get a notion of the figure I must present to my daughters and their generation. No doubt I am also a picturesque figure.

### OCTOBER 11, 1923 [ONTEORA]

THE country was glorious but someway I did not enjoy it. It makes me uneasy. I love it and yet it produces a kind of pain. The city calls. My mind is divided. I do not take the country reposefully any more. I feel myself on a hurried visit to nature. I have a sense of duties unperformed. The beauty of the hills and streams suggests the whole problem of country life. The question of domestic help, transportation, neighbors. It tempts me but it mocks me. It offers a tantalizing vision of something which must remain forever out of reach. My daughters are more than hills. My neighbors in the city are chosen, not thrust upon me by mere propinquity.

But deeper than all this lies something which I cannot quite define, a vague feeling of resentment or bitter sadness which the loveliness of the meadow and tree arouses. Perhaps it is a realization that my time for enjoying landscape is now too short to make a return to it worth the pain of sacrificing the city.

### MARCH 24, 1924 [NEW YORK]

THESE are days when I feel my years. I am not only lame but my brain is not of much use. All that I do seems of no use—all that I have done seems valueless. All that I have attained is pathetically thin and poor. A part of this is physical but some of it is mental. I no longer take keen interest or any joy in any task. As I think of Mark Twain at my age I get a sidelight on myself. I recall his sixty-seventh birthday dinner where I fancied him an old man. I am an old man, although at times I do not feel so. In the midst of certain memories, activities, I am as I used to be. But alas! these times are getting fewer—and at their best are deceptions.

### NOVEMBER 27, 1925 [NEW YORK]

THIS winter is to be a fight for me, a contest against fat, inertia, and the megrims. To exercise is a task. To set out for a walk is a bore and I find all kinds of excuses for not doing it. Loosening teeth, thinning hair and stiffening joints warn me that I *must* keep moving. In summer the case is easier. At Onteora there is physical work to be done and nature close at hand allures to action. Here, wind, dirt, ugly walls, dangerous motor cars and crowds of people discourage us from walking. The city is destroying us in one way, while if we were in the country we would be destroyed in another way. I doubt if I should find shoveling snow or splitting wood any more to my mind than walking in the city.

### JANUARY 31, 1926 [NEW YORK]

GETTING out today Zulime and I went to a tea at Mrs. Robinson Smith's and later to another at the Roulands'. It was my first appearance in society during the month and it would have been a pleasant outing had it not been for my crippled teeth which made speech a self-conscious effort for me. A man never knows the full values of his teeth till they begin to go. I did not know what an essential part they have played in my speaking. Without them I am self-conscious and hesitant. Whether the dentist can restore my confidence is [a] question to be answered before I can accept other invitations to public speech. For forty years I have been a platform orator of a certain sort. My ability to speak fluently and clearly has been, without doubt, a source of strength to me. I have said the wrong things at times but on the whole my speech has advanced my cause—whatever it may have been at the time.

APRIL 15-16, 1926 [HANOVER, NEW HAMPSHIRE]

*[David Lambuth and Kenneth Robinson were professors of English at Dartmouth.]*

IT was a cold, clean, wintry landscape—this Connecticut River Valley. Snow lay on the hills, the streams were surging with ice, a bare desolate country, one which I looked upon with sadness and dismay. Professor Lambuth, an alert, slender, gray-bearded man, met me at the White River Station and took me to the Inn. I lunched with Professor Robinson and young Borden, intelligent men but not in much sympathy with me. As the day wore on I wondered how I happened to be called to speak here. No one knew of me or cared to hear me. Why do I continue to go where I am in a false position? I have nothing in common with these young people. I am an old man celebrating the past—talking of men for whom they care nothing. Why should they? They have their own heroes and prophets! I am merely chanting songs in praise of the slain. My justification is in that loyalty.

*    *    *

Instead of going to Boston I came home on the night train, feeling that this trip was not a very profitable expenditure. It was not a very dignified approach or return. True the head of the English Department met me and showed me some attention but no one really knew much or cared much about my coming or my going. The boys were kindly but had evidently read nothing I had written. They are not really interested in elderly men like me and not at all interested in the authors I told them about. They listened because I made them listen by my method of approach. But why do it? I can live without accepting these dates that mean little. As a veteran and a member of the Academy I should not go where people are not in sympathy and full understanding, where the ground has [not] been prepared for me.

MAY 16, 1926 [NEW YORK]

[Trail-Makers of the Middle Border, *a semifictional account of the early life of Garland's father, was published in late 1926.*]

WHAT an illusory thing "my success" is! Here I am cooped up in a flat with a study about as big as a closet, without any seclusion or quiet. On one side the telephone and the vacuum cleaner—on the other an area with screaming babies, singing women, pianos, Negro porters, and barking dogs. There is no dignity in such a life and no inspiration to work. Comfort I have but nothing more. My work for years has been done under such conditions in the city and somewhat similiar conditions in the country, and now I am too old to assume the cost of better housing. The place in the country is filled with broken water pipes, boxes of books, and damaged furniture so that it may be two weeks before we can think of moving up there. I am in despair, today, of making anything worth while of the *Trail-Makers*. As I have noted before, it is a commonplace if not worthless book, and yet I must publish it or lose all the years of work I've put on it.

JULY 8, 1926 [ONTEORA, NEW YORK]

THESE are days of carpenter work. I have been toiling full days just as I did in 1912 after our old homestead burned. It is quite amazing the ability I still retain in this direction. We are putting the dining room in order and changing windows here and there to let in more light. As I work I find all of my former knowledge and some part of my skill returning. I can tell by the sound of the hammer when the nail is "going home," by the voice of the saw I can distinguish a knot, a sliver, or a nail in its path. I find myself anticipating many

of the carpenter's movements in setting a stud or making a joint.
I get tired but not weak. The work does me service and I enjoy the
sense of making things, of changing a poor thing into a better. There
is something creative in such work—something akin to writing a
novel or a play.

JULY 9, 1927 [ONTEORA]

*[Juliet Wilbor Tompkins, a New York editor and author, was
an old friend of the Garlands.]*

ONCE again, for the fiftieth time perhaps, we motored over to Wil-
low Brook to broil our steak and brew our coffee, as we have been
doing for ten summers. The girls are grown up. We ride in a better
car but something sweet has gone out of it. Our girls no longer depend upon us. They have young men in whom they have a keener
interest. We are older and Juliet is less well. She is frightfully thin
and nervous. Dr. Jones came late from a meeting of the Board and
was not very cheerful. I certainly am not cheerful these days. The
world is all going the wrong way for me. I don't like it and I refuse
to lie about it. An old man trying to keep the youthful point of
view is rather pitiful to me. I am old and see no reason why I should
pretend to any other state of mind.

APRIL 15, 1928 [NEW YORK]

IN the midst of this teeming island I find myself more and more
solitary. Invitations to go out, to speak, to meet people still come in
—though in lesser numbers—but my inclination is to remain at
home and read or work on my manuscript. Things that once seemed
important are no longer even interesting. Most events are repetitions, and hence of little value unless it be merely on the homely,
human side. Big dinners bore me, crowds of shrill-voiced women at
tea irritate me. I see all the dirt, flimsiness, ugliness of the city, of
America. Crowds appall or infuriate me. To walk dodging automobiles and cars is a weariness.

What does all this mean? Simply age and a growth in comparative ideas. A chair with lamp over my shoulder allures me. It is easy to stay at home, an effort to adventure into the town. I've had my miles of travel—two hundred thousand of them. Now, I suspect, I am to sail in an easy chair and ride a couch for the remainder of my days. Someone else must climb the mountains and explore the forest. My part in that activity is done.

### JANUARY 31, 1930 [LOS ANGELES]

As in New York I had my rut from which it was almost impossible for me to deviate, so here I have my routine. I rise before the sun each morning, go down to the kitchen, cook my coffee, toast my roll, and get back at my work at half past six. I work till the mail comes at 9:30. Then I am tempted to lay off for a few minutes but usually get in another hour or two before noon. Afternoons are spent in visiting our new house, going to market with Mebsie, and a walk. Evenings we dine with our in-laws or they dine with us. We see few strangers. This is not the outside conception of life in Hollywood.

### FEBRUARY 6, 1930 [LOS ANGELES]

*[Jesse Lynch Williams and Robert Underwood Johnson were New York friends.]*

LAST night I dreamed that I was back in New York among my literary fellows and was saddened to find them all old and gray and deaf—three out of five were so deaf that I could only communicate by shouting. Jesse Lynch was one of these (he is dead), Johnson, of course (he is deaf), and Irving Bacheller who isn't deaf but is old, and his brother. It was all very sad and I came away back to California much relieved at the thought of the sunshine and my daughters.

### MARCH 22, 1930 [LOS ANGELES]

I HAVE now reached the point where I debate the question of physi-

cal well-being and longevity versus activity and significant acquaintances and interests in a harsher climate where the risks are
more numerous. What is more value than physical well-being to a
man of sixty-nine? I am certain that if I fall sick while I am in New
York, I shall wish myself back in this equable and cleanly climate.
After seventy life is uncertain at best and out here, it would seem,
there are fewer attacks upon the poor old organism. This may be a
shirking of the battle of life, but I've done my share of the fighting
and am disposed to go on furlough. This does not mean a cessation
of work. I shall continue to work as long as I can wag a pen.

### APRIL 15, 1930 [LOS ANGELES]

As I go out into these perfect mornings day after day, I have moments of wondering whether it can ever be real to me in the sense
that my native valley, with its savage storms, violent contrasts of
sun and shadow, harsh winter, sudden spring with mud and dust,
is real. Will this suave and gentle climate bring a mental letdown?
Will I come to long for the savage winds, the dirty slosh, the whirling snow of New York? Here is the land of the lotus for old age, that
is evident, but does it nourish the genius of youth?

These questions are rising in my mind as I am about to establish
a new study in our new home. There is an undoubted letting go in
my case—a shirking of discomfort, a seeking of softer, longer life—
but at seventy I have a right to shirk.

### MAY 19, 1930 [NEW YORK]

I FEEL as never before the chill of the twilight zone into which I
have entered. John Van Dyke, Irving Bacheller, Augustus Thomas
and Albert Paine are all showing signs of swift decay. Van Dyke
came up to me at the club limping, suffering from varicose veins,
and confessed that he was seventy-four, four years older than I. As
I think of all these good friends so gray and sluggish, I am not sure

that I want to live where I can see them decay. Perhaps there would be less sadness in spending the remainder of my life in California where I would come in contact with the young friends of my children. It is hard to decide whether to grow old in companionship with my generation or in partial forgetfulness of it.

### JANUARY 22, 1932 [LOS ANGELES]

I RECALL going in one afternoon to see Mr. Howells in his later years —when he was beginning to feel "out of it"—and during my call, he said, "I have outlived my vogue." I could not believe this at the time but I understand it now. I have never had a "vogue" but I begin to realize that people, even my friends, are no longer interested in my books or in me. Outside the colleges no one gives me a thought. In my small way I in my turn have lost my "vogue."

This comes to every writer. Kipling is no longer in vogue. Edgar Wallace is the man of the hour. His books sell in millions. Vogues come and go more quickly now than ever before. The motion picture kings and queens come and go like rulers in South American republics. Hollywood is full of those who have outlived their vogue. There is only one precaution to observe—"make hay while the sun shines." Those who laid up their wages can at least live in comfort while in eclipse.

### SEPTEMBER 18, 1932 [LOS ANGELES]

[*The Radio Medal Committee of the American Academy awarded a yearly prize for good diction on the radio. Zulime Garland suffered from Parkinson's disease. Vol. IV is the fourth of Garland's literary reminiscences,* Afternoon Neighbors, *published in 1934.*]

IN definitely cancelling my lecture dates in the East, which I did today, I am cutting myself off from all my eastern activities and associations. I must now resign from the board of directors of the American Academy and from the chairmanship of the Radio Medal

Committee. In truth this is an almost complete letting-go of my hold on New York City and all that it means in a literary way, but it had to come someday and, as a man of seventy-two, I might as well admit the weight of my years and shift whatever official responsibility I have to other and younger shoulders. I don't like to retire in this way but it is my duty to remain here and help Zulime through her sad time. She was greatly relieved to know that I am to remain here till we make our Honolulu trip. She seems better and I must not do anything to retard her recovery, and my going just now would be a source of worry. Furthermore, I dreaded the long ride east and the homelessness of my stay there. Now I can finish Volume IV.

### AUGUST 6, 1933 [LOS ANGELES]

SOMEONE writes me to ask, "Do you feel old?" I have not answered but if I do, I shall say, "at times, not so much physically as mentally, and not so much in the working of my own mind as in the change of attitude toward the public. I am either a bore to be avoided or a venerable and wise old writer." I know I am dropping out of literary affairs day by day but that is inevitable. I imagine the elder men of letters suffered a similar neglect. Anyhow there is no remedy for it. The academic world still has regard for me. Tomorrow a dozen or more teachers of literature are coming to pay their respects.

### DECEMBER 23, 1933 [LOS ANGELES]

AT times I feel the emptiness of my position here and have a momentary longing to re-enter my more intellectual life in the East, but I am forced to acknowledge that this is illusory. I would be a forgotten man there. I would simply be another old gray beard at the Century Club. I would observe the city's life. I would not be a part of it. My experiences would almost all be disappointing if not sad. At seventy-three one should be content to sit outside the stir of life, but to one who has been especially active, such a departure is hard.

New York was for nearly fifty years my center of activity and as I listen to its voices over the radio, I suffer a pang of regret that I am no longer a part of its life. After all, it is our London, our Paris, our one really great city. Dirty, sleazy, amorphous, it is great in its almost savage power. It is not American except in its daring.

### AUGUST 22, 1934 [LOS ANGELES]

SITTING on my patio this afternoon with the olive trees all about me and the tall eucalyptus trees swaying in the cool sea wind, I found life, the mere living, very pleasant. I am like a man on some lovely alien island with no one of his old companions and colaborers about him, but at times, I am fully aware that this is about all that remains for me. Each year makes me less acceptable to people younger than I. To my neighbors I am just an old hunker pottering around my garden. My books are dying out of people's minds and my readers, never numerous, are each month silenced by death. Of such fortunes men of seventy-four are heir. Few are as rich as I am here in my California home.

### JANUARY 9, 1935 [LOS ANGELES]

MANY of my friends write in to deplore the recorded hours of my discouragement and this leads me to wonder whether Hawthorne and Emerson were always cheerfully philosophic or whether their editors cut such passages from their published diaries. It seems that a man may confess his vices but not his discouragement. No man is consistently cheerful and unperturbed and I have had many moments of bleak outlook. These I have allowed to enter into my literary record. The story would be incomplete without these confessions of failure. Then, too, I long ago lost all illusion of grandeur. I knew how slight my achievements were.

### JANUARY 28, 1935 [LOS ANGELES]

IT is probable that most old men grow solitary after seventy and some come to feel themselves a nuisance. I am reaching this state of mind myself. There is no help for it. It is a part of natural decay. The conventional action is to pretend a philosophy which considers the loss of teeth, increasing deafness, falling hair and other signs of disintegration as of no importance. Emerson and Hawthorne were tragic figures in their old age. So were Carlyle and Tennyson. I wonder how Herbert Spencer looked at death? A large part of Walt Whitman's optimism was, I now suspect, a literary pose. None of us likes growing old and our philosophy about it is a flimsy staff to lean upon. The worst of it is the realization that one's friends come at last to an open showing of indifference, deepening in some cases to a wish to avoid. Up to the present year, I held my friends fairly well. Now I feel their lack of interest, a feeling which leads to unconscious neglect.

### MARCH 3, 1935 [LOS ANGELES]

THE day cleared and the sky was like June, deep blue with great white clouds sailing about. The country is now so beautiful that I should be perfectly content but I am not. I feel separated from my kind. I think I could find them if I went back to New York, but they are either dead or grown indifferent to me. In going back I should carry my added years with me, and I would find them with an equal weight of added age. I should have gained a philosophy which would enable me to find solace in the flowers, birds, clouds and mountains of this marvelous land, but I haven't. I still feel the necessity of pushing ahead. I must be doing something definite each day.

Every faithful married couple must go through what we are now going through—seeing our partners growing old and gray and inert from day to day while we look helplessly on. No doubt Zulime sees decay in me as I must confess it in her.

### MAY 17, 1935 [LOS ANGELES]

AT times age bears heavily upon us both. I am growing "thick of hearing" at the same time that Zulime's voice grows weaker and, as a result, I am unable at times to follow her. We are both losing the power to initiate anything. I am no longer vitally interested in my garden. It grows ever harder for me to mow the lawn and I find it easy to put off all small jobs. I can only grind away at my desk for a few hours in the morning. Walking is a painful exercise by reason of my feet which become heated and sore. In other words, I am aware of my seventy-five years. There is no escape from these disabilities and not much amelioration is possible. My hardest task is to keep moderately cheerful in Zulime's presence.

### MAY 6, 1936 [LOS ANGELES]

SOMEONE is building a house next door and all day I hear the slap of falling boards, the ring of saw and tap of hammers. To some people these sounds would be an irritation but to me they are pleasing. They have many delightful associations. They suggest the building of new towns and more intimately my own share in the several houses I have built or repaired. I think of my father's house in Dakota, in 1881; of the additions I made to the house in West Salem; to my share in the enlargement of my Onteora homes. It all has definite meaning. I can tell by the stroke of the hammer whether the men are setting studding, laying floor or putting on roof boards. I can tell by the sound of the saw whether a plank or a beam is being cut. I enjoyed building. I do yet, and the smell of new lumber is still a joyous agent. It means homes, good wages, firesides.

### JULY 24, 1936 [LOS ANGELES]

IT is not pleasant to feel oneself growing toward futility but such is the lot of most men of seventy or more. The question arises in me, "What shall I do to fill out my days?" I saw this sadness come to Howells and Burroughs. They both kept on writing when the public no longer desired their books. There are books that I might write but I feel no urge to set about their composition. My eyes will not sustain the strain. I cannot take on a history or biography for the reason that too much reading and travel would be involved. I can only set down what is in my mind.

### AUGUST 21, 1936 [LOS ANGELES]

As I was dressing this morning, I realized as never before that this old body of mine must soon be delivered up to the flames. In the natural course of events, I shall cease to animate it. It has served me well for seventy-six years, but it is wearing out. To dwell on this side of life does no good but it would be foolish to ignore the inevitable. I would rather think of committing my body to the flame of a furnace than of surrendering it to the earth. We all know this change must come but we do not act upon that knowledge. We go on from hour to hour and day to day, as we should do, till the inevitable demand must be met. After all, the living—even the aged—are concerned with life, not death. To most of us life is worth living even at seventy-five.

### NOVEMBER 13, 1937 [LOS ANGELES]

THERE comes a time to every old man when he has little or nothing to look forward upon doing. If a writer, he must realize that he has no more books to publish. If a painter, that his cunning hand is failing him. This is the natural course of events. In such wise is the stage cleared for the action of the young. It is not well to hold the stage too long. Reverence for age is well, to a certain degree only. It may degenerate into pity or at best tolerance. This tolerance I begin to feel. I realize that I am no longer interesting, except to a very few. I know that I am nearing the end of my career as a writer. There is little to which I can look forward. Decay is certain. The best I can hope for is the toleration by a few of my friends and neighbors. This is the penalty of living too long. Zulime and I must now be content with a narrowing social world and a loss of respect. Our chief concern should be to retain the love of our daughters and our pleasure in the sunlight, birds and flowers. These by the magic of our car we can endlessly enjoy.

### JANUARY 21, 1938 [LOS ANGELES]

IT is so much easier, now, for me to loaf than to work that I do little writing. There are men who do good work at seventy-seven but they are so exceptional as to be miraculous. I am able to do a little in way of revision in the morning but nothing that can be called *creative* work. I find letters of continuing interest and I take pleasure in replying to those which have any substance. The garden does not invite me now. It is cold and bleak, and so we drive and visit the theaters and listen to the radio. I wonder what Emerson did at my age? Whitman, Hawthorne, and Lowell did not live as many years as I have reached. There is a shock in this. Whittier, Bryant and Holmes went to eighty or more, as did Howells and Burroughs, but mainly my illustrious predecessors died at seventy or under. Is anything gained by long life? Is it anything to boast about? Is it not a progressively bad habit?

### APRIL 26, 1938 [LOS ANGELES]

[*Frederick Peterson, a former teacher at Columbia University, was born in 1859 and died in 1938.*]

IT is difficult for me to abandon the hope of achievement. For more than fifty years I have arisen each morning in the determination to do something to make the day worthwhile. I am now facing emptiness and futility. I begin each day with a sense of dismay. "Another empty day!" The attempt to justify the mere living ends in failure. We walk of a morning. I do little writing. I doze often. I send a few letters. I work a little in the garden and end the day by taking Zulime to the theater which she enjoys, mainly, I think, because it enables her to forget her disabilities and her loneliness, for she also lives almost wholly within herself. Our daughters help us as best they can, but they cannot neglect their own affairs in order to comfort us. In this condition of mind and body men like Frederick Peterson and others of my friends undoubtedly spend those years beyond the biblical limit. I hope they have a philosophy which sustains them. I have none.

JULY 17, 1938 [LOS ANGELES]

SITTING on my patio this morning, I fell to reconsidering my life as compared with the great ones of America, and I was obliged to admit that my "successes" are pitifully small. This commonplace house with its worn furniture, my ragged garden, my meager income are hardly more impressive than the possessions of carpenter or mason, not to be placed beside those of a plumber. It is true that I have written nearly 50 books but they are all forgotten except one or two and those sell only a few hundred copies per year. I began with such high hopes of national fame and a measure of wealth and I am ending here like a sailor on the shore of a sunny island. If I compare my lot with that of Thoreau or Emerson or Hawthorne, I take some comfort in my house and my carriage but if I look up at the really great and powerful among my friends, I must admit my feebleness. No doubt those are right who say, "But think of the distance between what you are and the plowboy you once were." But that is [not] entirely consoling.

DECEMBER 8, 1938 [LOS ANGELES]

THE feeling, the *realization* of age was in my mind as well as my body today. My joints cracked and my brain was "fuzzy." I know that my work is nearly done. I do not precisely cumber the earth but I mean mighty little to it. This sense of age and vacuity was deepened by a visit to the Newsreel Theater where, for an hour, I saw the world in action, marching, flying, fighting, dancing and at work in field and shop. I am now out of it all with very little will to even travel to *see* what is going on. Zulime still on her diet of watery soup was almost equally depressed.

### DECEMBER 30, 1938 [LOS ANGELES]

[*Williams was seventy-five in 1938.*]

SIGNS of decay multiply. One eye is now useless. My teeth are growing thinner and hearing is impaired, and my feet are so tender that walking is a painful "process of falling," as Dr. Holmes called it. But can a man of seventy-eight expect but growing disability? The worst of it is I have no one to help me, no one to share the daily burden of maintaining this house and garden. My daughters have leaned so long on Daddy that they regard me as an everlasting prop. I have tried to arrange matters so that they can carry on if I should meet with an accident, but it is very hard to bring myself to it. Sorting papers and the use of my eyes in reading letters is now a wearisome business, and I do not feel able to have it done. Looking ahead is dismal business now. In all this I am but sharing the common lot of octogenarians. An amazing exception to this decay is Henry Smith Williams who has written over a hundred books and painted or etched a thousand pictures—and is still at it!

### FEBRUARY 13, 1939 [LOS ANGELES]

IT is customary with old men to minimize their years. They like to be called ten years younger than they are. They cling to positions of power and responsibility long after they have become inefficient. As writers they make no record of their growing lethargy of mind and body. We seldom find in journals of famous authors any mention of their deterioration. In Thoreau, in Emerson, in Hawthorne, so far as their printed records go, no mention of disability or death appears. Mark Twain looked ahead, saw certain decay coming and said so, but for the most part men and women even after seventy shut their eyes to the dark future, and this, I grant, is well. But I find it more natural, more in the spirit of Hamlet's "looking fore and after," to admit that my usefulness is soon to end and my body be gone to the flames.

APRIL 28, 1939 [LOS ANGELES]

As one reads the biography of an ordinarily successful man, there comes a point where, if the biographer is honest, tragedy begins. In a sense every biography ends in tragedy. Old age, neglect and death are in the natural course of most lives of distinguished men. It is the exception for the writer, artist or politician to "grow old peacefully." Even if he seems to be at peace in a comfortable home with his family around him, he is not at peace within. If he is honest with himself, he must admit that it hurts to be left out of aesthetic or civic affairs, to see younger men winning large honors and exercising greater authority—men whom the veteran does not esteem at public valuation. Then there is the pain of acknowledged decay, of certain feebleness and inevitable death. There comes a time in almost every man's life when he has nothing to look forward upon, when hope fades and expectation involves only failing power, lessening activities and ultimate extinction.

JULY 18, 1939 [LOS ANGELES]

*[John Bradley was a professor of geology at the University of Southern California.]*

As I was dressing this morning, I had a disheartening concept of what my aging body requires. It is not only a poor, fumbling, tremulous machine; it is a decaying mass of flesh and bone. It needs constant care to prevent its being a nuisance to others. It stinks. It sheds its hair. It itches, aches and burns. It constantly sloughs its skin. It sweats, wrinkles and cracks. It was a poor contrivance at the beginning—it is now a burden. I must continue to wash it, dress it, endure its out-thrusting hair and fingernails and keep its internal cogworks from clogging. The best I can do for it is to cover it up with cloth of pleasing texture and color, for it is certain to become more unsightly as the months march on. I agree with John Bradley, who calls man an absurd bundle of inconsistent survivals of his immemorial past. In age these outworn parts are a pest.

### AUGUST 11, 1939 [LOS ANGELES]

I AM fully aware that these later volumes of my diary bear witness to my growing loneliness and decay, but these admissions by their repetition are a part of my mental and bodily history. Whoever reads these books will not find in them any striving to be younger and gayer than a man of my years naturally is. Kicking up my heels and roaring out boastings of strength would not conceal my seventy-nine years. As I have repeatedly recorded in this chronicle, "It is my business to be old." If I cannot *naturally* be cheerful, I *shall* record my aches and pains. I shall try not to be a bore with statements of my decay, but I shall not disgust my friends with a factitious gayety.

### AUGUST 19, 1939 [LOS ANGELES]

IT is in the morning, before the routine of my day sets in, that I feel most keenly my growing weakness and the futility of my life from this hour on. I see all the sorrows and complexities which are certain to come, not all of them but so many of them that I am disheartened. As the sunrise comes on and one by one routine experiences and duties are taken up, I lose my sense of age, to a degree, and take up the illusion that all is well with me and mine. My desk, my garden, my car and the sunlight enable me to forget the deeper realities which age is thrusting upon me. I make my coffee, read the morning paper, and then set to work writing words which no one will ever read. This makes my day. The weeks fly. Saturdays come as if only half the number of days intervened, and yet certain hours of each day drag!

### SEPTEMBER 10, 1939 [LOS ANGELES]

SIGNS of age increase. I lose my glasses. I forget names and dates. I get tired early. I lack initiative. Decisions are difficult. Interests weaken and grow fewer. Each day is just another twenty-four hours. Shaving, bathing, changing my shoes are burdens. My main concerns now are correspondence with my narrowing circle of friends. I still enjoy an hour or two at the polo game, and a few biographic films make me forget my perplexities and the Old World War.

### JANUARY 30, 1940 [LOS ANGELES]

THE Beamans and Greever, good loyal friends, came to dinner but I fear they found us two very dull hosts. Zulime could not make them hear and I felt blank spots in my brain. It was an effort to keep my discourse connected. My memory is now not only "treacherous"—it does not exist at times. Familiar names suddenly drop out of my story. I am obliged to grope for a connection before I can recover the name of a place or a person. This seems to be due to some physical cause like indigestion or weariness, for at other times the name or place is easily recalled.

### FEBRUARY 25, 1940 [LOS ANGELES]

A LONG rainy day alone [in] the house gave me time for reflection and a summing up of my life and its achievements which are becoming more and more pitiful as my own vitality ebbs and I have no further hope of accomplishment. I marvel that so much honor is granted me. As a man dying on his feet [I] have lost all pride in my books and all expectation of further reward. For some obscure reason, I am suddenly unsteady on my legs and as I was feeding the fire tonight, I nearly fell into the fireplace. This dizziness may be due to indigestion and temporary but it is very disturbing, nevertheless. The youngsters came in for dinner but I succeeded in concealing my disability from them.

# THE GARLAND FAMILY

GARLAND maintained close family ties throughout his life. Initially these consisted of his mother and father and of the McClintocks, his mother's relatives. He had settled his parents in West Salem in 1893, and as long as they were alive he spent much time with them and with the many McClintocks who lived nearby. As this generation died and as his daughters matured, Garland's family world shifted its axis to them. Both daughters had artistic interests—Mary Isabel in the stage, Constance in painting—but both married young. Garland's hopes and anxieties about their careers and about their personal lives are those of any ambitious parent, increased by his distrust of modern life. His fears were confirmed in the mid-1930's when both daughters were divorced. These years were also darkened by the growing physical incapacity of Zulime Garland.

*     *     *

## APRIL 14, 1898 [WEST SALEM]

ARRIVING in time for breakfast I found the people well. The day was clear and bright, a genuine western spring day. I fell to work on the woodpile—the smell of the freshly-split oak brought back many memories of the past—of the woodpile, the hens, the men at work, the seeding.

It is all very familiar. Every inflection of my parents' voices is an appeal. I was instantly deep in the past—all my acquirements of no avail. Mother is getting older and so too is Father but she seems to show it more than he. She gets out so little! Her life is placid—all the life here is placid and uneventful. Yet it can be tumultuous. There was a fight between an old man and a young man—a volcanic outburst, so they say.

## APRIL 17, 1898 [WEST SALEM]

I SPENT the day over in the valley at Uncle Frank's and saw deep into farm life once more. These plain and hearty people in their plain little cottage have a strange charm. They know little of the world. Their point of view is difficult even for me. They have a sturdy independence. They are disposed not to yield a peg—not even to a nephew who has "made a big success."

Uncle Frank played the fiddle once again and its familiar scrapings echoed deep deep into my brain. I have a hundred memories of wistful youth which his "crooked" tunes touch and reanimate.

Father was quite happy. He enjoys such trips. Mother was worn with the ride. The women of the valley have less of joy than the men. They are almost all in poor health. Uncle Frank's story of his set of false teeth was very comical. He found everybody looking at him and laughing.

Cliff had his fiancée there, a nice girl. He is very crude and not very entertaining. I wonder how he wooed such a girl. She is a little older than he and much more refined. Cliff is a good boy, though. I could imagine the delight it gave him to have her there and to be free to go walking with her and to sit beside her—as he did, he on the floor, she in her chair.

## OCTOBER 10, 1899 [EAGLE'S NEST CAMP, ILLINOIS]

[The Hustler *became* Her Mountain Lover *(1901). Oliver Grover and Ralph Clarkson were Chicago artists. Garland and Zulime Taft were married on November 18, 1899.*]

WORKED on *Hustler,* began to think of leaving. Z and I walked and talked nearly all day, to some purpose. The sky was gray and the signs of rain. The Grovers and Clarksons left camp. Only Taft and I remain to guard the women. Days of singular charm to me. Zulime comes to interest me more and more, and grows more certain of her feelings toward the question in hand. We still walk to and fro on the wood road. Days of gentle debate and serious question, solemn and sweet at the same time.

NOVEMBER 19, 1906 [CHICAGO]

[*Mary Isabel had been seriously ill. Garland was working at this time on his novel* Money Magic *(1907).*]

BABY was awake bright and early this morning and looks very well but she can't speak much better. I was able to attack my work with a good deal of heart and pushed it ahead a bit. I feel like a man who has been lost in a black and narrow cavern and now feels the air and sunshine again. For two weeks the heart of me has been so torn with sympathetic pain that I could not write, could not think of anything but my baby.

Here is *Money Magic* in truth, for with the means to employ the best available medical and nursing skill I have saved my child. Had I been as poor as most farmers are, she would have passed into the shadow never to return to us.

OCTOBER 4, 1907 [CHICAGO]

LITTLE "Margery Xmas" is beginning to laugh and crow like a normal child and her mother is correspondingly relieved. Mebbe is growing into a little girl so fast it almost makes me weep. She is a great chatterer. Yesterday I brought her a comical book, *Noah and His Ark*, and she was tremendously interested in it. She begins to use the word "God" and "Jesus" caught from the other children. I suppose people would call us pagans, so completely is the Bible left out of our home. But we do not intend to burden our children's minds with worn-out theology.

JULY 9, 1912 [WEST SALEM]

As I hear stories of Aunt Deborah and Uncle Frank, I am filled with a sense of the essential tragedy of our lives—any lives. All the buoyancy, hopefulness, helpfulness of the early days here are gone. Father, who is growing each day more automatic, more difficult, more ungenerous (because less confident of the morrow) types the whole story of decay. Uncle Will is gone, Uncle David is gone, Mother is gone and Uncle Frank and Aunt Deb are cranky, indifferent, selfish—or self-centered—and so I will be soon if I am not so already. It is all decay, decay!

### NOVEMBER 14, 1912 [CHICAGO]

THE children went to the Art Institute today and enjoyed the pictures keenly. Afterward we went to a bookshop and Mebsie looked at books with me. This shows how swiftly she is growing up. She found *The Blue Bird* and I bought it. In the evening she read the first act to me. Her ability to follow dialogue is remarkable. The wonderful world of literature is opening to her, and closing for me.

### AUGUST 27, 1914 [WEST SALEM]

ZULIME was full of the wedding which has torn the local society in strips. She went away at four o'clock in low-necked gown and white slippers whilst I remained to paint the china closet and run the lawn mower. Her interest in what I am trying to do was never keen and now it is casual. But I suppose most wives are that way. The husband is a little mill grinding away turning out more or less money for the household.

### JUNE 30, 1916 [NEW YORK]

[*Lily Morris was the wife of Ira N. Morris, a millionaire Chicago financier and diplomat.*]

ZULIME went down to meet Lily Morris and I remained with the children. I worked all day on the book MS. of the *Middle Border*, and Mebsie started in to typewrite it for me. She copied a page and a half.

Zulime came home at six after a brilliant day at the Ritz and other places, to go into our little smelly kitchen and get a scanty supper for her husband and children. It was a sickening drop! Italian Counts at the Ritz Carlton and Italian spaghetti with her family in a 7 x 9 dining room. Such is our life. The kiddies see the humor of it.

<h2 style="text-align:center">MAY 27, 1919 [NEW YORK]</h2>

MARY Isabel against my advice but sustained by her mother went away to Palisades Amusement Park and did not get home till two o'clock. As we had no word from her and as her companion was a boy of no very great experience, we became very uneasy. It all seemed a criminally careless thing to do and I thought how easy it would be for her to go out this way and never come back—as thousands of young girls do every year. It made me realize, too, that my "Little Mary Isabel" was little no longer and that I should soon lose her altogether. We were terribly alarmed at two and I was just about to go to the home of the boy's father when I met the children on their way back. They had been held up by the ferry. We have been very happy together, Mary Isabel and I, but I foresee that she is now to take her divergent path. Her own life with some other man is sure to begin in a year or two more. This was a very painful night for me.

<h2 style="text-align:center">NOVEMBER 18, 1919 [NEW YORK]</h2>

THIS being the 20th anniversary of our wedding day, I gave Zulime a ring which I found at Vantine's. It cost twelve dollars more than the one I gave her as an engagement ring, a fact which just about gauges the change in my fortunes and also in my spirit of giving. I went down expecting to do the fine large thing and came home with this result. The children liked the ring and Zulime pretended at least to find it acceptable but to me it was an accusation.

It is hard for one who has been forced all his life to save (and who has lost confidence in his ability to earn money) to do the noble thing in a case of this kind. I confess to the failure.

ZULIME and I did a little shopping but (as usual) bought the cheapest things, not the things we really wanted. This is the way we have always acted—with caution. With us the thought of old age in destitution has been a never-failing chill to any extravagance. We never have been extravagant. We have never been able to buy anything we really preferred. We have always had to take what we felt we could afford. Our furniture, our pictures, our clothing has never represented our taste but only our poverty. In this we are typical of millions of Americans.

THIS was a blue day for my wife as well as me. She was down in spirit as well as in body. She is sick of housekeeping, sick of our ratty flat, sick of dish washing and house cleaning, and I don't wonder at this feeling on her part. My wonder is that she does not rebel and refuse to do any more of this endless, distasteful drudging. She was never intended for such work and her daughters are of her mind in the matter—the work must be done and they do it. At least they do enough to carry us along, but it is not an occupation with them. They do not think in terms of housekeeping but of art in some form. And they will each do something because they are thinking toward it and away from housekeeping. This may be wrong on their part as well as ours but they are surely on the way to trying out the larger work before marriage brings the other. I intend that she shall have a delightful summer in England—one summer free from worry.

ZULIME and I are entering on that stage of intercourse with our daughters where they not only question our judgment but resent our authority. This is, I know, the law of life. The young birds must leave the nest. The young animals as they mature cease to find companionship in their den, but it is a painful fact to us as to any other doting parent. Mary Isabel begins to resent our advice as well as our criticism, and Constance is developing a sense of humor which does not always spare her mother. Mary Isabel finds young men, most any young man, better company than her Daddy, and is easily "bored." If we mention these facts, she retorts, "You brought me to New York," and to that there is nothing for me to say.

They are both spoiled for "the simple life" but perhaps they will find out something to do in the complicated life of the city which we all love—Zulime as much as any of us. Up to this present year the daughters have not been given to the faults of their generation, but change is setting in. Even sweet little Connie breaks out now and again in the tone and diction of "the flapper." It saddens me, but it is the law! Youth must detach itself. Youth has its rights, its world.

JANUARY 25, 1923 [NEW YORK]

[*Mary Isabel and Garland frequently appeared together on the lecture platform during the 1920's, Mary Isabel in costume reading from Garland's works. William C. Glass was Garland's lecture manager.*]

LIKE thousands of other parents I have come to the point where all my hopes and plans for my children seem fruitless. Mary Isabel made manifest her boredom in platform work and I phoned Glass, my manager, to take her off my California trip. She has lost all interest in writing and seems to have a notion that the world owes her a good time and not too much work. She wants to go on the stage because it offers something brilliant and exciting, not because she hopes to accomplish anything by it. She has small interest in my work and little concern for my records and fame. She is entirely for herself—as is natural perhaps.

All these signs of uneasiness and loss of regard for her home, her mother, and me is sorrowful business but there is no help for it. She will soon go with some man anyhow and what she does in the immediate future is unimportant. She thinks she wants to act but she doesn't. She only wants the flare of it and the admiration of young men. As an outcome of all my teaching and all her inheritance, it is a bitter dose for me. When I think of my own position at her age on an Iowa farm without a cent of my own, without influential friends and contrast her opportunities, I am appalled at her careless unconcern.

In all this I am only suffering the fate of millions of other fathers. I am glad that I made most of the days when we were a united family. I have that to look back upon. Last summer in England was our highest point in our career as a family. The disintegration has now set in. For the first time the lack of a son makes itself felt. Sons do not necessarily abandon allegiance to their parents when they marry.

The story of the Granddaughters of the Middle Border must eventually end in separation and sorrow for Zulime and me. In this as in all else that I have written, there is a typical story of fatherhood.

### AUGUST 7, 1923 [LONDON]

As the end of our stay approaches I have a sense of failure. I have not succeeded in doing as much as I had hoped to do. For one thing my daughters have absorbed more of our time in social hours and we have not been able to entertain as many of our literary friends as we did last year. We have gone out more and among titled persons but this has not had the direct literary result which I had hoped to attain.

Now, too, the daughters have not taken the same interest in sightseeing and in meeting distinguished folk. They are more and more concerned with meeting young people, especially young men, and theater, dinners, and parties have filled their minds. They have abandoned sightseeing altogether. They manifest no keen desire to go anywhere or see anything. They like to lie abed till ten o'clock and "rest" till the time comes to go to some party or the theater. No doubt this is a normal girl's attitude but it is a bit disappointing to me after my hopes and plans for them.

### DECEMBER 1, 1923 [NEW YORK]

THE plague of suitors for the favors of my daughters continues. Constance now has at least three and Mary Isabel a dozen and their interest is registered in calls, inquiries over the telephone and invitations to the theater. Zulime and I are fairly submerged in this tide of young life. There is hardly room for our friends at the table and at times we are driven out upon the streets or into a back room of the flat. To all this beleaguerment Zulime gladly submits but I am less compliant. I don't enjoy having my work broken in upon and I am not entirely pleased by the young men who sit about our front room and make themselves at home at our table. They are all nice young fellows—as young fellows go—but they are not absorbingly interesting to me, and (naturally) the ones which interest me least are the ones who are most regular in their attendance. They are mostly very young and some of them are still students. They will be less pervasive after tomorrow.

### OCTOBER 25, 1925 [NEW YORK]

ZULIME and I are facing the same problems which parents have faced for centuries, the guidance of our girls who have entered upon that stage of development where they are critical of their elders, resentful of advice and especially of correction. Then, too, I am aware of a disillusionment as to their ability. Mary Isabel, who has been my pride and my confident hope, appears to have no desire to write, or act, or read. She tells me that she does not want a "career," that she wants to be a wife and mother, which is not only natural but laudable. Meanwhile, however, she is unhappy because of nothing to do but housework. She wants a job only to earn a little money while waiting for marriage. She has no wish to study in any way, merely to read interesting books. Constance is more ambitious. She wants to be an artist and a singer and she is willing to work towards these ends but she dresses like a shopgirl and dresses her hair till she looks pert. Neither of them will consent to wear sensible shoes and inconspicuous stockings. They must paint and powder like chorus girls—and yet—and yet they are sound at heart. They are following a fashion. I hate to think that my girls are so slavish in their adherence to vogue but so it is! Seemingly they are quite as apish in this regard as their friends. It is an ugly age, an age unhealthily obsessed with sexual matters. It is true all ages have found this the main object of life but usually with more decorum about it. This is like the age of the Restoration or like that of Napoleon's Consulate when the dress of men and women made much of the physical side of love. It will give place to a saner period, a more modest behavior, but meanwhile it is an irritating and saddening age.

JANUARY 9, 1926 [NEW YORK]

[*Hardesty Johnson was a professional singer. He and Mary Isabel were married in May 1926.*]

MARY Isabel came into my room today and with shining face showed me a lovely ring on her engagement finger. It came from Hardesty Johnson who has quite won her consent to an early marriage. She seems entirely happy in him and his prospects and they make a handsome pair. She asked me to have a "scene" with Hardy, as I call him. She was roguishly intent on my dramatizing the situation like this: "Young man, sit down. I want to talk with you. I want to know what your intentions are—or rather, knowing what your intentions are, I would like to know what your prospects are. Can you support my daughter in the luxury"—here I wave my hands toward the walls of our minute apartment—"to which she has been accustomed," etc., etc. Hardy is as reluctant as I am to this interview. Liking him and believing in him as I do, I am inclined to take the thing for granted. Zulime is much affected by it all but I am saving up my disturbance for the actual day of separation, which is likely to be in May. Hardy has so many things in his favor that in these days of atavistic morals I must count myself fortunate. He is a highly gifted singer, a man of fine physique and winning modesty and appears quite untouched by the cynicism which is attributed to the youth of today. He has a prosperous future, of that I am quite sure, but better than that I feel that he is a man who will deal patiently as well as justly with his wife. I have been very ambitious for my first-born daughter. I have held a firm faith that she would develop into a woman of unusual power and I still believe this, although at present she has no keen desire for a career. She has a capacious brain and in it are stored latent powers which a few years more will develop.

MARCH 7, 1926 [NEW YORK]

FOR some reason, perhaps owing to my lameness, perhaps to the dominance of our daughters' interests, Zulime and I have had a dull and narrow social round this winter. We have a wide circle of acquaintances but a small circle of friends. We have entertained very little, and we have gone to few dinners. It begins to look like a narrowing down of social activity for us both. However, we have had our share. Few women of her means have had such a pleasant career as Zulime has enjoyed for thirty years. Since our marriage, especially, she has gone everywhere and met almost everybody, hence cannot complain. Nevertheless we feel that change which has come with graying hair and slowing pulse. There is less reason for including us in lists of dinner guests, for we cannot furnish the interest we once carried. Those who have us now are tried friends rather than new acquaintances. I, at best, am only an elderly man of letters, respected but not sought.

MAY I, 1926 [NEW YORK]

THIS was our day for a conference with Dr. Turck and the results of it were favorable. The doctor told Hardy very little, but he gave me just what we wanted to know. On my return I found Mary Isabel with a look of white anxiety on her face—a look I had hoped never to see there. It was a ghastly look—a look of a woman who expected a death sentence. She stared at me with great wild eyes, and her brow was corrugated into the agony knot. It was almost impossible for me to connect this tragic face with the little Mary Isabel who was my comrade in the happy years of her childhood and girlhood. She is living the pain as well as the joy of the expectant wife. Is it all worth it? Sometimes I think the old maid has the better part. She may have less of the honey of life but she also avoids much of the sting. I cannot comfort my daughter as I used to do when she was hurt. I can only look on and suffer myself hereafter.

JUNE 16, 1926 [ONTEORA]

[*Garland was awarded an honorary degree by the University of Wisconsin in June 1926. The Dudleys and Eastons were old West Salem and La Crosse friends.*]

As the time approaches for me to start for Wisconsin, a feeling of sadness and reluctance comes upon me. If it was a mere visit to Madison to receive the degree I could go with at least a show of pleasure, but the thought of visiting West Salem gives me a pang. It is so full of ghosts of my people! And those who are alive are but tottering wraiths of themselves. I have built into my books a monument, a true monument, to my family and I do not feel neglectful of any member of it. I do not care to see the graves of my progenitors. If I could be accompanied by one of my children or by Zulime the case would not be so melancholy but to go there alone. No. No! What is gained by a few minutes' talk with an old uncle who is deaf and sad—sadder than I—to whom I would also be a shocking reminder of the passage of time? A visit to the Dudleys or the Eastons would leave a heartache.

### JUNE 14, 1927 [ONTEORA]

*[Constance was married in September 1927.]*

CONSTANCE was away at West Point and so Zulime and I were alone in the house—a foretaste of the future when both our girls leave us for homes of their own. I had a disturbing realization of the folly in making improvements for our children who will want—and are entitled to have—their own homes. It is all rather dreary, and brings to mind Howells' poem "Father and Mother." We have run our circle and come back at the end of twenty-eight years to the twain of us and a home that has only the promise of occasional visitors to mitigate its loneliness. There is not much that I can do now but think of the past and write of it. Millions of other fathers and mothers, other generations, have lived through this identical experience and I must do the same with such grace as I can bring to bear.

### JANUARY 30, 1933 [LOS ANGELES]

ALTHOUGH reduced to point of seeing only my immediate family, I am not at all unhappy over the situation. That is to say, I am adapting myself to it with such philosophy as I can bring to bear. Zulime will not visit anyone, not even our closest friends, because of her inability to use her right hand at the table. The least excitement renders it unmanageable. We are refusing all invitations of any sort—dinners, teas or even calls. The sad part of it is in comparing this isolation with her former love of people. When she was well, we enjoyed a wide circle of friends. We dined out frequently and mixed with receptions and teas, but all that is now impossible to her and I do not feel like going out alone. Our amusements are few. I get recreation out of building or work in the garden or in riding. She plays the radio or works on puzzles or reads. We walk together whether the skies are bright [or not] and so each day passes.

JANUARY 1, 1935 [LOS ANGELES]

[*Mary Isabel was living in New York.*]

WE enter upon the new year in fairly good health but feeling the weight of our years. Zulime still suffers from the nervous tremor in her hands and painful crampings in her feet but she eats well and sleeps well and takes great joy in motoring. We miss Mary Isabel but we have our grandchildren who visit us every day and Constance is a comfort. We enjoy our roomy house in which we are more than comfortable. We are luxurious. We have never been so free to buy what we want. We have decided to spend our money as we need it, leaving our daughters to shift for themselves, a procedure which they not only agree with but recommend. A sense of the insecurity of our lives makes saving of less account and the enjoyment of our little income an obligation.

NOVEMBER 9, 1936 [LOS ANGELES]

CONSTANCE informed me today that she and Joe, after eight years of wedded life, had agreed to separate, and so I, who have stood for decency and loyalty in social life, find myself with two daughters seeking divorces! There is every prospect that my final years of life will be clouded by these daughters who were for nearly thirty years my pride and joy. There is nothing to be done. They are both grown women and have all the character Zulime and I could give them. If they elect to see "freedom" in the way of the women of today, I cannot prevent them. I am too old and, at this moment, too sick to even argue the matter with them.

All this, as I said to Zulime, is just more evidence that our world is disintegrating. Lorado's death and this sudden declaration of purpose on our daughters' part coming together while we are both weakened and disheartened is almost more than we can surmount. However, we shall probably go on very much as usual.

### NOVEMBER 11, 1936 [LOS ANGELES]

*[John Wesley Harper was the son of Constance and Joseph Wesley Harper.]*

JOE is a pitiful figure now. He is beginning to see what he is giving up. I went over to sit with John today and the thought that he is losing his Daddy was poignant. He looked so little and so angelic in his bed drawing busily. He says nothing of his Daddy but he must know that he is losing him. No one will know till many years just what is whirling in his small brain. That is the curse of these divorces. They are comparatively harmless when no children call for righteous care. If I ever have a biographer, he can take this as one of my darkest weeks. Both my daughters separated from their husbands, my wife an invalid, myself threatened with pneumonia and unable to see even the few friends I have left.

We took our walk, however. The genial sun, the purple hills and the springing grass offered comfort. I said to Zulime, "That is all we can hope for now, physical comfort and the lovely home."

### JANUARY 23, 1938 [LOS ANGELES]

ZULIME'S illness makes any aid to Constance impossible. Seven years of her invalidism has cut us off from all of our acquaintances and most of our friends. A few still remain loyal but even these we see but seldom. As a family we have "frazzled out" sadly but this, too, is a result of age. Zulime and I as heads of the family are now too inert to keep up the connections we once enjoyed. Constance and Isabel must fight their own battles soon. I do not look forward to their future with pleasure, not even with confidence. I see only war and taxes.

### APRIL 8, 1939 [LOS ANGELES]

WITHOUT the radio and the moving pictures, Zulime and I would have a hard fight against boredom. We listen in on the European war talk and keep informed to the minute on what is going on. No weeks of waiting as in the days of the Civil War. Whether there is a gain in this or not is a question.

At night I played some old songs on our Victor and found them very moving, not because they were inherently beautiful but because they were weighted with memories of my mother and her musical brothers and sisters. Some of the records brought back the days when our daughters were eager little maids to whom these simple records were delightful, or deeply moving marvels. I do not even smile as I play these foolish melodies, for I long to re-enjoy their wonder and the love they bore me.

## PSYCHIC INTERESTS

GARLAND acquired his deep interest in psychic matters during the 1890's when he was introduced to psychic experimentation by B. O. Flower, the radical Boston editor. At this time such distinguished scientists as William James and Sir William Crookes were also absorbed in psychic phenomena. Psychic research was one of Garland's varied interests until the mid-1930's, when it became his principal concern. In the 1890's he had defended his interest as that of a detached scientific investigator. In his old age, however, he admitted a deeper commitment, that of the man soon to die who was seeking information about life after death.

\*   \*   \*

### JUNE 1, 1908 [NEW YORK]

WORKED busily all day at the office, lunched with Augustus Thomas and talked psychics. Called on Ehrich, found him deeply immersed in business. At dinner I had Palsey as my guest and I tried my best to get at the process by which these specters are born. We then went to Dr. Turner's to a sitting. Not much happened but what did happen was remarkable. His undershirt was removed while his hands were nailed to the chair and writing appeared on a pad. The writing was utterly out of his normal reach. Even if his undershirt were concealed on his person he could not handle it.

### AUGUST 23, 1910 [WEST SALEM]

LAST night for the first time in my life—so far as I know—I dreamed of making psychic tests. It is curious that with all my experiences I never dreamed of them before. I have often dreamed of writing, of talking literary affairs with Howells or Roosevelt, but up to this time no slightest trace of my spiritualistic investigations came into my dreams. There is no explanation of this. In my dream I was able, by holding my hands above a table, to cause its rising from the floor. It seemed very simple and natural. As I am inclined to think it really is in fact, with nothing to do with the return of the dead.

### OCTOBER 27, 1910 [CHICAGO]

I HAD this night the most extraordinary dream. I dreamed I had suddenly become a psychic and was able to "emit" the astral substance which is capable of being modelled into semblance of human form.

I was for the time a medium and gave some remarkable exhibitions of my powers. I was a kind of wireless receiver, catching and restating fugitive words and phrases. This is the second time in all my life that I have dreamed on this subject.

### OCTOBER 13, 1920 [PITTSBURGH]

[*Dr. Arthur Hamerschlag was president of the Carnegie Institute of Technology. Henry Hubbell was a portrait painter; Thomas Wood Stevens was head of the Carnegie School of Drama.*]

PITTSBURGH was hot, dirty, dark, and hideously unkempt as I came into it at nine but at Dr. Hamerschlag's house all was harmonious. I spoke to some sixteen hundred of the Tech students at noon and spent the afternoon with Henry Hubbell and Tom Stevens. At night I talked informally to Dr. H.'s guests (some fifteen or twenty) on psychical matters. Interest was intense, and went on till 12. It was an audience of experts—physicists, psychologists, mathematicians. Hamerschlag said I held my own with them because I had no thesis to uphold. I was only telling what I had seen. "It is not a question of religion with me," I repeated. "It is a question of fact, biological fact."

### APRIL 16, 1936 [LOS ANGELES]

[*The book was* Forty Years of Psychic Research, *Garland's account of his psychic experiments. It was published by Macmillan, of which Harold S. Latham was an editor.*]

MY psychic book, a handsome four-hundred-page volume, has come and I am delighted with its appearance. It is the handsomest book on psychic I have ever seen but this does not mean success for it. I do not expect it to interest any considerable number of readers. The scientific will depreciate it and the spiritualistic folk will detest it. As in my lectures on the same subject, I shall find myself in wrong with both houses. However, Latham is confident that it will be read and that the firm will lose nothing by it.

### JUNE 19, 1937 [LOS ANGELES]

NEWS of Barrie's death came today. That leaves only Shaw to represent the group with which I was connected. They are all gone—Doyle, Conrad, Galsworthy, Kipling, Zangwill, Parker, Hewlett, Hardy. Only Bernard Shaw is left. The *Times* called for a tribute and I shall write one for [the] *New York Times* also.

Each of these deaths brings the gulf a little nearer to me. I am headed for it and the way is all downhill. At times I forget this but now and again I know I am to go soon. I shall ask for Barrie on Monday. Perhaps like Kipling, he will respond. Albert Paine responded only a few days after his death. Kipling came, apparently, after only a matter of two weeks. It is not true, then, that "a long sleep takes place after death," as some mediums report.

### DECEMBER 31, 1937 [LOS ANGELES]

[The Mystery of the Buried Crosses *was finally published by Dutton in 1939. Mrs. Sophia Williams was the medium involved in the discovery of the buried crosses.*]

WE end this year in much better case than we began it. Zulime is in better health. Mary Isabel is at home and Constance is serene. It has been a moderately successful year for me, for in addition to my annuities and book royalties, six or eight anthologies have paid me for the use of short stories or poems.

In a literary way I have given most of my time to writing the record of my experiences with a clairvoyant who has led us to the finding of twelve ancient crosses. This book, which I am calling *The Mystery of the Buried Crosses*, is now in the hands of Farrar and Rinehart. I have no confidence in its acceptance, for three other firms have found it "incredible." It has not been a waste of time, for it has interested me at a time when I needed diversion. Sometimes I doubt it myself but at others I recover confidence in Mrs. Williams, my psychic co-worker. I shall go on into another summer if necessary to complete my demonstrations.

### APRIL 29, 1938 [LOS ANGELES]

I AM revising and condensing the MS. of *The Buried Crosses* with the thought of substituting it for the one now in the hands of Dutton's editors. I feel more inclined to take time to make this book an important contribution to occult literature. Losing interest in politics and business and, in lesser degree, in literature and art, I am giving an increasingly larger part of my thought to the question of death and the question of survival. It is a foolish man who puts off all consideration of this profound and inevitable change. It seems a logical employment of my remaining years—or year. At times I feel that the change may come soon. If I can make this story as significant to others as it now seems to me, it will be worth all the time I have put upon it.

### SEPTEMBER 17, 1938 [LOS ANGELES]

I HAVE moments when I doubt the evidence of my senses in this psychic campaign. It stands so apart from the ordinary interests of life and is so antagonistic to the ambitions and ideals of youth that I sometimes feel its futility. But when I face the fact that in a few years, perhaps in a few months, all the business of my life here will be finished, I see a strong reason for taking the problem of life beyond death into consideration, not in any religious sense but as a matter of adult thinking.

### APRIL 3, 1939 [LOS ANGELES]

LIFE with its cares and duties becomes each day more difficult. I am losing interest in my garden. I dread the going up and down the stone steps. The sticky adobe soil irritates me. The care of my clothes and my person is more and more a task. I find it easy to lay down my pen and I have lost the zeal with which I came to it at dawn. I am not much interested in current literature. I foresee that I shall be more and more interested in the Fourth Dimension. No matter what the readers say of my book, I shall continue to study the problem which is, after all, the most important of all problems to an octogenarian.

## LITERARY WORK

DURING 1898-1899 Garland maintained the amazing productivity which had characterized his career since 1890. But with his marriage and with his complete turn to mountain fiction, both his output and his creative drive began to decline. By 1911 he acknowledged that his career as a novelist had come to an end, and it was with relief that he turned to autobiography—perhaps his most natural medium—and began the long process of writing and rewriting which culminated in *A Son of the Middle Border* (1917), perhaps his best single book. Immensely encouraged by its success, he undertook the series of autobiographical volumes which dominated the closing years of his career.

\*    \*    \*

SEPTEMBER 14, 1899 [EAGLE'S NEST CAMP, ILLINOIS]

*[Garland had made an overland pack trip from British Columbia to Skagway in the Klondike, out of which came his* The Trail of the Goldseekers *(1899).* The Eagle's Heart, *a mountain novel, was published in 1900, and* Her Mountain Lover *(the final title of* The Hustler) *in 1901. This second novel was based partially on Garland's London trip of 1899.* Boy Life on the Prairie *appeared in 1899, as did the revised editions of* Rose of Dutcher's Coolly, Main-Travelled Roads, *and* Prairie Folks.]

SINCE leaving Skagway a year ago I have visited London and Paris and written 90,000 words on *The Eagle's Heart* and 30,000 words on *The Hustler.* I have thrown into totally new form upwards of 70,000 words on *The Trail of the Gold Seekers.* I have written a group of poems and I have written (or rewritten) nearly 100,000

97

words on *Boy Life on the Prairie*. I have read proof on *Rose of Dutcher's Coolly, Main-Travelled Roads* and *Prairie Folks* and put together several articles, not to mention innumerable letters and several articles of biographic content. I am in better health than when I began my trip into the Northwest but I am distinctly older. It is the best year I have ever had in a creative sense.

### APRIL 6, 1900 [WEST SALEM]

I FELT today a little stirring of a desire to write some verse, the first for a long time. I have not felt the concentration either of thought or emotion which I had before marriage, the moods which produced poetry. The distraction of travel and other things has prevented me from doing any big creative work. I am less alone and less contemplative. There is loss as well as gain in this new relationship. At times I fear its effect on my writing, at other times I say, "no matter, the gains outweigh the losses."

### JULY 19, 1902 [WEST SALEM]

A COLD gray day, autumnal in feeling. I wasted the whole day in one thing or another of no consequence to me or anyone else. It is singular how completely the past is shut away from me. I do not find stories here that seem worth my while. I seem to have exhausted the fields in which I found *Main-Travelled Roads*. In what direction I am to turn now I can not tell.

### SEPTEMBER 16, 1905 [WEST SALEM]

I AM forty-five years old today and I feel my years. I have accomplished something but not as much as I had hoped to do—more than I dared dream in my youth, not as much as I planned at thirty. My critical faculty is now dominating my constructive or originating powers. That I feel keenly.

### DECEMBER 27, 1907 [CHICAGO]

[*The articles were published initially in* Everybody's Magazine, *edited by John O'Hara Cosgrave, and then as* The Shadow World *(1908).*]

IN answer to Cosgrave's request I started today to write a series of articles on my experiences in psychic affairs and drove ahead on it pretty well but all on a commonplace level. Fuller and Browne came to dinner and I read it to them. "It is interesting," was all that Charles would say, and that is all it is.

### SEPTEMBER 14, 1909 [WEST SALEM]

[*Published in 1910, the novel was eventually titled* Cavanaugh, Forest Ranger. *Buffalo and Dayton are in Wyoming.*]

I AM almost forty-nine years old and I feel like 69. The rain fell in torrents all the morning and I could not write or even read with any comfort but I braced up in the afternoon and began what may develop into a novel to be called *The Forest Ranger* or *The Sign of the Tree*. I wrote about a thousand words on it. Into it I shall put a large part of the studies I have made of the forest during the last eight years with special reference to my recent visits to Buffalo and Dayton. I shall make the Big Horn range the scene of my story.

### FEBRUARY 23-25, March 1, 1910 [NEW YORK]

[*Garland was seeing* Cavanaugh, Forest Ranger *through the press.*]

I WAS pretty shaky and tired when I got through work at eleven a.m. and went down to the office but I kept pegging away—got at it again in the evening and worked several hours. I don't quite see my way out of it yet but I'll pull through someway. I generally always do.

⋆   ⋆   ⋆

I kept at the copy of the story which grew less and less worthwhile as I stared closely at its structure. I worked away morning, afternoon, and night and pulled it together till it had a sort of flow but it was by no means a joy to me as it ran under my pen.

\* \* \*

The proof began to come in and I feel a little better about it. It ran off very well but it all seems very inadequate and shallow. I could do better by it and yet sometime I shall take time to do a really good piece of work again. I am seeing no one and doing nothing but this book.

\* \* \*

Each day I think I shall be able to get away from this intolerable book and go home but the sense of fear that it may not be as good as it ought to be moves me to keep at it. I am seeing no one and I work night and day on it. It is an obsession. I am afraid it is a foolish book and yet I work on with it.

### DECEMBER 27, 1911 [CHICAGO]

[*The plays were by F. J. Hallo and Louis N. Parker. Garland's father died in 1914.*]

WE all lunched at the club as usual. Frank and father went to see *A Gypsy's Love* and father liked it very much. At night Frank went to see *Pomander Walk* and I remained with father. I spent a good part of the evening getting dates and figures regarding his early life. He talked very well indeed as his brain began to stir deep down. He had a clear notion of it all up to his Civil War experiences. I realized that he must soon pass and that I should get as much of his history as I could. He was touched by my interest and talked eagerly and well. I kept him moving in the right lines by questions. All this will have place in *The Middle Border*.

## JULY 7, 1917 [NEW YORK]

[*Garland had dictated an autobiographical story to a Washington secretary before he made his Klondike trip. Mary MacLane wrote a sensational best seller,* The Story of Mary MacLane, *in 1902. "Up the Coolly" is one of the stories in* Main-Travelled Roads.]

As I near the end of the last chapter of *The Middle Border* I am in a panic. At times I have a feeling that the book is of no value whatsoever. Then I think of certain passages and find them good. Probably it is good in spots and bad in spots. My brain is pretty clear now—too clear I am afraid—enabling me to see the faults in the book. So long as I was "tired" my thinking kept to the grooves. Now I cut across them. It is nearly twenty years ago since I wrote the first version of the MS. just before I went to the Klondike. I called it "The Story of Grant McLane." This was before Mary MacLane. I used the same Grant McLane in "Up the Coolly" in 1888. I disliked this first version of the story in the third person. It was faulty but had the facts. Since three years ago it has been my chief care.

## DECEMBER 19, 1921 [NEW YORK]

[*Both* A Son of the Middle Border *(1917) and* A Daughter of the Middle Border *(1921) were published by Macmillan. Harper's had published Garland's mountain novels, many of which were still in print.*]

LUNCHING with Latham today I made it very plain to him that I was desperately dissatisfied with the way things were going. I told him that if there were no other means of getting the Middle Border books advertised I would waive my royalties—provided these royalties were put into advertising. "The plain truth is my sales are pitiful. With the aid of Howells, Roosevelt, and Burroughs and all my good friends we have sold less than fifteen thousand copies of the

*Son* and less than ten thousand copies of the *Daughter*. This is no sale at all if the books are what we are told they are. This must be remedied. We must get out of our rut. We must advertise the book where it will count. I will pay this myself if you don't feel like doing so." I was in truth almost in despair over the whole situation. Latham went away promising to do something about it. I then went to Harper's and told them about the same thing concerning their books. I am willing to forego royalty for the sake of advertising. "That is what I need at this stage of my career." They were much impressed and something will come of it.

OCTOBER 22, 1923 [NEW YORK]

[*Garland published* Back-Trailers from the Middle Border, *an account of his family's experiences in the East and in England, in 1928, two years after the appearance of* Trail-Makers of the Middle Border, *his semifictional history of his father's early life.*]

A LETTER from Macmillan's offering a contract for *A Pathfinder of the Middle Border* brings me to a decisive point—whether to push ahead on my *Granddaughters of the Middle Border*, the third volume of the present series, or to finish and put forth next spring the prologue—this is my problem.

While mulling upon it I painted the woodwork in our little hallway and wiped up the paint—a part of it—which I splattered in my haste and preoccupation.

In talking with MacNeil yesterday I came at a clearer vision of what this last book of the series is to be. It will round the cycle by showing Zulime and me, two old people alone, representing our pioneer people, in the East, with our daughters adventuring on new paths—all of us representatives of the Back-Trailers of the Middle Border. This movement is quite as historic and quite as full of drama—of a different kind—as that movement westward which I have celebrated in the other books.

### APRIL 12, 1925 [NEW YORK]

IT becomes more and more apparent that writing is a dwindling power with me. I have gone so stale on the *Trail-Makers* that I cannot finish it. It appears entirely worthless to me at present. I doubt if I can end it on any successful note. When I see the magazines filled with the literature of sensual love, I feel entirely out of the running. No other subject just now seems to interest our writers— mainly because it succeeds.

### NOVEMBER 18, 1926 [NEW YORK]

THE reception which my *Trail-Makers* is having is an astonishment to me. I have had moments—many of them—when it seemed of no account, but now there is every indication that it will be more popular than the other books, more popular than any of my books except *The Captain of the Gray Horse Troop*. This, I suspect, is not due to the book but to the psychology of the hour. We are developing an appreciation of the romance of our early history. Our historic sense is deepening and my books of the Border are accepted as casting some light on the character and doings of the humble folk who laid the mudsills of the western states.

### JULY 14, 1927 [NEW YORK]

GETTING out a volume of my MS. copy of my diary, I worked all the morning on 1902-3 correcting its slight inaccuracies, reliving as I did so the lovely days of our first seasons together in New York City and in Colorado. It was a pleasure mingled with bitterness, for scores of our companions of that day are gone: Howells, Norris, Mabie, Herne, Warner, Kate Douglass, Ruth McEnery Stuart. Only a few remain. It is history now, this record of mine, and may turn out to be my most important contribution.

### AUGUST 19, 1927 [ONTEORA]

ALTHOUGH the valley was beautiful and the house quiet, I did not succeed in doing any work. My brain was like a mass of macaroni—no vitality in it. Sometimes when I look ahead I am appalled by the shortness of my span of possible life. What I do must be done quickly. The fourth book of the Middle Border series lies under my hand but gets on but slowly, and I am going over my diaries once more striking out the repetitions and valueless entries, indicating what can be done with the various lines of record. There is a volume dealing with my children and their development, a second dealing with my meetings with notable people and my estimate of their work, and a third dealing with the family fortunes and the changes in life and thought during the last thirty years. Of the value of these records I cannot speak with certainty. Sometimes they seem important, at other times they seem faded and the persons I admired have grown remote and pale.

### OCTOBER 18, 1927 [NEW YORK]

MACMILLAN'S are disposed to print my diaries in sumptuous form and Latham is to submit to me a proposition which will involve the whole series. If we come to terms we will print two volumes next year and this means a long and careful preparation. At the club I met Hobart Chatfield-Taylor who said, "I've found a job for my old age." This, he explained, was a history of fashion in which each chapter was complete in itself and could be written any length at any time. I told him that I had found a task which would fill my closing years but I did not tell him what it was. If my diaries prove of value—as Latham seems to feel they will do—I shall have a long series of them—a lengthening chain, one that will fill my declining days with a mild interest.

## APRIL 8, 1930 [LOS ANGELES]

[*Garland closed* Roadside Meetings *with an account of his first trip to England in 1899, including in his account a visit to Henry James at Rye. This interview actually occurred in 1906, during his second visit to England.*]

As I near the end of *Roadside Meetings,* I perceive the need of something more than just a statement of fact. If the book is to stand alone, as Brett wishes it to do, it must round up into some sort of historical climax. This I tried today to supply by adding a chapter out of its chronological order—the one dealing with Henry James and Bret Harte. It gave me a chance to say what I have long felt about expatriation, and I think it will add a mild climax to the book. The success of this volume will open the way to another sheaf of my dated records.

## MARCH 6, 1938 [LOS ANGELES]

MORE and more clearly I recognize the shortening of the way before. Each month I have less to look forward to. Another possible book, an occasional address, a tour here or there—nothing really worth living for. Most men of my age, if they are honest with themselves, admit that they cumber the earth. We are hobbling along in the path of younger and more capable men. I have had all day to consider these facts. In going over my files and my letters, I find my justification—such as it is—in the past.

In these forty volumes of my diaries, in my notebooks and letters, there is, undoubtedly, much material for literary history but who will dig it out? I can no longer do it. My eyes will not stand the strain, and I have no one to do it for me.

FEBRUARY 17, 1939 [LOS ANGELES]

MORE and more I realize that my work is nearly done. Few men of my age continue to write anything vital except possibly in a reminiscent mood. I have little to look forward to—my book in April and possibly an article or two. I could, perhaps, give an occasional lecture but committees know that I am old and that my talks may be boresome. With my writing urge dying out and my lecture field narrowing to an occasional address at some school, I am already taking my place as one who has lived his life and is only waiting for the bugle to blow "Lights Out."

APRIL 23, 1939 [LOS ANGELES]

[*The book was* The Mystery of the Buried Crosses.]

As the date of publication of my psychic book draws near, I find myself in divided thought concerning its effect on me and those who are still disposed to honor me. When I consider that I am an old and nearly forgotten man, I realize that not even criticism matters. But, at times, when I feel some slight resurgence of thinking power, I am not so confident of the value of this work. In theory nothing should so matter to me now as the question, "Am I to survive the change called death?" but the habit of living, of writing, of carrying on from day to day my life's routine persists and may go on for several years. I ask myself, "Is it wise to enroll myself among those whose chief concern is the seance?" This new book of mine may bring many of these "cranks" to my telephone.

JUNE 8, 1939 [LOS ANGELES]

[*Garland was writing* Fortunate Exiles, *a fifth volume in his literary autobiography, dealing with his California experiences.*]

A LETTER from Latham asking my permission to "dump" my unsold books on the market marks the end of my career. I have outlived my readers as well as my fellow writers. There is no use of my writing another page. I have nothing that the public of today wants, unless perchance my psychic work finds a public. What is the use of working on my *Exiles*. No one would publish it no matter how well it was written. All my fellows are in substantially the same situation. White and Bacheller still have a market, but a failing one. They too will soon reach the end of their vogue. We all come to it. Our only hope is in our historic aspect. Some of our books may chance to be valuable for reference.

### NOVEMBER 12, 1939 [LOS ANGELES]

[*The "young biographer" was Eldon C. Hill, who was preparing a doctoral dissertation on Garland's life.*]

In looking back over my life from this vantage point of octogenarian hopelessness of further striving, I see nothing that is great and little that is admirable in my work. Here and there are worthwhile paragraphs, perhaps pages, but as a whole, my career is mediocre. My friends insist on honoring me as one who has achieved something more than success, but of my achievements, I am less and less inclined to boast. I have been active in [a] weak man's way and I have had ambitions to be of some lasting account in my nation's history but I can no longer delude myself into self-satisfaction. I cannot see my young biographer winning rewards or even attention by his book. And yet, I cannot refuse to aid him when he writes for material. I cannot bring myself to discourage him, although I feel that he is wasting his time.

PART TWO

AMERICAN LIFE AND LETTERS

---

## PERSONALITIES

GARLAND was a pursuer of literary and other lions from the time he
sought out Edwin Booth and Walt Whitman in the 1880's to his
interest in Hollywood personalities in the 1930's. One of his un-
realized motives may have been the desire to increase his own
stature by the stature of his associates. But Garland was also fas-
cinated by the genius and strength which make for success and
fame. His pen portraits thus often possess the verve and insight of
the writer intensely absorbed in the essential characteristics of a
human personality. And like much good biography from Boswell
to this day, his portraits are frequently autobiographical as well.

\*      \*      \*

## FELIX ADLER

### DECEMBER 12, 1917 [NEW YORK]

*[Adler was the founder of the Society for Ethical Culture. A
brilliantly persuasive practical moralist, he had a large following for many years.]*

WE dined at Mrs. Hilman's, meeting the Felix Adlers, Mr. and Mrs.
Paget and a Mr. Content. It was fine, thoughtful but rather slow
company—all Hebrew. They had read my *Middle Border* and professed to like it very much. Zulime pleased them—that was certain
—and as she sat beside Adler she had an excellent chance to be instructed. He is a vastly learned man, and a man of highest purpose,

but quaintly ugly. Small, almost hairless and of bloodless complexion, he has an unwholesome appearance. He speaks well, very well, and has done a fine work here in New York City.

## IRVING BACHELLER

### MAY 1, 1929 [NEW YORK]

[*Garland had written for the Bacheller newspaper syndicate in the 1890's. Bacheller's novels were far more popular than Garland's.*]

In dining with the Irving Bachellers, we entered the Barclay for the first time, finding it a spacious home of the rich, characteristically American in its ornate lobby, its wide halls and its efficient service. The prices of food are appalling to such as I but Irving finds it's a nice convenient home between seasons. He doesn't seem to belong in such a place but I suppose his wife likes it. He was busy on a new book and also on a series of articles attacking the foul moving pictures of the day. He is a bit inconsistent here, for he is a hot opponent of prohibition. If you can't "make people good by law" then what is the use of trying to cut "the boob" off from his favorite bedroom farce? It was not a pleasant evening. After more than thirty years of association, I begin to feel that in growing old we are growing farther apart. He is a fine old figure but like myself he is losing edge.

## GEORGE GREY BARNARD

### NOVEMBER 17, 1928 [NEW YORK]

[*Barnard is remembered principally as a collector of Gothic and Romanesque art. John D. Rockefeller, Jr., built the Cloisters to house the Barnard collection.*]

My wife and I visited Barnard's cloister again today, and called on Barnard himself. He was just moving into his new studio, and as we entered the door, we heard his voice—a marvellously rich and flexible organ yet—booming out directions to his men. He looked small and not very well, and his collarless shirt was not very clean, but he was as full of theories and poetic fancies as ever. His house is a museum, packed with Gothic, Japanese, Chinese, and Spanish junk. He showed us some ancient Chinese cave frescoes that were new to us, and discoursed upon them in his accustomed way, vaguely eloquent and occasionally profound. He is an almost great man and sculptor but he is without [a] balance wheel. As we came away, Zulime said, "He *is* crazy, isn't he?" She did not mean insane but just befogged by theories.

### APRIL 25, 1938 [LOS ANGELES]

NEWS came this morning of the death of George Grey Barnard, an old friend, a very powerful and original sculptor. He was so vigorous when I saw him last that I considered him good for ten years. He was not large but he was physically very powerful and as handsome as Lord Byron, so far as his head and profile could be counted. He loved Lorado Taft and I think he had a very real affection for me. I hope he took time to record his story but I fear he did not and that it has gone into silence with him. He told it to me one day at luncheon, in his home, and I found it most dramatic and humorous as well as pathetic. It was, in outline, typical of the ambitious American student in the eighties, only a little more dramatic as he himself was more dramatic. He leaves some large work unfinished and I fear he died in disappointment. He died suddenly, the report said, of heart failure. A good way to go.

## JAMES M. BARRIE

### JULY 27, 1923 [LONDON]

[*Lady Hawkins, an American, was the wife of Sir Anthony Hope Hawkins, the popular English novelist. Barrie had not had any children by his wife, whom he divorced in 1909. In 1910 he adopted five orphaned boys, George, Jack, Peter, Michael, and Nicholas Davies.*]

LADY Hawkins came in to tea and talked much of Barrie whom she called "Jimmy" in a way which I doubt he would approve. She also said, "He is a true Scot about money, you know." She estimated his income at twenty thousand pounds a year, and as his expenses are small, he is without doubt a very rich man.

She told of his sons, "He adopted five and educated them all but some of them do not get on with him. They resent his niggardliness."

She told of his saying to one of the sons, "Your ties and waistcoats cost more than my entire expense at Edinburgh University." "Michael is the one he loves but the one that was drowned. Michael comes into Peter Pan as a baby and Peter is the actual name of one of his boys, all grandsons of Dumousie." I have long known that Barrie was "careful" but I did not enjoy hearing him called mean. I led Lady Hawkins to admit that he gives away large sums. "I find him generous for charity's sake."

## JOHN BARRYMORE

### DECEMBER 11-12, 1930 [LOS ANGELES]

[*Barrymore had married Dolores Costello, herself an actress, in 1928.*]

WE climbed up to John Barrymore's eyrie today—nearly a thousand feet above Beverly Hills. He has two separate houses on this hilltop, one a curious little bungalow with a grass-grown tiled courtyard, and a handsome Spanish type of two-story house just beyond with a pool and fountain between. From the moment we entered the gate we were surrounded by "trophies" and "treasures." Both of the houses are museums with old furniture, old books, primitive weapons, paintings, drawings, prints, models of ships and all kinds of other queerities of no value to anyone else. Below, on the hillside, he has an aviary with some sixty varieties of rare birds fluttering and chirping there. In another lower room were crocodiles—stuffed —trophies of his shooting. He told us with pride that his wife killed one of them and also caught a fish nearly ten feet long. She, a blonde young girl, took us about carrying her baby on her arm. She did not seem at all the moving picture actress as she did this. She was very maternal and spoke with charm and intelligence. I do not wonder that my daughters like her. After we had seen the house under her care, she took us up to see John who was in bed convalescing from a tropical fever. He was not far from my concept of him but appeared more interested in art and literature than I had anticipated. There is something exotic in him, however, something not quite real. I think he felt in me and in Lorado something equally alien. We didn't really coalesce at any point, although with more time to talk we might have discovered more things in common. He has no illusions and so far as I know no ideals. He has a collector's enthusiasm but how much he owns in addition to this remains for me to discover. He has a handsome head and good profile and speaks well but not noticeably well. He was respectful in tone.

*        *        *

In talking over our visit to Barrymore with others, I learned that while he receives an enormous salary as a talking screen actor, more than five hundred thousand dollars per year, more than a lifetime of Hamlet on the "legitimate" stage, he has not laid up a dollar. This may be an exaggeration but they say he owns nothing but this house and its curios and an immense yacht in which he sails for a considerable part of every year. "He knows nothing of money" is a remark of all who know him. He was once—not so long ago—the man who appeared to be Edwin Booth's successor on the Shakespearian stage but he is now almost forgotten in that role. He is now doing "Moby Dick" and "Svengali" and other sensational roles. I could not detect in him any keen regret. Perhaps he has no reason for regret. He is now reaching millions instead of thousands and is being recorded as he could not have been recorded as a great tragedian on the traditional boards.

## REX BEACH

### OCTOBER 19, 1917 [NEW YORK]

*[Beach's popular Yukon novels celebrated the manly virtues.]*

AT a meeting of a committee today I met Mrs. Rex Beach who has always been a remote personality to me. She turned out to be a rather pretty blonde woman just past her youth. She told me many curious things of herself and Rex. She went into Alaska when a child, walking hundreds of miles over the pass down the Yukon to Dawson and finally to Nome. She said, "I was in Nome when there were 25,000 men and only ten women. I met Rex there." She said that Rex, so big and burly in appearance, was not in the least like that. "He is always taking medicine," she said, but swore me to secrecy about this. "He does hunt big game," she added, "but he is not the rugged athlete people think he is." She laughed heartily when I told her of some wonderful stories of her husband's prowess. "No man is a hero to his valet or his wife," she ended. Zulime, who came in, also liked Mrs. Beach. She is no blank page.

## POULTNEY BIGELOW

### AUGUST 17, 1930 [ONTEORA]

*[Bigelow died in 1954 at the age of ninety-nine.]*

POULTNEY BIGELOW and lawyer Nichols came to call and we had an hour's lively talk. I like Bigelow. He is vivid, delightfully humorous and incisive. We talked of Ford, the Kaiser, and other strange matters. He is seventy-five years old. He had not seen or heard the motion picture which he had made for the newsreel, but I assured him of its excellence. This pleased him. He confessed to being entirely out of the modern world. He spoke of an MS. he had prepared for the publisher and asked me for a commended agent. His writing has so many sharp angles against Jews, Catholics and other thinkers that it is hard to find a publisher for it. He is brusquely honest in all his heresies and prejudices, and yet I find him pleasing.

## GEORGE P. BRETT

### MAY 27, 1924 [NEW YORK]

[*Brett was the head of Macmillan's for many years. The books referred to in the closing sentence are* Trail-Makers of the Middle Border *and* Back-Trailers from the Middle Border.]

BRETT belongs to the old-school publishers who regard the author not as an equal partner but as a kind of inferior to whom it is not necessary to refer any matter concerning the book in which each have an interest. Fortunately I am not forced to put up with the kind of cold resentment which Brett always manifests when anyone disagrees with him. He is a capable man but I have never been able to deal directly with him. In the first case it was Marsh, now it is Latham. Latham is friendly and would do all that I ask but Brett thinks *he* is the sole arbiter. This attitude must eventually give way just as employers of labor have been forced to admit that their "hands" are not peons but partners in the industry. Brett's arrogance goes back to "Grub Street" and the days when writers were poor cattle on the edge of hunger and humble in the face of publishers. Fortunately I have won substantial freedom from him and his like and have no need of publishing at all. These books can all wait till I am out of the reckoning.

SEPTEMBER 24, 1930 [NEW YORK]

AFTER a busy morning at my desk and in putting things in order, I went down to Macmillan's to lunch with Brett and the heads of his departments. It was highly instructive to see how that cold, calm little man kept his young men in subjection. No one hazarded a remark but myself. Each man there waited for "the chief" to direct the conversation. No one expressed an opinion unless requested to do so. Brett had his customary jest about the publisher struggling in poverty in order to maintain the author in luxury, and they all laughed but me. Presuming on my age and long friendship, I countered by calling to mind the stories of the palace he was building in Florida. I could have no quarrel with him, for he said of my *Roadside Meetings*, "It is the best book of the year—one of the best books of a decade," and as the judgment of a cold, keen commercial publisher this remark had weight with me.

## VAN WYCK BROOKS

NOVEMBER 3, 1938 [NEW YORK]

[*Brooks's new book was* New England: Indian Summer, 1865-1915, *published in 1940.*]

VAN WYCK BROOKS came to see me at 2 p.m. and we had a talk of nearly two hours. I liked him as much as ever. His clear eyes, resonant voice and his charming smile were quite as I remembered them. He told me of his marriage in California and his teaching at Stanford University but explained that he was a native of New Jersey and of Dutch ancestry on his mother's side. We talked much of Howells and of his delicacy of mind as well as of his courage of conviction. He told me of the book on which he is at work which deals with the period immediately following *The Flowering of New England* and that it will take the better part of a year to finish, but his eyes are bright and keen and he seems unwearied and confident. I said to him, "I feel no confidence in my own opinions now. I am dying out of a world which no longer represents me and which has already forgotten me."

## JOHN BURROUGHS

### JULY 29, 1919 [ROXBURY, NEW YORK]

[*Clara Barrus was Burroughs' biographer.*]

THESE three days have been a revelation of the simplicity, the dignity, and the tragic philosophy of John Burroughs, who has been my friend for over thirty years. He opened his heart to me during these quiet hours in the old house. He ran over large spaces of his life, and as he talked Dr. Barrus took notes furiously, for he talked to me with a spirit and interest which he could not sustain with her. She had been at him so long that her questions bored him. She had been digging out his boyhood experiences, and her book is mainly made up of these memories. It is a boy's life and not a biography.

There is no need to conceal the facts in regard to this home. It is a poor, bare, ugly little house, hardly more than a shack. It is the kind of house that a poor man builds. It is not like mine—a summer camp. It is a flimsy farmhouse to which a rustic porch has been added, and John's life is as bare of the graces of table and toilet as a farmer's life. He thinks deeply and writes with power and precision but he lives like a renter.

### AUGUST 9, 1930 [ROXBURY, NEW YORK]

[*Mrs. Grace D. Vanamee, Vida Sutton, and Colonel Frank*

*Crasto were Onteora residents. Burroughs had died in 1921.*]

WITH Mrs. Vanamee, Miss Sutton, and Crasto I drove over to Uncle John's old summer home. We found Clara Barrus in possession, or rather we found her obsessed by the lodge and its memories. She reported that people still come to visit the spot, four thousand last year, and she is on hand to receive them and take them into the dining room and the little study in which he worked. It was a little more ragged, a little more musty than when he lived in it, and all rather painful to me. I went in reluctantly. It was as if he were present and yet the knowledge that he was not made the vivid memories of him the more poignant. It is a futile task, this keeping dim fires going on the altars of our dead. Few read John now, and next year there will be fewer yet. It is inevitable that his fame should fade like that of Emerson and Howells and Thoreau. This display of his poverty is rather shocking, like that of Joaquin Miller on Oakland Heights. His monument is in his books, not in this flimsy cabin.

## WILLA CATHER

### NOVEMBER 14, 1930 [NEW YORK]

[*Miss Cather was being awarded the Gold Medal of the American Academy for her* Death Comes for the Archbishop.]

I WAS dead with fatigue and so was Zulime at seven but we dressed and went out again to the concert. Willa Cather was on the platform and I did not recognize her, so changed was she. She is a plain, short, ungraceful, elderly woman. She did not speak to me and I made no attempt to greet her. It was a surprise to me to find in her such a type. I had remembered her in quite different guise. She spoke without force or grace, with awkward gestures, but she did a noble book in *Death Comes for the Archbishop.*

## HARRY CHANDLER

### JANUARY 1, 1931 [LOS ANGELES]

ALL the family went today to see the big football game in the Rose Bowl at Pasadena but I remained at home. Part of the time I listened in on the radio and part of the day I spent in an interview with Harry Chandler, proprietor of the *Times*. I found him a very simple, unassuming man of about my own age, gray, cherubic of countenance, thoughtful and able. He told me he was a native of New Hampshire but that he had been here for many years. He said, "I remember you as a man with a dark beard in 1891."

The purpose of my call was to present Lorado's plan for a vast museum and he became genuinely interested. At the end he asked me to ride home with him and on the way became quite friendly and agreed to lend the aid of his paper and his own personal influence to the plan. As we parted he said, "Let me know if you get any more ideas on the subject."

He promised to have one of his men write a page article and did not refuse when I asked him to write an editorial about it.

He was not at all the kind of man I had expected to meet. He is in truth elderly, country-bred, and midwestern, a kindly man—able in many ways but nonliterary. He is without subtlety or pretense. I liked him and I think he took to me. I understand his paper better now that I have met and heard him.

## FRANK CHAPMAN

### MAY 26, 1929 [NEW YORK]

[Chapman was for many years Curator of Ornithology at the Museum of Natural History in New York. His book on Barro Colorado Island appeared in 1929 as My Tropical Air Castle.]

FOR the first time in a month or more I was able to go out to dinner.

We had a family meal with Frank Chapman and his wife in their lovely apartment overlooking Central Park. Chapman's melodious voice was a joy to hear, especially as he read me some parts of his book on Barro Colorado. He has done here—I believe—the most popular book of his life, for it is a record of a joyous outing—several of them in fact. The island on which he has a winter home is in the government zone of the Panama Canal. He is therefore a privileged guest in a paradise of tropical life with all the comforts of a home. He spent the winter writing this leisurely book which is scientific in its observation but popular in its tone. He has written it with loving care, delighting in reliving its delights, for he loves the place not in spite of its howling monkeys, ant bears, spiders, snakes and lizards but because of them. Oh well! Each man to his taste. I prefer California or the Catskills. He was a charming host, one of my most valued companions.

## WINSTON CHURCHILL

### MARCH 9, 1922 [NEW YORK]

LORADO met some more men at the club including Winston Churchill who is full of what he regards as a discovery concerning the nature of the subconscious. It is curious to find this novelist so involved in psychical analysis. He seems to be completely given over to the consideration of "The Primitive Mind" and "The Creative Mind" and their interactions. I can not believe that he is adding anything very real to the discussion. He is, in truth, rather tiresome.

## WILLIAM ANDREWS CLARK

### MARCH 24, 1932 [LOS ANGELES]

MRS. STRUBLE came for me at two and took me to the Clark Library. Clark owns a square block of land on West Adams Street. On it is an old vine-covered house. A high brick wall encircles the block giving silence and privacy. On the east of the house at the end of a garden he has built a lovely little library which houses his collection of Dryden's works and related books. It is an exquisite little building with lovely murals, elaborate carvings and many rare books in fine bindings. Clark came in to see me and we had some easy friendly talk. I found him attractive. He is a small, dark man with clear, candid glance. The talk about his being a dissipated man is not borne out by his appearance. He looks the scholar and the art collector. While in this building I had no sense of being in the West or in a democracy. Here was the kind of beauty which is possible only when one mind directs and sustains.

## STEPHEN CRANE

### JUNE 6, 1900 [CHICAGO]

*[Garland's reminiscence, "Stephen Crane: A Soldier of Fortune," appeared in the* Saturday Evening Post *on July 28, 1900. He last saw Crane in 1898.]*

SEEING in the papers today the news of Stephen Crane's death I was reminded of his early struggles and his contacts with me; and during the day I set down some reminiscences of him as I knew him. I always considered him a man of short life, a kind of Keats or Shelley. He took little care of himself and his death is due to his own habits of excessive smoking and I fear the use of opium. The last time I saw him he looked yellow and thin. An unwholesome type.

### AUGUST 2, 1922 [LONDON]

*[Mark Barr, an engineer, had known Crane in England in the years before Crane's death. Garland had seen Crane frequently in New York between 1892 and 1894. During 1896 Crane was*

*hounded by the New York police because he had come to the aid of a prostitute who was being unjustly arrested. In a subsequent raid on his rooms the police claimed to have found an opium pipe, and it was soon rumored that Crane was an addict. It is generally believed that Crane and Cora did not marry.]*

AT night Mr. Mark Barr and his young son came to call. Barr again spoke of Stephen Crane's marriage. He quoted Crane as saying, "I brought Cora back." He married her over here in the presence of [H. G.] Wells and one or two others. "Conrad wrote about him saying that he was surrounded by a lot of third-class people." He was never given to really fine associations. Barr considered Cora Crane a woman of education, "an ample 'negro mammy' sort of person." The fact of Wells being a witness at the wedding would not add anything to its legal aspect, for so far as I know he does not believe in the home or marriage.

In looking back on Crane, I can now see that he had not the power of growth. He had a gift but not the attributes of a big writer. He made no advance over *The Red Badge*. In truth he retrograded. With all his endowments he was not an admirable character. He gave out the effect of being an alley cat so far as habit went. And during the days when I first knew him in New York City he was living like an outcast. Although not a drinking man, he smoked incessantly and I sometimes thought used a drug of some kind. Of this I was never sure, and though the police found an opium pipe in his rooms, there was no proof that he used it for himself.

## CLARENCE DARROW

### MARCH 19, 1911 [CHICAGO]

CLARENCE DARROW and his wife came over to supper and we had a great deal of talk. He is a big personality and a most interesting one, but bitter, bitter and essentially hopeless. I can not find that he has any ideals or convictions left. His deep voice booms along on a minor note, a plaintive note, as though life were a mere mechanical going on for him. Part of this may be pose but much of it is, I fear, the truth. What he gets out of life while travelling in this mood I can not understand. His philosophy is essentially destructive, and yet there is something admirable about his honesty of statement.

### MAY 19, 1913 [CHICAGO]

[In 1911 Darrow had defended two labor leaders, the McNamara brothers, against the charge of dynamiting the Los Angeles Times building. During the trial they changed their plea from innocent to guilty. Darrow was then indicted for suborning perjury but was ultimately acquitted.]

WE dined at night with the Shannons. The Darrows were there and we heard a good deal of the trial through which Darrow has passed. He seemed very well and carefree so far as this trial is concerned. He said he was to get forty-four thousand dollars out of the Mc-Namara case but his own trial had cost him twenty thousand so that for two years' work and all his worry he had only twenty-odd thousand dollars. He was in debt, too, he said. He did not look old or broken; on the contrary, he was vigorous and full of fight. He is fifty-six, so he said. He talked books altogether. He loves books and authorship.

### APRIL 18, 1914 [CHICAGO]

WE dined at night with the Darrows. Darrow himself was as usual on the rampage. He is getting more and more anarchistic. He is on the "off" side of everything—woman's suffrage, prohibition, white slavery. He is for "freedom" with all that it might mean, and especially savage against Christianity.

## NOVEMBER 4, 1920 [CHICAGO]

REACHING Chicago at dinner I found the Darrows at supper with them [the Shannons] and again felt that Clarence was by no means as bad as he made himself out to be. He loves books and talked on and on about the books he had been reading. He particularly dwelt upon Mark Twain and his savage attacks on the Christian religion. It was all rather wearisome to me. What is the use? Why attack any religion?

## THEODORE DREISER

### FEBRUARY 7, 1904 [NEW YORK]

[*Dreiser had been recovering from a nervous breakdown by working with a railroad gang on the upper tip of Manhattan. Throughout his life Dreiser accused Doubleday, Page of suppressing* Sister Carrie *after publishing it in 1900.*]

BACHELLER and Theodore Dreiser lunched with us. Fuller was also present. Dreiser turned out to be a tall, thin, ugly and very uncouth fellow of serious not to say rebellious turn of mind. He was bitter over his treatment by Doubleday and disposed to take the world hardly—a vivid contrast to big sweet-minded Bacheller who is the personification of success. Fuller was very gay and witty and seemed to enjoy the whole day. M. Aubert, the young French traveller, came in late and I gave him some letters to men in Washington. Dreiser stayed on and on, telling us of his struggles. He became a bit tiresome at last and we were glad when he went back to his work as boss of a gang of excavators. I admired his *Sister Carrie* but not deeply enough to become an advocate of it. It is good work but plodding and graceless of style.

### JANUARY 21, 1913 [CHICAGO]

[*Dreiser was in Chicago for research on* The Titan, *the second novel in his trilogy based on the career of Charles Yerkes. In*

*1916 Garland refused to sign a statement protesting the sup-
pression of Dreiser's* The "Genius," *and the two men were
enemies from that time.*]

THEODORE DREISER met me downtown—queer, silent chap—and I
took him to Lorado's studio and then to the university and so round
about home. Nellie Walker and Miss Hogan came in and spent the
evening. Dreiser seemed much impressed with Chicago, the university, and Lorado's studio. He caught the deep sadness of Lorado's
work and liked the sadness. He is a pessimist—don't believe the
world can be made any better. "A mad world, my masters," is his
favorite quotation. A big, awkward, blundering yet amiable mind,
with a certain largeness of perception and honesty of purpose. Not
highly polished but sturdy and bold in action.

## RALPH WALDO EMERSON

### SEPTEMBER 2, 1935 [LOS ANGELES]

I READ Emerson's essays in the afternoon and evening, finding them
less important than I had remembered them. His references to
"God" and "Nature" bored me, I must confess. They seem the utterances of a preacher turned scholar, such as he really was. His
scholarship was confined to the classics, however. I saw his library
and a dreary expanse of faded and lifeless authors it seemed to me.
All the covers were a weather-worn brown, nothing of contemporaneous science or literature, as I recall it. Every book published
previous to the Civil War, most of them eighteenth-century classics.
His essays reflect this library with here and there a flash of intuitive
wisdom.

## JOHN ERSKINE

### JULY 26, 1939 [LOS ANGELES]

JOHN ERSKINE came in at four and we talked of literary affairs in

New York City and of old magazines in contrast to those of today. He agreed with me that the old *Century*, *Scribner's* and *Harper's* had a lasting quality which the mere "snappy" journals of today do not have. He is out here to make an article on certain phases of the moving picture industry, but I suspect he is being drawn into the maw of the machine. My daughters remembered him pleasantly as their instructor at Columbia many years ago. They thought him an extremely ugly man but that he had [a] beautiful voice. He was kindly, almost respectful of me and we gossipped of the Authors' Club, the Century Club and the men who used to frequent them. Most of those I knew are gone.

## DOUGLAS FAIRBANKS
### JANUARY 11, 1930 [LOS ANGELES]

WE saw Douglas Fairbanks and Mary Pickford do *The Taming of the Shrew* as a "talkie" today and we had a good time during it, and they seemed to have a good time performing the farce, for they frankly made it slapstick comedy. It was Shakespeare in a new guise, but many of his lines were retained—more of them than I had expected to hear. Fairbanks was a joy—so young, so gallant, so humorous in effect. He is nearing fifty but no one would suspect it, so slim, agile and powerful is he in the picture. She looked very small, very lovely, but very determined to be the Kate of the text. Within her limitations she was an artist. She did it much better than I anticipated. Knowing her for the sad little lady she is, I realized all the more fully the art which went into this characterization. It was so delightfully amusing that we were surprised when it stopped at the end of an hour.

### MARCH 28, 1930 [LOS ANGELES]

AT Fairbanks' invitation we went out to the studio again today. He met us in most friendly fashion. A small very brown man. His coat of tan superimposed on his naturally brunette complexion made him look like some kind of Oriental—a Spaniard at lightest. He introduced us to a group of Germans who were, they explained, on a tour around the world. Two of them were women, one a pretty little American girl, wife of one of the Germans, and the other a Countess, a worn-faced much made-up woman who had once been beautiful. Led by Fairbanks we all drifted into one of the studios where a short scene from the new play *Abraham Lincoln* was being taken. For an hour we studied this process. The mob of camera men and electric light men with their machines, wires, screens and lamps made a confused and confusing mass, and all was converged on a group of four actors at a table, one of whom was enacting the role of Wilkes Booth. While we were standing about, Fairbanks introduced Ina Claire (John Gilbert's wife) and Louis Bromfield, and we had some little talk with them. Bromfield, in rather rowdy dress, was chewing gum. His face was rather unpleasant, eyes a little too near and his expression a bit smart-aleck. As we were walking out, I saw him give Ina Claire a poke, as if to show that they were very good pals. I have never read one of his books, but from what Fuller wrote of them they are like his face and eyes. I don't intend to do the man an injustice but his utterances out here are not of high character. There is something cheaply egotistical about him.

We had tea in the Mary Pickford bungalow, but she was not there. The little place was filled with superb roses, and Fairbanks told us they were in honor of the tenth anniversary of his marriage to Mary Pickford. Aside from the Germans and English, we were the only guests.

## MARY WILKINS FREEMAN
### [1920-1925]
### [MEETINGS WITH AUTHORS. LECTURE NOTES]

[*The group of minor Boston authors described by Garland in-*
*cluded Louise Imogen Guiney and Gertrude and Minna Smith.*
*The visit to Randolph occurred in 1886 or 1887, when Miss*
*Wilkins was in her mid-thirties. Her companion was Mary*
*Wales, with whom she lived until her marriage to Dr. Freeman*
*in 1902. Dr. Freeman was an alcoholic, and the marriage was*
*tempestuous. Mrs. Freeman died in 1930.*]

IT is more than thirty years ago since I met Mary Wilkins, as we
called her then. I was a student and teacher in Boston and she was
just beginning to write her stories of New England. She was at that
time a small, shy, yellow-haired, blue-eyed girl just reaching the
old-maid stage of life. She was reticent, low-voiced, plain of dress—
a kind of brown thrush of a woman, one who fitted into a company
so quietly that few noticed her.

She was a member of a group which used to meet at the home of
Joseph Edgar Chamberlin, one of the editors of the *Transcript*. He
was "The Listener" of the *Transcript* and greatly beloved of all
who knew him. Miss Guiney, the poet, the Smith sisters, Alice
Brown, Bradford Torrey, Sylvester Baxter, and I made up the most
usual membership of these parties. Occasionally Mary Wilkins
came. We all enjoyed her coming, although she added little to the
noise. No one could have been less assertive and yet she was always
smiling and happy. She liked to be part of the merriment by sharing
in the enjoyment of it.

She lived at this time at Randolph, a village a little way out of
Boston, and there I visited her. Her house was typical of the cottages described in her stories—a small, low structure facing on an
elm-shaded street. It was quite as inartistic within as the interiors

she so often described—comfortable but not harmonious. Her housekeeper was also her companion, almost her jailer and taskmaster, for Mary laughingly described to me how relentless her housekeeper was. "She shuts me in my study each morning and won't let me out till I have written at least fifteen hundred words." She then confessed that writing was a drudgery for her. The stories came to her almost complete so that putting them down on paper had none of the joy of creation about it.

She was writing almost entirely for *Harper's Magazine* in those days, as Alice French was writing for *Scribner's*, and obtained about $300 for each short story, which seemed a good deal to me, for I got only about one-third of that sum. Alice French was supposed to get more.

Our supper that June evening was very New England. Several kinds of cake, berries and cream, and hot biscuits. Mary was almost as much a guest as myself. Her resolute companion and housekeeper was in full charge and sat with us to see that we ate of each cake and that our cups were replenished.

Mary was quietly, almost roguishly humorous. She was "an old maid" in appearance and movement, but her keen laughing blue eyes and quizzical smile denoted the novelist who saw everything and remembered what was of value to her. I was a big brown-bearded Westerner at this time and must have seemed a bit like a Wisconsin lumberman to this prim little woman. But she bore the ordeal of my visit very well and we parted better friends than ever.

Often at our meetings around Chamberlin's open fire Mary would respond to calls for a story by telling a ghost story or a mystery story, and she told them well, in concise, vivid diction, sitting quietly in her chair with two or three of her girl friends grouped about her feet. She was like her stories, plain, simple, humorous. She made no claims as a writer, although her work was meeting with the widest acceptance.

Moved by something which she did not understand, she kept

steadily at work depicting a society which was passing, a New England gone to seed, a race dying out in old maids, eccentric men and deserted farmhouses. It was not a grateful task but she did it with an art which is as fresh and vivid in its appeal as it was in 1890. Her sense of character was so keen that she was able to write on and on without repeating herself till in the volumes of her short stories she had completed her record.

We do not see her any more in literary circles in New York and I fear her work is done.

She lives at Metuchen about thirty miles west of New York. Her husband is Dr. Freeman, a physician, I believe. I have visited her home, which is spacious and attractive but the village is most unattractive.

Of late she has dropped out of all our circles. No one ever sees her. No one speaks of her. What this means I do not know. Some say she has become difficult in her old age and that she is a recluse, bitter and resentful. I do not know.


## ROBERT FROST

### SEPTEMBER 29, 1915 [NEW YORK]

AT the club I met Robert Frost, the *North of Boston* poet. He is a man of forty-four, quiet, self-contained, clean and gentle like his works. He spoke of my work and how much my *Crumbling Idols* had meant to him.


### SEPTEMBER 27, 1916 [NEW YORK]

CHARLES TOWNE, Harcourt of Holt's, and I talked of Robert Frost and planned ways to help the sale of his recent book. Harcourt told us of the lonely farm on which the Frosts live at Franconia Notch. They have been very poor, and are so still, but he has earned over two thousand dollars this year so that he is feeling less worried. We talked of a dinner to him and shall probably do something of the sort.

[*Frost's daughter was also ill with tuberculosis. The Frosts had visited her in Colorado before coming to stay with their son, Carol, and his wife, Lillian, in Monrovia, just outside of Los Angeles.*]

WE drove over to Monrovia to get Robert Frost and his wife. We found them in a little yellow cottage near their son and daughter who were in another cottage of a little better type. Robert was looking much older than when I saw him last and Mrs. Frost was plainly worn and anxious, for her son's wife is lying helpless on her bed, a victim of tuberculosis. Robert is a fine figure of a man not quite sixty. He has the appearance of a handsome New England judge, clean-shaven, rugged and dignified. On the way over he told me the story of his son's struggles. The daughter-in-law has been unable to walk for a year and they have brought her out here in the hope of bettering her condition. Robert and his wife have been here for a month in order to support and comfort the son who is distracted with anxiety for his wife and desperate for lack of employment. He had had to leave the farm in South Shaftsbury and cannot plan to go back.

In his slow, calm way Robert admitted that the situation was tragic. As for his own case, he is quite secure of a living. He is a part-time lecturer at Amherst College on liberal pay and for life. He is not writing much. He does not write out his lectures and has no notes from which to begin. "I just talk," he said. "I like to talk and I never repeat a lecture. I have never written any prose but sometime I may do as you have done—write out my reminiscences."

He spoke of going to San Francisco to see the place in which he lived as a child. "I could not find it. My father was a newspaper man. He was editor of a paper on which Henry George was a typesetter. He had a warm admiration for George and I often saw them together. We are New Englanders, of course. My ancestors like your own came to Maine some three hundred years ago. Do you realize that we are half as old as the English language! It is not true that we have no background." We had several hours of good companionship, discussing all sorts of problems, for his mind ranges wide. He hates the pornographic school as strongly as I do. His opinion of the men who represent it was quite as definite as my own.

The more we talked, the more singular his position among American writers became. He is unhurried and has no urge to acquire money. "One book in eight years is fast enough for me," he said. "I am busy all the time mentally," he explained, "but I write very little." I could not discover that he was at work on any theme. "I find I carry my problems about in my mind, work 'em out there, then give them to my audiences in talk."

There is no other writer quite of this self-contained, unworldly character. We were all delighted with him. He seemed almost a member of the family.

### OCTOBER 2, 1932 [LOS ANGELES]

WE motored over to Monrovia to get Frost and his wife and son but only Robert was able to come with us. His son's wife is a helpless invalid. His daughter is not strong and his wife is suffering from the strain of it all. Robert himself is more concerned about his son who has been forced to give up his farm and come here to nurse his wife. She cannot sit up and she is partly deaf so that the whole family waits on her.

Robert enjoyed his ride with us and his luncheon and the polo game and on the way told us much of his adventures. After eight years on a New Hampshire farm, he sold it for three thousand dollars and took his wife and four small children to England. He lived for three years on this three thousand dollars. Part of the time at Beaconsfield just out of London, the remainder of the time near

Gloucester in a cottage for which he paid fifty dollars per year. His money gave out in 1915 and he came back to Boston. "I had fifty cents in my pocket," he said, "and I bought another farm in Franconia for a thousand dollars—paying nothing down. I sold it several years later for four thousand dollars and bought the farm I still own in Vermont." He had no ease or security till he was made a resident poet at Ann Arbor. He is now endowed by Amherst College and is secure. He writes nothing in prose and only now and again in what he calls verse. He is much greater than anything he has written. He talks well—wisely and humor[ously]. We enjoyed every moment of his stay. He is loyal to New England, however, and this is right. He made me feel recreant to my tribe as he spoke of going back.

## MAY 6, 1933 [NEW YORK]

ROBERT FROST lunched with me at the club and we had a good talk of an hour or more. He was looking well and cheerful, and well he may, for his salary had not been affected by the depression. He told of his slowly operating muse and named some of the general themes on which he was at work. I urged a book of prose but he disclaimed all wish to do so but confessed a desire to do a long poem in his kind of verse. It would be a kind of condensed novel.

## NOVEMBER 29, 1938 [LOS ANGELES]

[*Frost won the medal.*]

THE ballots for choosing the Gold Medal for Poetry came in from the National Institute today, and I found three candidates on the ballot, Robert Frost, Stephen Benét, and Edna St. Vincent Millay. I voted for Frost, although he hasn't a touch of lyrical poetry in his six or eight volumes. His lines are poetic thought but not poetry. He is a fine rugged New England character and a rustic philosopher. I know his work and like it, but it is not poetry. Benét's work I do not know and Edna Millay does not seem to me quite worthy of the

Medal. In fact, there are no outstanding poets at this time. We have a multitude of singers of pretty songs, personal sonnets, but nothing large, so far as I know. We are a scrappy lot—all of us.

## HENRY B. FULLER

### JANUARY 1, 1901 [CHICAGO]

[*Fuller was one of Garland's closest friends for over thirty years. Between 1890 and 1901 he published eight books, including two important Chicago novels, but did very little writing for the remainder of his life until just before his death in 1929. A bachelor, he frequently visited the Garlands in West Salem and New York.*]

WE spent the day in work and in reading till eight when we went to the Nixons' to meet our Eagle's Nest friends in a little party. It was a charming little group of people. Fuller was there quaint as ever and easily the most interesting of all the men. He was, however, looking worn and haggard. His health is not good and he takes no great care of himself, especially as to his eating. He remains as remote as ever so far as his actual home life is concerned. No one calls on him at his rooming place—for the reason that no feels sure of a welcome. He lives in one little room and without the dignity which should be his.

### JUNE 26-27, 1908 [CHICAGO]

FULLER and I are cooking our own food here and getting along so well that women and hired girls seem superfluous. I am working on *The Shadow World* and Fuller is aiding by his suggestions and interest.

*     *     *

I cooked the steak at night and Fuller washed up the dishes. We sat talking the motives of life till nine o'clock. Fuller seems not to have any incentives left. Nothing interests him deeply. He said that he only lived in the hope of getting away to Italy. "I'd never come back." His attitude is absolutely hopeless. He has neither wife, child, nor home. He has no real interest, nothing to engage him and he is rapidly degenerating into a funny, slovenly old man, censorious of everything. I left at 10:30 for West Salem.

### SEPTEMBER 20, 1909 [WEST SALEM]

FULLER left at 8 a.m. He went in a rather depressed mood as if his trip up here had been a failure. Little things annoyed him: the katydids, the children, the noises of the trains, and the lack of heat in his room. He is getting more and more "notional" day by day and knows it and knows he can't help it.

It is a sorrowful thing to us, not humorous. He is quite pitiful in his loneliness and essential hopelessness of outlook. He regards himself as a failure.

### NOVEMBER 24, 1911 [CHICAGO]

[*Frederick Richardson was a Chicago artist.*]

THE Little Room was slimly attended today. I brought Henry B. and Fred Richardson home with me to dinner. We rallied Henry about his clothes and he said he was thinking of buying a new suit. At this I pretended to an attack of heart failure and Richardson dryly remarked that he would like to see that resolution carried out. Fuller admitted that he had not bought a new suit for ten years or such a matter. We thereupon remarked that it was all of ten years. We succeeded in making an impression on the old seed.

## ZONA GALE

### MARCH 25, 1900 [CHICAGO]

CAME home at five and took things easy till seven-thirty when we started for the South Side to take supper with Mrs. Herman Hall.

Zuliema went home with the Brownes and I came home alone. Zona Gale was there, a slender little woman of quiet rather wistful personality. She seemed so slight to make her way in a city. Her home is in Portage but she is meditating going to New York in some newspaper capacity. She told me she had reviewed some of my books for the Milwaukee papers. Her own work I do not know.

### DECEMBER 28, 1938 [LOS ANGELES]

[*Miss Gale's play*, Miss Lulu Bett, *won the Pulitzer Prize in 1921.*]

THE death of Zona Gale is announced in the papers this morning. Thus ends the life of one of our most beloved friends, a gentle and yet brave spirit. She was our neighbor in Wisconsin and a frequent visitor in Chicago and New York. We saw her last here, a few years ago, on her way back from Honolulu. She was loyal to her little native village and was never long away from it. She was a devoted daughter and remained unmarried till after they were gone. Her stories of village life have never been surpassed in some qualities— their sympathetic understanding and their quaint humor. She had a surprisingly effective method on the platform. Her quiet voice reached every ear, even in a large hall. She read her stories delightfully. As a member of the committee for the Pulitzer Prize one year, I was delighted to vote a prize for her *Lulu Bett*, a quaintly realistic play of village life. Her longer novels were less successful to my thinking.

## JOHN GALSWORTHY

### JANUARY 31, 1933 [LOS ANGELES]

JOHN GALSWORTHY has gone. He was only sixty-five but his work was done. His books of late were rather stodgy, heavy and repetitious. I lost interest in them some years ago. He was a fine, dignified, able writer, an altruist in feeling. He was *too* grave and philosophic. All his plays were, in effect, propaganda for something or some one. We met a few times here and a few times in England to my enrichment, for he was always thoughtful. He had no power to entertain, as Shaw always did. He was neither witty nor humorous. He told no stories and seldom uttered a picturesque phrase. He spoke with grace and precision but always in level tone, subdued, smoothly flowing and without emphasis. His eloquence was quiet. He had enthusiasms but never voiced them. A gray man, gray in dress, in comportment and in expression. A large figure but I doubt if he will last as long as Shaw.

## R. W. GILDER

### NOVEMBER 19, 1909 [CHICAGO]

[*Gilder had edited the* Century *from 1881 to his death.*]

WORD came this morning of the death of Richard Watson Gilder and I feel that a friend as well as a literary guide has been taken away. He was the first among the great editors to give me substantial encouragement and he has since been my adviser and elder brother.

I met him first in 1890—or possibly 1889—just after he had accepted *Flaxen* and one or two other of my short stories, and his letter to me was an inspiration.

He was an ideal American citizen in that he lived purely and helpfully as well as ambitiously. He was always the public spirited citizen, the patriot as well as the editor and the poet. He was a literary landmark. Of the old time editors, only Howells remains.

I sent greetings in the name of the club and put his black-bordered name on our wall, for he was an honorary member of our club.

## WILLIAM GILLETTE

### FEBRUARY 4, 1932 [LOS ANGELES]

*[Gillette died in 1937 at the age of eighty-two.]*

AT William Gillette's invitation we all saw *Sherlock Holmes*, his play written some forty years ago. It is a good, tense, well-played "yarn" of the detective sort so popular now in book form. Gillette concealed his age amazingly well. He read the lines as well as ever and was heartily cheered at the end of each exciting episode, but when he said, in Holmes' character, "What does it matter? What does anything matter?" I felt that he was expressing his own philosophy, and then, a little later, Holmes said, "In a short time nothing will matter." I forecast Gillette's own shortening span of life. This is undoubtedly his farewell to the stage and almost the final year of his life. He is a lonely man. He has no family, no close relatives. He will go back to his hermit-life on the Connecticut River and there await the sunset. He said over the phone, "I was glad to meet Mrs. Garland. It was love at first sight with me," and as he was going away he said, "I'd like to adopt this family but I'm a dodderer and I should dislike being a nuisance."

## ELLEN GLASGOW

### FEBRUARY 4, 1899 [NEW YORK]

AT 10:30 I went over to Hoboken to see Ellen Glasgow off to Monaco and Rome. She was looking rather pale but very pretty and joyously alert. The boat was a queer over-decorated stuffy little steamer. I would not go on that boat eighteen days for a thousand dollars. It made me ill to look in on the smelly little dining room.

DECEMBER 5, 1921 [NEW YORK]

[*Mrs. Frank Duke was Ellen Glasgow's closest friend. Joseph Hergesheimer and James Branch Cabell had achieved considerable fame because of their sexually provocative novels. Here and elsewhere Garland used "yellow streak" to mean raciness rather than cowardliness. In 1901 Cabell's cousin had been found dying on a Richmond porch not far from Mrs. Cabell's house. There were persistent rumors that Cabell had been involved in his death, and it was not until many years later that it was revealed that the cousin had been killed by the brothers of a seduced girl.*]

ELLEN GLASGOW and a Mrs. Duke (also from Richmond) were guests with us at Edwin Winter's last night. I had not seen Ellen for several years and I rather dreaded the ordeal for she was reported to be very deaf. She looked very well but the moment she spoke I perceived that she was less sensitive than when I talked with her last. Her voice had the flat tone of a deaf person.

Like many southern women she uses a shrill staccato, an excited tone which is unpleasant, but she manages her sounding box cleverly and remains cheerful withal.

She is a powerful personality, a brave thinker, one of the best in the South. She told me a good deal about Hergesheimer and Cabell. "They have formed a mutual admiration society," she said. Hergesheimer she does not like. She finds him cynical and a *poseur*. For Cabell she has a tender spot but considers him overrated and possessing a yellow streak. She declared that he had not killed the man who was found in front of his mother's house but Mrs. Duke differed. She said the circumstantial evidence was all against Cabell. The mother was a "gay" woman and the man a beast. "He ought to have been killed." Cabell was expelled from college and has been a recluse all his life. "Nevertheless, I like him," said Ellen. "His family had a degenerate side. He has some of this. His work shows it, especially *Jurgen* which I consider a base book."

## ZANE GREY

[*The office was that of Harper and Brothers; Harry Haynes was a Harper editor.*]

ZANE GREY was in the office when we went in, and I had a few minutes' conversation with him. I liked him better than I like his books. His eyes were fine, clear, and frank, his manner unassuming. He spoke of Tahiti where he has been to fish. He is much given to fishing. He has a home in Pasadena and another at Catalina Island. Haynes told me that he made more than a half-million dollars last year—more money than any other living author and more than any novelist of any time or place. His vogue is astounding and yet he appears to avoid publicity. Haynes said that he lived very quietly and that he avoided comment and social honors. He spoke of my *Back-Trailers* and said it made him eager to see England himself. "I've never been."

GREY was walking on deck as I came up at seven this morning. I introduced myself and for an hour we walked and talked about whales, sharks, swordfish, and finally of Arizona and New Mexico. The deeper I got into his thinking, the more I liked him. He is like his books, manly, adventurous, clean-minded and wholly American in his excellencies as well as in his faults. He lacks in literary subtlety and grace of speech just as in his writing. He was not in the least boastful as he might very well have been over men who like myself are failures from the commercial point of view.

It is plain that he feels his isolation from his fellow writers and is a bit bewildered by the failure of the critics to value his work for the excellence which he believes it to possess. He seemed to regard me as an elder and wiser brother and treated me with candid respect.

As for me, I regarded him as an amazingly significant literary phenomenon. He confirmed all his publisher's reports of his royalties and they were enormous, more than any other fictionist in our time or in any other time. He admitted immense losses during the last two years, "a million dollars" he said. "I used to get seventy-five thousand dollars for the serial rights of a novel and as much more for its rights as a motion picture. This year I have been offered as low as five thousand for the picture rights of a story. I refused and just before I sailed, I was offered forty-five thousand dollars for three of my stories."

He spoke of his early struggles, "I was in New York, hard pressed for money when I heard 'Buffalo Jones' lecture. I decided to ask him to take me west as a kind of chronicler and witness. He took me because of my *Betty Zane*, the story of a pioneer woman. This was my start."

He told me of his mother's asking him when a lad to sign the Francis Murphy pledge. "I did so and I have never tasted whiskey or any other intoxicant. I don't smoke and I don't tell smutty stories." These peculiarities increased my respect for him. They explained his stories, which are without offense in this way. He admitted that he found little companionship among the Hollywood men. "I hate all this pornography of Hollywood, as you do."

The longer we talked the more we had in common. We are both what would be called "puritans." He knows much of the Hollywood corruption and keeps clear of it. That he is a man of power of resolution, no one can deny. He has made his great sales as Edgar Wallace did, without resort to pornography, and what he lacks in literary taste and charm, he makes up in sincerity and vigor. Though a small man, he is astonishingly vital. "I work all the time." He told of writing his first book in a bare room with a chair and stove. He described his present study, forty feet square. "I now have a place to work," he said, "but most of my work was written in barns and huts or on a fishing boat. Now I have a real workshop and I feel like writing in it." There was something very attractive in his candor.

## SIMON GUGGENHEIM

### APRIL 25, 1926 [NEW YORK]

*[The second Guggenheim brother present was probably Daniel, who also lived in Port Washington.]*

MRS. S. R. GUGGENHEIM sent her car for us and took us out to Port Washington to her million-dollar home. Simon Guggenheim and his wife and Elmer Schlesinger and one or two others were present. The house, enormous, elaborate and filled with costly furniture, was rather appalling in its effect on me. It did not awe me as in other days it might have done. It wearied me and disheartened me. So much useless luxury, so much striving, so much to be explained. If I had a million dollars per year, I would not live in such a house.

The two Guggenheim men were pleasant and patient with me, and Simon and I enthused over Colorado together. It was not easy for me to realize in any degree the power of these two quiet, under-size Jews whose firm is known all over the world. They were smiling, quite unassuming and plainly dressed, but they talked of interests in Alaska and Chile, and of plans for cheaper production of copper and nitrates with the note of certainty in their voices. They live in ducal homes but they are really very simple men in other ways. Their women go in for splendor but they are less concerned with it.

## GEORGE ELLERY HALE

### JANUARY 7, 1929 [LOS ANGELES]

*[Hale was one of the founders of the California Institute of Technology. He and Garland had probably met during the 1890's when Hale was at the University of Chicago.]*

A SPECIAL delivery letter came in the afternoon inviting us to call upon George Ellery Hale at his solar laboratory in Pasadena at five o'clock. This we did. His work shop, a two-story white building, stood amid a grove of orange trees, and when we knocked at its rather forbidding front door, it was opened by his secretary. On entering this, the front hall, we caught a glimpse of Hale, a gray-haired man, sitting in a low easy chair reading by the light of a lamp before the fire. A delightful picture of scholarly ease. He rose alertly to meet us, a slender, medium-sized man of delicate and refined aspect, cordial, simple, hospitable. His moustache, clipped close above his mouth, made his smiling lips a prominent feature. His glance through his spectacles was direct and genial. There was nothing austere or remote about him. Nothing of the great astronomer. On the contrary he spent nearly half an hour telling us of the Huntington Library and its marvellous collection of books and MSS. In truth he had been instrumental in organizing this library and is one of its directors now. He told of the almost haphazard way in which Huntington began his collection and of how it had grown upon his hands. He spoke of one enormous collection of English papers—nearly a million pieces—which they had not had time to examine or list, of incalculable value. Also of American papers and letters.

At last he began to tell us of the great new telescope which is coming, double the size of the largest now in use, but coming too late for him to use. He is seventy-nine and will be eighty by the time the new lens is in position. He can not hope to look through it, and he knows this. He is starting on a cruise tomorrow to secure a complete rest. He admitted a physical breakdown some years ago and I could feel in his voice a conviction that his work was almost done. He has made a world-wide reputation and must now retire from the line.

## BRET HARTE

### MAY 5, 1899 [LONDON]

COMING back to my hotel I met Kinross and then called on Thring of the Authors' Society. He was also very friendly. Spoke of meeting the Authors' Club. I then went to call on Bret Harte, whom I found living in the West End. Lancaster Gate. Bachelor apartments. He was affable and polite but looked old and burnt out, his eyes clouded, his skin red and flabby. He has lived hard and fast, that is evident.

## JULIAN HAWTHORNE

### JANUARY 17, 1930 [SAN FRANCISCO]

[*The son of Nathaniel Hawthorne, Julian had been a successful writer until he was convicted of mail fraud in 1913 and spent six months in the penitentiary.*]

To find myself confronting Julian Hawthorne was like meeting a ghost out of the past. I had not seen him for over thirty years and I remembered him as a powerful, confident, and happy man. Here now came a small, thin, gray octogenarian with dim eyes and uncertain memory. At first I could find nothing familiar in his features, but gradually I detected remembered lines and movements. We talked of his noble father, of his family, of Emerson and Concord but carefully avoided all mention of his trouble over the Lowell interview and his punishment as an accomplice in a fraudulent scheme, concerning which I hold him to have been an injured man. His career is almost tragic in its contrasts. When I went to Boston in 1884, he was one of the most brilliant and promising of the younger men of that time. Son of a most illustrious father, he was a successful writer in his own way, and then things went wrong or he went wrong, and he was checked in his upward course like a bird shot on the wing. For forty years or near it he has lived obscurely, almost forgotten, yet here he is an active mind in a fairly vigorous body at eighty-four. I liked him in those elder days, and I found him admirably gentle and controlled and understanding today. He is both the man of letters and the gentleman, and not embittered.

### AUGUST 28, 1933 [LOS ANGELES]

PAUL JORDAN SMITH and his former wife, Sara Bixby, came for me and drove me down to Newport Beach to have tea with Julian Hawthorne. He and his devoted younger wife are living in three rooms over a garage, a very humble place indeed for a son of Nathaniel Hawthorne. It was incredible—and yet this man is the link between Tennyson's age and that of Robert Frost. He has failed in mental strength and physical vigor since I saw him last. He has shrunk in size and has in the face the shadow of approaching death. He cannot stay long and I took his hand in parting with a feeling that we should not meet again. I urged him to let me come down and fetch him home to lunch someday soon, but he definitely refused. "I hate to motor," he said, "and it tires me." He said he was writing busily on his autobiography and I urged him to put it all in. "Don't leave out any recollection of the writers of that time. No one else can take your place. You are the last." He said he could still peck at the typewriter and that he often did a thousand words at a sitting.

## WILLIAM RANDOLPH HEARST

### JUNE 14, 1923 [LONDON]

*[Shearn had been a justice of the New York State Supreme Court.]*

THE Shearns came to dinner, and Mrs. Shearn, after the children had all gone to the theater, gave us an hour's talk on W. R. Hearst and his wife's trials and good works.

"Hearst made five millions of dollars from his papers last year," said Mrs. Shearn. She likes Mrs. Hearst and as she knows her well this judgment has weight. She said, "Judge Shearn and I have travelled with the Hearsts many times and for months at a time so that I know them."

She said, "Hearst does not drink or smoke and he loves fine and beautiful things but he is a libertine in thought and act." He believes in giving the people what they want. "If they want obscenity I am for putting it into my magazine."

She said Judge Shearn remonstrated with him about this and that he cynically replied, "That's what they want and that's what I am going to give 'em." "He really thinks that he is on the side of the people," Mrs. Shearn said, "and he takes that way to get at them." He is now concerned with another woman so openly that every one knows it. He is the most corrupting single soul in America.

## JAMES A. HERNE

### MAY 13, 1901 [WEST SALEM]

LATE mail today brought report that Herne was dying in Chicago. I at once got off a wire of sympathy to Mrs. Herne. I fear the worst. The old man had felt the effects of his hard drinking each time more keenly and his superb constitution was undermined and laid open to the grippe. He seemingly could not come to Chicago without falling into the hands of some one who could and did destroy him. Who they were I do not know but they belonged to the underworld.

He was his own worst enemy. A man of great powers and of great charm even when in liquor, which he used too frequently. He was, after all is said and done, the most original of our dramatists.

## ROBERT HERRICK

### FEBRUARY 18, 1906 [CHICAGO]

[*Boston-bred and Harvard-educated, Herrick had come to the University of Chicago in 1893. Although frequently critical of Chicago life in his fiction, he remained until 1923. He suffered from a weak heart most of his later life.*]

WE dined with the Judsons meeting Robert Herrick and two or three other of the University people. Herrick has grown older but his self-restraint is quite as marked as ever. I liked his unemotional manner. With us he seemed less grouchy than he sometimes is at receptions and dinners. He appears unhappy in Chicago.

### APRIL 1, 1906 [CHICAGO]

WE dined at Lorado's, called at the Hales's for their musical, and took supper at the Halls's. I had some talk with Herrick at the Hales's. He was sitting apart, looking like a tired boy, his face rosy and impassive, his eyes clear, his brow smooth, and yet I knew that he was not at ease. He lightened at our coming and seemed quite another spirit as he talked with us. I don't think he is deeply interested in his fellow educators.

### MAY 16, 1907 [CHICAGO]

HERRICK called looking very well but not feeling at all himself. He talked of a stay on a ranch. He has been suffering like myself from growing old and finds his work going hard. I felt my own gray hairs quiver on my head as we talked together.

### APRIL 30, 1908 [CHICAGO]

IN the afternoon we went to tea at Salisbury's house and I took a walk with Herrick and Lovett. Herrick looked thinner and older, strange, too, as the bones of his face showed plainer. He said he felt well, better than for years. It is rather curious but I do not find either Herrick or Lovett congenial. There is something in their thought which is alien and repellent.

### MARCH 28, 1921 [NEW YORK]

I WENT to the club to meet Brander Matthews and talk things over. Robert Herrick came in at three just as I was going out. He looked like a handsome old man—familiar yet remote. He has finished his work for the year at Chicago and is East to work on a new book. He has not quite lived up to his promise. He has been too hard, too un-sympathetic, and his writing has lacked charm. Since the war, and indeed before the war, he had become in a sense the journalist. If he were to do a really fine work now it would bring him back to a place where he might be considered for the Academy.

## BRONSON HOWARD

### MARCH 24, 1906 [NEW YORK]

[*Theodore Roosevelt had accused a number of nature writers of sentimentalizing their semifictional accounts of animal life. Howard's last important play was* Shenandoah (*1888*). *He died in 1908.*]

AT the club at dinner Bronson Howard and I fell into talk on John

Burroughs and Seton and the nature-faking controversy. He seemed very well and very alert, but his work is done. He writes no more and has no desire to do so. He had "lost the knack of it," as Hamilton Wright Mabie said of Cable.

Some men go on into age with the creative power glowing but Howard, even while he is physically vigorous, can no longer make dramatic characters live. This is natural and in order.

## WILLIAM DEAN HOWELLS

### DECEMBER 29, 1898 [NEW YORK]

AT the Herald Square Theatre I found the Hernes rehearsing in a new play. They were all glad to see me—apparently. Then went to call on Mr. Howells. He looks old and sad but laughter is ready yet. He went from grave to gay so swiftly it made his dark moods seem fleeting. Yet I feel under all a growing weariness of the world and of striving. His family ties him down to the city, which he detests.

### OCTOBER 24, 1899 [CHICAGO]

[*George Ade was a humorist, Will Payne a novelist, Holmes a travel lecturer, and Field (brother of Eugene Field) a journalist.*]

INTENDED to breakfast with Mr. Howells but did not get down in time. I found him in, and we had a good talk. He was profoundly interested in Z. and made most minute inquiries about her. He went to see ex-governor Altgelt at 10 and I came home.

At one I met Ade and Payne, the novelist, Burton Holmes and Roswell Field and we all sat at Fuller's lunch, with Mr. Howells as chief guest. A very pleasant party indeed and Howells charmed them all by his kindly, alert humor, his interest in them, and his modesty. He was one of us, absolutely unaffected and simple.

### JANUARY 3, 1900 [NEW YORK]

*[Mildred was Howells' daughter.]*

ALTHOUGH I rose late I did some work on the *Hustler* while Z. went to call on some of her friends in the art world. We met at Mr. Howells' at lunch. Mr. H. was very more than usually charming and interesting, for he liked Z. Mrs. H. did not appear.

This is as near as Howells ever comes to entertaining. A couple of friends at lunch. I have never known him to give a dinner or a formal lunch. Mildred receives at tea of an afternoon but nothing more. Whether this is due to Mrs. Howells or to the Dean himself I do not know. I suspect to both. They dread the burden of such entertainment, not so much in the cost perhaps as in the care and worry and planning. Perhaps when younger they felt otherwise.

### MARCH 26, 1906 [NEW YORK]

I FOUND my way to Mr. Howells during the morning and we had a good intimate talk of old times and new. He is growing old rapidly but his mind is clear and his humor ready—not as ready as it used to be but on tap nevertheless. He strongly advised me to write a story based on my Boston experiences and to do it now. Nearing seventy he still is hale and sound of wind and limb and yet I could not but realize that he is aging and that ten years more would make him an octogenarian. He was most kind as always and most penetrating in comment.

### DECEMBER 11, 1910 [NEW YORK]

I HAD tea with Mr. Howells who talked and laughed with vigor. I spoke of the times when men and women had no nice warm underclothing and did not run away to Bermuda to avoid the cold. "I had no underclothing at all," said Howells, "and neither did my father. And yet I set type in winter in a thin-walled shanty with coat off. We suffered terribly with chilblains," he added.

MAY 8, 1918 [NEW YORK]

ZULIME and I called on Howells—or rather I called first and she came later. I found him looking very old and tragically sad. He feels himself to be at the end of things. I tried not to let down in his presence but I had a feeling that this was the last time I would see him. He seemed but a ghost of his former self as I saw him last on the street corner waving to me. He looked ninety years old. It filled my throat with pain. He goes to Kittery but when comes back?

NOVEMBER 16, 1919 [NEW YORK]

*[Howells died on May 11, 1920.]*

WITH the children I called on Howells at noon. They looked very handsome and he was pleased with them. He was, as always, kindly, considerate, and tactful. As we came away, Mary Isabel alluded to the fact that while John Burroughs spoke like a farmer, Howells talked as beautifully as he wrote. Burroughs has built up an art of writing but he speaks as he was instructed when a boy. Howells grew up in a home of good English. As we came away I had a feeling that we might never see him again but he may come through the winter, after all, for his heart is in better condition than last year, so Mildred told us, but he is fading out of the web of American life.

[1920-1925]

[MEETINGS WITH AUTHORS. LECTURE NOTES]

*[Howells had begun moving frequently in the mid-1880's. Garland first met Howells at Lee's Hotel in the early summer of 1887. Howells' letter on the Chicago anarchists appeared in the* New York Tribune *in November 1887. The Quality of Mercy was published in 1892 rather than 1894. Howells' contract with Harper's for a fixed yearly income began in 1900. Garland's*

article on Howells' Boston, "William Dean Howells' Boston:
*A Posthumous Pilgrimage," appeared in the* Boston Evening
Transcript *on May 22, 1920. "Red Top" (it had a red roof) was
designed by Mrs. Howells' brother, William R. Mead. Howells'
wife was increasingly an invalid after the death of their daughter Winifred in 1889. It is unlikely that* The Minister's Charge
*(1886) was written at Red Top.*]

MY first meeting. Lee's Hotel, Auburndale, Massachusetts. Meeting
at Little Nahant. The talk on the hillside. He brought me down to
the little rustic gate which let into the road across the marsh to the
station. "There lies your way," he said with a smile. And as I turned
and made off it was a way of lighted stars and gleaming water, a
way of glory. However, I did not consider it prophetic. The meeting
on the hills at Watertown. "The sawposts." The old Brooks place.

Howells was always moving and no matter where he moved I
visited him. In Belmont, in Watertown, in New York City on 59th
Street, at Far Rockaway, at Kittery Point, at York Harbor, at W. 57th
Street and at innumerable hotels. At times he was surrounded by
books and appeared the scholarly literary worker, but mostly he
was in temporary quarters—Hotel Albert—dining at French cafés.
He had many callers and was genial but contrived to have them do
most of the talking.

On these visits he often read to me something he was at work
upon. Often I sought his advice on something I was at work upon.
Our talk was never frivolous or casual. Sometimes we went for a
walk talking incessantly on all kinds of topics, but not infrequently
upon social reform, for he was very deeply impatient of injustice in
those early days. He read Bellamy and Morris, but I could never get
him to read Henry George, although he admitted that there was
much in the land question. He was a gentle theoretic socialist.

He used to go abroad almost every summer, often to Carlsbad,
sometimes to Italy, and he was more and more outspoken against
the growing despotism of the military party in Germany. He gave

me my first conception of that menace. He read German and Italian and Spanish, and he was one of the first to introduce Russian writers to us. He wrote of Tolstoy and Gogol and Turgeneff and sympathized with the radicals in Russia who were resolute to destroy the tyranny of the Tzar.

He influenced Mark Twain to take up these reform ideas, and *The Prince and the Pauper* [and *A Connecticut*] *Yankee* [in] *King Arthur's Court* were due to Howells almost directly.

He was the recipient of innumerable volumes of poetry and fiction by young writers and when one came with the breath of life in it he acknowledged it and wrote of it in his department in *Harper's Magazine*. He was most generous and kindly but where his interest was not engaged he could not be brought to palliate or gloze.

He was always of a quiet unassailable dignity and yet was unassuming, almost shy. At a hotel he avoided notice as much as possible. He came and went silently, unobtrusively, almost humbly, and yet he was not humble. He was merely modest and tasteful. His sense of humor made all pretense childish. He pretended to nothing. Gentle as he was, modest as he seemed, he could be granite where a principle was involved. He could not be scared or put down. In the case of the Chicago anarchists he spoke out because he felt they had not been justly tried. His letter, short but of scorching power, was widely copied. Some of his friends regretted this letter but those of us who knew him understood it. It was a righteous protest in his way of thinking.

Even when he lived most spaciously he lived very simply, almost meagerly. He liked good food but not feasts or banquets or show viands. He was a gourmet and not a gourmand. He often spoke of some special dish which he had found at this or that obscure French or Italian restaurant. He enjoyed a dish with exotic savour, something which revived old memories of France or Spain or Italy but he groaned when invited to long, drawn out, smoky banquets.

He used no tobacco and no liquor except wine and this he drank sparingly and for its association.

He was careless of dress, not slovenly but just negligent. He kept in the conventional styles of coats and collars not because he cared, only because on the whole it was easier.

He dreaded public appearances. To preside at a meeting, or to lecture, was distasteful. At a time when everyone wanted to see him he shrank from going upon the platform, and from going to large parties or receptions. His face would cloud and his tone become petulant when importuned to preside at a meeting, or to be a guest of honor at a dinner. Almost the only times I ever heard him speak sharply was in protesting against some such demand on the part of his admirers. Part of this arose from comments of reporters.

He loved to mix with people who paid no attention to him as a celebrity and many times he said to me with a certain mournfulness, "If only I could go about as I once did, unnoticed, and study people without finding them on dress parade." Once he said to me, "Make your studies while you can. By and by it will be impossible for you to go to a boarding house or country hotel without being found out." He never permitted people to make a "lion" of him. He showed more temper about this than any other.

His habits of work were methodical. He sat at his desk every morning. Lunching at one he usually went for a walk. As he grew older he took a nap after lunch. At five he was nearly always at home and served tea to whoever might come in. He made few calls and those he made were brief and ceremonious, but humorous. He never permitted himself to enter upon a long argument or harangue.

In all my long experience I never heard him monologue. He conversed. He loved witty, humorous, touch-and-go yet penetrating conversation. He would listen patiently to my harangues but never argued at length. He had the faculty of putting his dissent into a paragraph, or even into a line, which left me silent with confusion.

For all his gentleness, his kindness, he remained remote to me.

He appeared a lonely soul after all. He had few friends in the sense in which Bacheller and I, or Paine and I, are friends. He neighbored with no one though kindly with all. He was not a boon companion with anyone. His courtesy was exquisite and never-failing, but he was never familiar. It is hard to define the quality which defended him from those who would call him "Bill" or "Will." No one in his presence presumed. He was not reticent but he never told a long story or held the floor for a long exegesis. His remarks were concise, to the point and usually humorous. He loved quick retorts. His mind seized on what his visitors said before they could finish.

I have heard him tell with gentle humor of Holmes and Long-fellow sitting at the head of the table and talking for all the others.

Whether his wandering habit arose from the restless spirit of his invalid wife or not I cannot say, but he seldom spent a second winter in the same place. But his summers for many years were spent either at York Harbor or Kittery Point, Maine.

He cared little for music. At least I have heard him speak of opera as the most unreal of arts and while he likes certain songs, I do not recall that he cared about orchestral music. His interests were literary and sociologic.

Undoubtedly his short body and large head had much to do with keeping him from the platform. I recall once that he was hurt by some jocular reporter's reference to his figure. He was always at a disadvantage in a throng and he felt it. He was a poor presiding officer and of late never appears in that capacity. He knew little of parliamentary procedure and was impatient of ceremony.

He had no settled creed and though he believed in immortality he confessed that it was more an act of faith than of reason.

Without his humor he was a sad man. His mind was too keen, too inclusive not to feel the folly of human wisdom. His moods were Celtic, for he was of Welsh descent.

He earned a great deal of money and lived well but not lavishly. He never gave dinners or receptions. He seldom gave a lunch, but was regularly at home at five o'clock when he served tea. I don't know why he so seldom gave dinners or luncheons, whether it rose from a feeling that it was a useless expense or from a distaste for company. I could never decide. He seldom invited one to lunch or dinner, though he several times asked me to visit him at his summer place.

He told me once that he had many relations dependent upon him and as he travelled a great deal, he felt the necessity of care in the matter of expenditure.

He loved the theater and often went, especially to the first-night performances.

He was never a generous host. Perhaps his early training in economy has given him so strong a habit of saving that he cannot break it, even when he became rich. He loved to discover curious out-of-the-way restaurants like "The Black Cat" and certain Italian places, largely for their old-world flavor, for the associated memories which they called up. He usually went with his wife and daughters. I never knew him to take more than one or two guests.

His highest point was at about 1894 when he sold the serial rights of *The Quality of Mercy* for $10,000. It seemed a large sum then but is small compared to prices paid popular writers of today. He never made large sums from his writings but when Harper and Brothers reorganized they agreed to pay him ten thousand dollars a year for fifteen years. At least this is my understanding of the contract.

For many years his home was in Kittery or York Harbor, Maine. His life there was very simple. He worked every morning at his desk; in the afternoon he walked or worked about his garden. His home at York Harbor was a plain brick cottage of the simplest American type without architectural charm. It stood a little back from the sea. In taking me about the place he expressed a humorous yet tender interest in the trees and shrubs. It was all very bare and meager—like my own home. Books, magazines indicated something of the owner's interest but there was nothing distinctive in the house.

Although instructed in the Swedenborgian faith he was, so far as I know, of no special religious conviction. He was humorous but he was tragically sad in his later years, as was Clemens.

On the 17th of May, [1920], in company with two old friends, Thomas S. Perry and Joseph Edgar Chamberlin, I set out to discover the various houses in which Howells had lived in and about Boston. Perry, the most authoritative of all the survivors of Howells, was able to point out the places for us, and I entered each place and made inquiry.

Forty years and more had made great changes and few remembered anything about Howells, for he was only a slight, unobtrusive sub-editor in 1870. Even when he lived at Belmont, I don't imagine many knew him. He lived first in Sacramento Street, 1866 to 1870. Three Berkley Street, 1870-1874. Gave reception to Hay there, also to Bret Harte. Had a miserable study. No way of heating it. Two parlors. A small dark dining room. Fiske a neighbor.

Moved from there to Concord house in 1874. Red Top built in 1878. He had a real home at last. It was lonely for Mrs. H. Hence he left it. He planted all the trees and watered them all one summer with his own hand. Had two mulberry trees, one he called "William" and the other "Elinor." Elinor died some years ago and William died last year. "From Venice as far as Belmont is my married life." He called his study "The Cabin" and the north porch "The Deck." He called this "the prettiest house I ever saw." He loved it but it had no telephone, no railway nearer than Belmont. His wife was ill and so was Winifred. He sold it in 1882. He wrote here:

> Dr. Breen's Practice
> A Modern Instance
> A Woman's Reason
> The Minister's Charge
> Undiscovered Country

Nothing could have been more unlike Venice than these bare com-

monplace little frame cottages in Cambridge, but the Red Top
home had charm. The Cambridge houses utterly commonplace, not
in the least like Howells. They were like the homes of working
people.

He never entertained partly on account of his wife's health and
partly because he could not afford to do so. She was very nervous
and entirely unable to cope with the preparations for a large dinner.

He was of Christlike patience with her, always waiting upon her.
She was always asking him to close a window—or open it.

His life is contemporaneous with the real American literature. It
began with him and Clemens, Bret Harte, Joaquin Miller, Cable
and John Hay. 1871 is the date, approximately.

He had few intimate friends, none in the sense in which most
men speak of their intimates. He was singularly aloof. Perfectly
amiable, he did not inspire intimacy. He was the onlooker. He took
a kindly interest in many people. He acknowledged an affection for
a few but it was not easy for him to show it.

He had many admirers, many callers, many acquaintances but
few intimates. He was singularly aloof even in his intimate circle.
Never stiff, never formal, ready to laugh or jest and quick to retort,
he nevertheless did not invite familiarity. He called no man by his
first name. It was never "Ned Stedman" or "Dick Gilder" with
him. I think he did speak of Thomas Sergeant Perry as "Tom" but
he had known Perry since 1867. This regard for the personality of
others was deeply characteristic of him. He was just and fine
though keenly critical.

## ARCHER HUNTINGTON

### MARCH 9, 1926 [NEW YORK]

*[The adopted son of Collis P. Huntington (one of the "Big
Four" of the Southern Pacific Railroad), Archer Huntington*

*was an art collector, a Hispanophile, and a philanthropist. He
and Anna Hyatt were married in 1923. Both he and Garland
were on the Board of Directors of the American Academy during the 1920's.]*

As Anna Hyatt Huntington had expressed an interest in Lorado, we
arranged a date when he could go in to tea at the Huntington
palace on 5th Avenue. Lorado had never been in the house before
and marvelled over its size, its curious arrangement of rooms. Naturally the sculpture and painting caught his eyes, as we walked
through, but his interest was in the tall, blonde, plain woman
whom he considers one of the chief woman sculptors in America.
She held his interest, for she has dignity, keen intellectual powers
and remarkable directness of diction.

Huntington was very humorous and uttered many gay paradoxes.
He likes Zulime and sparred with her over the charge of "arrogance." Lorado quite won him, too, and in truth Lorado was at his
best, unassuming but self-contained. He talked well and just
enough and was not (as he sometimes is) deprecatory. He is a great
figure and I hate to see him "meaching" in any presence. It was a
pleasant and intellectually gay hour. We all enjoyed it. Huntington
has a wide interest in the arts. He reads much and I am told writes
verse, although I do not know that. His wealth is enormous and the
translation of Anna Hyatt from her studio in Greenwich Village
to this palace is as romantic as a fairy story. I have seen her studio
and the room in which she and Archer Huntington were married
and the contrast between that workshop and the rooms in which
she received us is as great as that between the conventional woods-
man's hut and the royal palace of story. Furthermore, she now has
ample studio space in another building and the complete privacy
which she has so long needed. "Why is it," she asked, "that people
break in on an artist's privacy? Is it because, as we work with our
hands, they think our minds are not employed?" She smiled as she

said this but I could see that she had lost many days for such inter-
ruptions. She now has full opportunity to do her utmost and while
she is rather secretive about it, she suggested that her imagination
was active and that small forms were rising round her in the big
studio.

## MARCH 8, 1927 [NEW YORK]

HUNTINGTON and his wife came to the studio to hear Hardesty and
Isabel give a part of their program. They were deeply pleased with
my youngsters. Zulime could not go but Constance was on hand to
give the comedy touch—a mood in which Huntington joined. He
was amusing as a college wag. He joked and made fun of his book
*The Cid* and bantered me as well as the girls. He was deeply
moved by Mary Isabel's reading and had many fine words to say of
Hardy. Anna Hyatt was less demonstrative but none the less
pleased. He told us about his translations and of the Cid. He helped
on the pronunciation of the words and suggested other Spanish
songs and poems. No one could have been more delightfully informal. We forgot his vast house, his many millions, his museum
of paintings. He was just a big kindly neighbor. He brought us all
home in his car keeping up his mood of jocularity.

## MAY 17, 1930 [NEW YORK]

[*Garland was planning to resign from the Board of Directors of
the American Academy because of his projected move to California.*]

HUNTINGTON called up and asked me to come in at 1 E. 89th, and
this I did. As he had told me to come to No. 3, I did so and found myself at a door which looked like the door of a garage. I was met by a
woman who took me up to the great hall filled with pictures and
pieces of sculpture. There I waited till she came and took me one
story higher. What a maze of houses and rooms his home is! He met
me heartily, and we had an hour's talk on the Academy, on his

museums, on his latest benefactions. He said, "I've done nothing but give money—that's easy. You fellows have done all the work."

He has founded nine museums, so he told me, his latest a naval or marine museum. He has a museum obsession. He believes in storing the records of the nation. He has amply provided for the Academy's action but does not much believe in action. He is content to have it be rather than do. He was frank to say that he didn't like the idea of my resigning from the board. "Wait awhile," he said.

## W. W. JACOBS

### SEPTEMBER 8, 1922 [LONDON]

THE daughters were up early but not very eager for a trip to Wheathampstead. We found Jacobs waiting for us at [the] station. He had aged greatly in sixteen years. He is now a thin, gray, sharp-faced man of exactly fifty-nine. It turned out to be his birthday. His home, a substantial and pleasant brick house, is about a half mile up the road to the west. I found Mrs. Jacobs greatly changed but still a lovely woman. Her black hair is touched with gray but the greatest change is in her expression. She is very sad under her smiling. She had grown quite deaf so that she missed much of what was said, but this is not what saddens her. I think she feels that her husband and children do not care enough about her to make her hear and so she retires into herself. Jacobs is an ailing man, or perhaps only a failing man. His vitality, always small, is ebbing. He realizes as does Kipling and Hewlett that he is a passing man. This whole generation of men, my contemporaries, is ceasing to produce. They still loom high on the horizon but they are figures largely. Will the generation behind us do as well? I suppose every generation has made the same comment upon its succeeding wave.

## ROBERT UNDERWOOD JOHNSON

### OCTOBER 14, 1937 [LOS ANGELES]

[*Garland and Johnson had been closely associated in the National Institute and the American Academy.*]

ROBERT UNDERWOOD JOHNSON is reported to have died last night. He has been a factor in my life for nearly half a century. He was assistant editor for the *Century* when I began to write for it. He was a tall, bearded, handsome fellow with full, red lips, and I disliked his supercilious manner when dealing with me. He was in truth kindly and appreciative but he had an insufferable air of authority, an attitude which Gilder never assumed. Later we became very good friends. He was [a] reformer who never lost zeal.

## HOWARD MUMFORD JONES

### JULY 14, 1912 [WEST SALEM]

[*The novel was eventually titled* The Forester's Daughter *(1914).*]

A YOUNG man from La Crosse came up in the afternoon and I revised *Not in the Service Book*, going over the earlier MS. It was very hot work but we stuck to it.

Later comment: This young fellow, the son of a poor widow in La Crosse, developed a considerable power as a writer and later published a book of verse. He became a teacher of literature in a southern university and continues to write. He was an expert typist and was of pleasant service to me for several weeks.

### OCTOBER 11, 1932 [LOS ANGELES]

HOWARD MUMFORD JONES, a young man who, some twenty years ago, did some typewriting for me in West Salem, came to luncheon today, a man of forty, tall, bald and sandy-haired. After some fifteen years' experience as a professor of literature, he has won the Guggenheim scholarship and is here to make research in the Huntington Library. He is to go to England and Ireland soon and has undertaken to write a life of Tom Moore, a singular commission. He is a fine, scholarly, dignified midwestern product with almost no local accent of any sort. He is at work just now on some such thesis as this: "The Influence of English Thought on America in 1800." And when I think of him as the tall bare-headed youth with his typewriter under his arm striding across my garden twenty years ago, I find difficulty in making the personalities coalesce.

## OTTO KAHN

### DECEMBER 10, 1921 [NEW YORK]

THE School Art League luncheon was a rather interesting affair but my own part in it was not important. I came last and by the time I was called upon the audience had thinned out. I spoke but a few minutes on matters not clearly connected and felt like the failure that I was. I doubt if I could have said anything with a half-hour allotment. Otto Kahn who lives in an enormous Italian palace on Fifth Avenue spoke to me of my talk at the Town Hall and wanted to know where I lived. I told him. He was quite interested. "You are a neighbor of mine." It made me laugh to think of his probable notion of *where* I lived and *how* I lived. His home is one of the largest, the most magnificent, the most lavishly, foolishly grandiose of this new world, and yet as a Jew he feels the lines drawn against him. Moreover, many people regarded him as a pro-German during the war. Of this I am not competent to speak. So far as my knowledge of him goes, he is a kindly, cultured little man, especially interested in the drama and in art matters of all kinds.

## RUDYARD KIPLING

### JULY 18, 1929 [ONTEORA]

[*Garland was preparing* Roadside Meetings, *which has a chapter on Kipling. The entire Kipling family had come down with pneumonia when visiting New York in February 1899. Kipling and his wife survived, but they lost their daughter. Frank N. Doubleday was at that time a member of McClure and Doubleday, Kipling's American publisher.*]

IN writing about Kipling and his illness in 1899, I was reminded of the present condition of those three men. Doubleday is in bad health and letting go of the great business he has built up. Bok, immensely rich, has quit editorial work altogether and has ceased to write so far as I know. He, too, is said to be in wretched health. Kipling is an old man who writes no more and is seldom noticed in the press. And I, not much better off physically, sit here making record of my betters. Doubleday's devotion to Kipling during his illness in New York was heroic. He gave up his days and his nights to the sick man's service. Whether Kipling still retains grateful memory of this or not I cannot say, but my impression is that he does not. Bok has just erected a great bell tower in Florida and imported for it a superb chime of bells. A lovely thing to do but a singular extravagance. Of Doubleday I hear nothing. He, too, spends his winters in Florida—and we were all so young and confident thirty years ago.

## SINCLAIR LEWIS

### JUNE 15, 1923 [LONDON]

[*St. John Ervine was a popular English playwright. Lewis was visiting England and the Continent after the great success of* Babbitt.]

AT four-thirty we took a bus round to Ervine's where we had tea in most informal fashion. Ervine looked rather tired and dispirited. Is going away soon. He told of Sinclair Lewis' antics here. "He is a dreadful bore!" said Ervine, "He swears, talks interminably, shouts across the room. He is drinking a lot. He went down to visit Wells for a week end and nearly drove Wells insane. We don't care what he said about us last fall but he thinks we have it in for him on that account. We dislike him because he is a bore and has no manners."

## ALICE AND IRENE LEWISOHN

### JULY 17, 1917 [NEW YORK]

WE dined at Walter Ehrich's meeting the Lewisohn sisters, two very thoughtful, very wealthy and very philanthropic women. Of immense wealth, unmarried and rather plain, they nevertheless have a great deal of dignity and charm. Alice told me much of Lloyd George, whom she knows. One of her sisters lives in England and their wealth enables them to meet many people of distinction. I liked both the girls very well. They are able and sincere, though lacking in humor. They made up for that by a kind of frank radicalism and broad sympathy. Both are undoubted feminists.

## ABRAHAM LINCOLN

### FEBRUARY 12, 1926 [NEW YORK]

AT the Town Hall Club luncheon to Sir Arthur Currie of McGill University, Ely called on me to speak. I said very briefly what is my conviction in regard to Lincoln. He is now a kind of vague universal figure into whose life and words each of us can read his own interpretation. In truth he was a very simple character without subtleties, shades, or mysteries. He was just what he claimed to be, a country lawyer and politician with deep love of country and a neighborly feeling for all men. He wrote only moderately well and his position was not always free from expediency but in the eyes of our hero-needing age he is endowed with all wisdom and all patriotism. He has become a subject of orations, historic theses, and subtle essays. Nevertheless he remains the same country lawyer who acted from the simplest motives and saw no mystery in his course.

## VACHEL LINDSAY

### MARCH 23, 1915 [NEW YORK]

*[Juliet is Juliet Wilbor Tompkins.]*

AT night Juliet came down to dine with me and to see the portrait. Afterward we went to the MacDowell Club and heard Vachel Lindsay recite his poems, which he does with great spirit. A small audience enjoyed his singular exhibition. The "Congo" and "Booth" poems were the chief numbers to most of the hearers but to me they were the least valuable of all the pieces. He was well dressed and looked quite citified but nothing will ever take a certain open air quality from his performance. He is a stump speaker in manner and voice.

## AMY LOWELL

### FEBRUARY 23, 1916 [NEW YORK]

AMY LOWELL spoke at the MacDowell Club on "The New Verse" and made the occasion a lively one. She is huge physically but her mind is keen and her spirit undimmed. At the close of her address she sat down with a challenge to all, "Come on—now for the fray." Helen Gray Cone made an eloquent rejoinder and kept her poise admirably when Amy came back at her. Margaret Widdemer was very lovely to look at and very humorous. May Robinson was fine, but we men were all intimidated. MacKaye said a few halting words and Untermeyer glibly argued with Amy. It was an amusing time. Certainly poetry is looking up when it can show so much humor in its advocates. The women came off especially well.

## MRS. HAROLD F. McCORMICK

### MAY 19, 1911 [CHICAGO]

[*Mrs. McCormick, the daughter of John D. Rockefeller, was married to the son of Cyrus McCormick. Bert L. Taylor was a Chicago journalist, and S. Weir Mitchell a Philadelphia physician and novelist. Mrs. Potter Palmer had been the grand arbiter of Chicago society for many years.*]

AT night we went to dine at the McCormicks' on the North Side. It was a pleasant enough party but the only people who interested me were the Taylors, Herricks, etc. Mrs. McCormick, a quaint ugly little woman, was a bit upset by Dr. Weir Mitchell's failure to come to the dinner. He came in late, however, and made all things well. It is a curious thing this attempt of the daughter of millions to put herself into the place occupied of old by Mrs. Palmer. She has no presence and not much tact but she is vivacious and interested in the social struggle, and with millions she may go far.

### JUNE 14, 1911 [CHICAGO]

[*Mrs. McCormick was helping support the Chicago Theatre Society, an independent theater group of which Garland was secretary.*]

IN the afternoon Mrs. McCormick came to the club to sign the contract. She was very plainly dressed and looked like a serious-minded professor's wife. Her long thin plain face was very like her father's, and it was hard to realize that she was one of the richest women in the world. I didn't realize it. Her suggestions were again very pertinent and I took advantage of them. She is becoming deeply interested in the whole idea.

## EDWARD MacDOWELL

### MARCH 10, 1906 [NEW YORK]

*[MacDowell had suffered a nervous collapse in 1905.]*

MRS. MACDOWELL asking me to go to a rehearsal of MacDowell's music, I joined her at 9:30 and we went to Carnegie Hall. Mrs. Deyo came in, slim and self-contained, and played for the orchestra in the 2nd Concerto. It was fine. And the Indian Suite was mighty. It is bigger than I had believed it to be. It grows. . . .

Edward is very well. He knew me and talked with me quite naturally but slowly. He was quite gay at times. At others sad. He is gaining in mental power, it seems to me. We talked of his music, of its Celtic-American quality, and he said, "Yes, it can be so described." I begin to hope.

### JANUARY 31, 1908 [NEW YORK]

*[MacDowell was buried at Peterboro, New Hampshire, where Mrs. MacDowell later started her famous artists' retreat.]*

I CALLED to see Marian MacDowell. She looked old and sad, her brave brightness almost clouded over. She told me in detail of the burial of Edward among the pine boughs in an airtight vault. "He was very beautiful to see," she said, "and his hands were as supple as yours as I took hold of them for the last time. The country people turned out in great numbers. It was an exquisite winter day. The cement vault was filled with pine branches and when the coffin was lowered the green boughs sprang up around it. It is as if Edward were sinking into a bed of boughs, all green, no earth apparent. I think of him sleeping there like an old Norse God."

## MAURICE MAETERLINCK

### DECEMBER 30, 1919 [NEW YORK]

*[Nicholas Murray Butler was president of Columbia University and chancellor of the American Academy.]*

THE dinner at Dr. Butler's house was a jolly one. Maeterlinck was in good spirits and after dinner got to telling us stories of his life in Belgium. He was older than I had expected to see him and not at all a mystic in appearance or conversation. He is tall and strong and round-headed. He had white hair drawn in a wisp over his brow. He was helpless in the midst of the jesting but could understand English when it was spoken slowly. He told us that he had no ear for music at all. It was all "noise" to him. He was shocked at the way men and women danced here in New York City. His face expressed disgust. He spoke of his young wife, not of his old one. He thought the Woolworth Building a cathedral. He told of his interviews with the king and queen where neither knew how to begin, or how to quit. He was very funny about this. He asked the king if he boxed. "Oh, no," said the king. "How would it look for a king going about with a black eye." He seemed a fine, serious man but no sign of the mystic.

## EDWIN MARKHAM

### MARCH 27, 1918 [NEW YORK]

*[Markham's poem "The Man with the Hoe" had made him a national figure when it was published in 1899, but his later poetry was seldom read. He was born in 1852 and died in 1940.]*

At night I presided at a meeting of the Poetry Lovers at a little book store on 31st Street. It was a singular collection of folk. I saw no one I knew and so far as I could see it included no poets, except Markham and Florence Wilkinson. There was a great deal of talk about poetry and many definitions were read, all of very little value so far as I was concerned. Markham was long-winded and repetitious, showing the garrulity and the gusto of a man who eats, sleeps and lectures in the atmosphere of "Literature." Admirable in many ways he has no sense of proportion. He doesn't know when to stop, but then perhaps I won't have any more sense when I am as old as he. I came home at midnight pretty tired and rather disgusted with having wasted so much time.

MARCH 17, 1919 [NEW YORK]

*[Edward J. Wheeler was president of the Poetry Society. The testimonial for Markham occurred in April 1919.]*

At lunch Wheeler and I discussed a "testimonial" to Markham. It seems that the old poet is getting down to a very narrow income. He has lost his place on the Hearst papers and is left in a precarious state. His boy is growing up, however, and will soon be of use as a breadwinner. Poetry is an uncertain staff on which to lean, and I fear Markham has put too much time on work which has no value as a means of subsistence. He is getting old and is not adaptable as an editor or hack writer. His situation is not a cheerful one. Wheeler's notion is a dinner and subscription for the poet and it may work out to his advantage.

[1920-1925]
[MEETINGS WITH AUTHORS. LECTURE NOTES]

*[Wheeler died in July 1922.]*

MARKHAM is a handsome figure and in some ways an admirable

personality, but his manners are eccentric. He is loud-voiced and pompous of phrase, self-centered and pretentious. His table manners are very bad. He crumbles bread and eats it out of the hollow of his hand. He sucks his coffee with loud noise, leaving his spoon in the cup.

He always carries a bag filled with papers on which he works while at the banquet. He pays no attention to other speakers, wets his pencil in his mouth, uses it to scratch his head, ignores his companions at the table and otherwise acts like an egotistic child.

With all these amusing and repellent peculiarities he is a noble character. He is reverting to his Oregon bringing up. As he grows older he becomes more and more blundering and pompous and self-conscious. His spoken English is very bad. He has no sense of values in anything relating to himself. I would go across the city to avoid hearing him lecture and yet other people enjoy him.

His presiding at the Edward Wheeler memorial meeting was offensive to a degree. He was so taken up with himself that he showed no real respect for the man he was supposed to honor. I was disgusted with his self-conscious egotism and his lack of tact.

He was less offensive as I met him in Florida—1924. He now wears a tuxedo at parties and evening clothes at dinners. There is something fine and hearty about him for all his blunders in grace and tact.

NOVEMBER 14-15, 1933 [LOS ANGELES]

[*Millard was a San Francisco author and editor.*]

MARKHAM was at the University Club for dinner and I sat beside him. He was a "show." He roared and jested as he ate. He drank out of his ginger-ale bottle notwithstanding the glass. "Take away that dead duck," he said to the waiter when a chocolate éclair was brought. When his host asked, "What would you like?" he replied, "watermelon." When a piece of cantaloupe was put before him, he attacked it at arm's length with spoon and fork. He said, "I never eat white bread. I never drink tea or coffee. Otherwise I eat any-thing." His energy is astonishing. He lectured and read his poems for two hours, bellowing, booming, shouting. He was pompous, pedantic and vain in his conceit. He boasted of the number of books he had written and of the number he had sold.

He boasted of the prizes he had won, of the tributes to him as the greatest poet of modern times. Before reading a poem he de-livered a discourse upon it, no matter how slight the lines were. And yet the people liked him. They laughed at him but they also laughed with him, for he saved himself by occasionally laughing at himself. He would have been a grotesque old braggart but for his candid manner and his humorous remarks.

He admitted his verbosity. He threw himself on the mercy of his auditors. "I'm so happy tonight with these old friends beside me"—here he smiled at Bailey Millard and me—"that I feel like reading all my poems, but I won't." He boasted of his brilliant son till we began to wince, then saved himself by saying, "and what do you suppose the wonder son of mine is doing?" Here he paused for effect. "He's writing mystery stories." This unexpected and comical ending relieved the tension.

He was at once childish and pedantic, tasteless and yet essentially fine. I have never seen a stranger performance. Through all his bragging, platitudes, pomposities, his kindly, scholarly self ap-peared. He has grown into a showman, consciously or unconscious-ly. Without his grotesque antics, he would be a platform bore. His success lies in his eccentricities which permit his auditors to laugh.


FEBRUARY 9, 1937 [LOS ANGELES]

NEWS comes that Edwin Markham has been declared incompetent to manage his affairs. Loss of memory and other mental derange-ments are given as the cause of the court action. So this is the sad end of a glorious career. Starting as an unknown public school teacher in Oakland, California, he flamed over the world as the author of "The Man with the Hoe." This led him to abandon California for New York City. He wrote one or two other notable poems, one on Lincoln, but he remained the author of "The Man with the Hoe." He may be said to be a poet of one poem, for this overshadowed all else in his books. He read it on every occasion and talked of it before and after each reading. He was almost childishly boastful of it and of his Lincoln. He was a pedant in his lectures but a boisterous boy in conversation. He often disgusted me but he was, after all, a sweet and noble nature. His candid admiration for his own work was not an offense, for he always boasted with a smile, as if he didn't quite believe himself. He may linger on for months but this is the end of Edwin Markham.


## DON MARQUIS

### JANUARY 25, 1931 [LOS ANGELES]

[*Marquis had written a widely read column for the* New York Sun *from 1913 to 1921. In ill health for much of his life, he died in 1937.*]

ON my way back from the polo game, I stopped to have tea with Don Marquis and his wife. I found him looking very well but very gray. He is no longer even middle-aged, he is old. He has been ill and is only just recovered to the point of walking up stairs—"heart trouble" the doctor calls it, caused by a germ.

As I studied him I wondered why he had not achieved a more enduring place in our literature. Like so many other newspaper men, he has an immense amount of work and some of it has been brilliant work, but it all seems scrappy, scattering, illusive. He was one of our best "colyumnists" at one time. He has written several plays, two books of verse and many stories and yet if he goes he will not leave any solid achievement behind him. He has had—like all his fellows—a certain kind of success as he went along and perhaps that, after all, is the best form of success. Perhaps this striving for a literary monument is an inherited folly and that to win the applause of those around you as Marquis has done is a far more satisfactory form of fame. Despite his career as a newspaper man and club habitué, Marquis remains essentially fine and manly. I have always liked him.

## EDGAR LEE MASTERS

FEBRUARY 7, 1919 [NEW YORK]

[*William Marion Reedy had published Masters'* Spoon River Anthology *in his* Reedy's Mirror.]

EDGAR LEE MASTERS was at the club for lunch and we had a good stretch of talk. He is a boyish-looking man with a round head and a sturdy figure. He has humor but it is essentially bitter. He sees the dark and doubtful side of life. He talks well but rather slowly and his accent and his tone are both curiously of the small western town. His *Spoon River* book is precisely his character. He is a poet in feeling but a poet very nearly soured by adverse influences. He has no enthusiasms so far as I can discover, and his hatreds are many. He naturally sees the yellow streak in his neighbors and it is due, partly, to his practice as a lawyer but more to his temperament. He said he was making very little as a lawyer, was in despair and disgust of Chicago. "I am completely isolated, so lonesome sometimes I don't know what to do. The town is getting worse in a literary way. Reedy feels the same way about St. Louis. Everybody is in New York."

MAY 5, 1919 [NEW YORK]

EDGAR LEE MASTERS was in the club as I entered at noon and later he and Marsh and I sat together. He was full of his new book which according to his own statement has the same yellow streak in it that is in the *Spoon River* pieces. He has a liking for the illicit. Lawless women seem to be his chief theme. He is a big burly boy in appearance but is no longer young. His new book will be a test of his quality. He has not yet proved his capacity for growth. His books are all alike. If he can not swing out into a new form he will retrograde. There is nothing really original in his idea. Hardy made use of it long ago and something like was used by the Greeks. America, as usual, has overvalued a novelty.

JANUARY 17, 1920 [NEW YORK]

*[The occasion was the annual dinner of the National Institute of Arts and Letters. Masters had been elected to the Institute in 1918.]*

AT the dinner we elected eight or ten new members, among them Irving Bacheller and Ray Baker, whose names went through with a good margin. In Irving's case there were no votes in opposition at all. It was a pleasant dinner but not worth the four dollars, considered as a dinner.

Edgar Lee Masters came in, loitered about for a few moments and went away. I saw him standing a little [to] one side with a look on his face resembling that of a boy who has strayed into a strange company, and a little later when I looked he was gone. Whether he felt peeved or just lonely I can not say but I was sorry to have him slide out so quietly. I could have introduced him to men who would have known of him. It only shows how lonely a man from "the provinces" is, after all. Chicago is a long way off.

## BRANDER MATTHEWS

### OCTOBER 27, 1918 [NEW YORK]

AT night Zulime and I went over to Brander Matthews' and found the Spragues, Odell and one or two of others doing the usual things. We sat and talked around the library table for a while. Then we all went down to the dining room where we ate gingerbread and drank ginger ale or whiskey, or ate nuts and drank White Rock, in the usual way. I have been doing just these things at Brander's house for over twenty years. It is a very simple form of entertainment and refreshment but it is pleasant. He was looking a little better than he was when I saw him last, but he walks very badly.

### MARCH 31, 1929 [NEW YORK]

AT night the *Times* called me up to tell me that Brander Matthews had died at noon. I was surprised but not shocked, for he has been lying between life and death for a long time. He and I were old friends, but I have not seen him since his stroke. I could not endure seeing him reduced to helplessness and vacuity. For a long time he was reported to be unable to speak and unable to recognize his friends. This made it impossible for me to call upon him. I wanted to remember him as he was—witty, acidly critical and humorous. He was never entirely sympathetic with me. There was something unjust in his witticisms that repelled me. He was loyal to Howells and Roosevelt, however, and that helped me to continue on intimate terms. He was always kind to me even when he might have been humorous at my expense. He had many violent dislikes, not to say hatreds, but he was always comic in the expression of them. He was never a handsome man and in his later life after he had lost the use of his legs from the knees down he was almost grotesque, but he never complained or apologized. His scraggly beard and his habit of opening his mouth with a snap after some witticism made him a curious gnome-like figure. Immensely scholarly in some directions, he carried it all lightly and was never boresome even in his monologue. He loved storytelling of the brief, witty, and sometimes off-color type. He was in truth much simpler and more genuine than he gave himself out to be. He was a most loyal husband. As a writer, he has not much in permanent form.

### APRIL 3, 1929 [NEW YORK]

BRANDER MATTHEWS' body was brought in by hired pallbearers in the conventional way, and we all stood to see them pass. I sat beside Augustus Thomas and W. L. Cross. Cass Gilbert, Blashfield and several others of the Academy were present. It was all rather out of character for Brander. I don't believe he would have permitted just this sort of service. Augustus voiced it when he whispered, "I suspect Brander would like to make some marginal notes on this ceremony." I said, "I don't want my poor old body carted around like this. I want it to go straight from me to the flames."

We were all old, even Cass Gilbert looked old, and Butler was too sick to make the address announced. In a few years and we will all be done with duties and done with life. I limped back down the street feeling my years heavy on my shoulders, leaning on my cane, my ankle very painful.

## JOAQUIN MILLER

### DECEMBER 2, 1898 [CHICAGO]

*[Garland had visited Miller in Oakland in 1892.]*

I HAVE spent nearly the whole day with Joaquin Miller. He impresses me again with his simplicity, his power, his prophetic earnestness and his gentleness. He has been deeply abused and misunderstood for he does not readily yield to the wishes of those who would exploit him. I dragged him out and showed him to a few of The Little Room people. He was deeply impressed with the elegance, gaiety, and refinement of the building's inhabitants. He was deeply impressed by Miss Lucy Monroe and Miss Bell. Both seemed to him very beautiful and charming. He kissed their hands in the old way. He looked rugged and handsome. Like Neptune or Walt Whitman. His gallantry disturbed me. It was a little affected. Not like him.

### DECEMBER 8, 1898 [CHICAGO]

AFTER a fairly good day's work I went down to find "the poet of the Sierras." He was in fine form and well pleased with the short lecture tour he had just made. I dined with the Brownes and Tafts and then we hustled to the lecture in the teeth of a keen wind, the keenest we have yet had this year. The poet's lecture came on. He looked very fine and quite irreproachable, except his boots. His language was well-chosen always and his points sound and well-received. He urged simple language, urged men not to hurry and to study nature, enforcing it all with bits of exquisite poetry. He was nervous at first and not at his best; he only made his points by leaps and bounds. Afterwards he became freer, more himself, and held his audience to the end. He was a superb picture in his Klondike dress.

### FEBRUARY 10, 1929 [SAN FRANCISCO]

[*Captain Arthur Garland was a cousin who lived in San Francisco. Miller had died in 1913. He had married Abbie Leland in 1883, and they had moved to "The Heights" in 1886.*]

ARTHUR, his wife, and I drove to Oakland and to "The Heights" to find Joaquin Miller's home, which I had not seen for thirty-six years. I could not have found it alone, so dense is the forest that has sprung up around it. The room in which he received me in those days seemed smaller and there was only a rusty pipe to remind me of his shower. We went to the house in which his mother then lived. We found Abbie Leland, a poor old woman, disorderly, loquacious, surrounded by dusty, faded portraits, MSS. and other mementoes of Joaquin. It was a dark little den of a place, incredibly cluttered and hodgepodge. Once beautiful, she is now a fat little old woman living in her glamorous past. I could not decide whether to give her a dollar or not. After she knew who I was, I could not offer her money. There was something sordid as well as unkempt in this confused collection and in this minute little camp. It was hardly more than a wooden tent. I came away with a sense of dismay that in so short a time Joaquin's remains should be so few and so ratty.

## HARRIET MONROE

### MAY 6, 1922 [CHICAGO]

[*Miss Monroe had founded* Poetry *in 1912.*]

FULLER met me at the University Club and we had lunch together. Afterward he took me to see Harriet Monroe in her office on East Erie Street. It was a sad-looking place and Harriet's condition was rather pitiful to me. The litter of backnumbers of *Poetry* was especially distressing. To see her thus struggling to maintain a poetic center in a prosaic town was another cause for congratulation that I am out of it. The only people to survive are the newspaper folk or the sensationalists.

## KATHLEEN NORRIS

### JANUARY 16, 1930 [BURLINGAME, CALIFORNIA]

CHARLES G. NORRIS and his wife Kathleen came to dinner along with a Mr. Fuller and his wife. I had not seen either of the Norrises for some years and I found them both gray. She is much the more important of the two, and much more attractive also. She has done much good work and some hasty and shallow work, but she made a most favorable impression on me. She told of her early life in a little town over across the bay and of her early struggles to earn a living. She spoke of her first success, a short story called "Mother" as based substantially upon her own mother's life.

I was pleased to observe that she did not drink cocktails or smoke or take wine at the table. Evidently she is a believer in prohibition. She is a tall woman, handsome from the front view but having a nose with a curve which is not beautiful. No doubt she is aware of this. She lives in a handsome home in Palo Alto and declares she goes out hardly at all.

## ALBERT BIGELOW PAINE

### JUNE 10, 1929 [NEW YORK]

I FELT so much better today that I went to the Town Hall Club with Zulime for luncheon. As we were coming out we saw Albert Bigelow Paine sitting at a table near the door. He looked old and thin but appeared in fairly good health. He talked with us for a few minutes entirely without stammering, and presented us to his speech doctor, a man named Greene. He said he was going back to Bronxville to live for the summer but did not say whether he had come back to stay or only for a visit. He has been away three years or more; indeed, he has not lived here for five years. He is enamoured of France and especially of the Riviera. He said three years ago, "I shall never come back," but old age may have changed his attitude. He looks eighty years of age but is gay and humorous of speech. A great old philosopher. He knows his time is short.

## GILBERT PARKER

### SEPTEMBER 6, 1932 [LOS ANGELES]

[*Born in Canada, Parker was a historian and novelist of Canadian life and an English M.P.*]

NEWS of Gilbert Parker's death came today. It was a surprise to learn that he was three years younger than I—his age is given as 69. He was a good man and a forceful man. He won great distinction, lived a full and happy life so that it is not necessary to say that he has gone to his reward. He had his reward here. He was almost uniformly successful. He went up steadily. No doubt he had his sorrows and disappointments but looked at on the arc of his career they are slight stains. He was always the orator, the preacher in manner, but kindly and considerate. He never tried to say the smart thing or the humorous thing and to some he was "heavy" but I liked him. We had much in common and as I see his smiling face in the newspaper, I have a real pang of sorrow. How fast they drop away. Shaw, Barrie, Kipling must soon follow!

## ROBERT PEARY

### SEPTEMBER 8, 1909 [CHICAGO]

[*Peary reached the North Pole in April 1909. On his return he discovered that Frederick Cook had just announced that he had reached the Pole in early 1908. The controversy raged for some years but eventually there were serious doubts concerning the authenticity of Cook's account.*]

THE Cook and Peary controversy is just beginning. I predict that Cook will fail to prove his case. No one but an insane man would put himself in the fix he now presents. It looks as though hearing that Peary was about to announce his discovery Cook had been tempted to forestall him, even if he had not been near the Pole.

Every intelligent human being on this globe is tonight discussing this case, and the Esquimaux who made it possible are forgotten. In all cases of this kind, the redman, the native on the spot, is given little credit when, often, he deserves the chief credit.

### DECEMBER 15, 1909 [NEW YORK]

AT night as I sat in the hallway of the hotel I saw Peary go by to his dinner. He looked thin, serious and rather "foxy." His keen eyes glanced from left to right as if expecting recognition. No one cheered or remarked upon him. He should have been mobbed with admirers. Cook has taken all the romance out of the discovery of the Pole.

## FREDERIC REMINGTON

### JANUARY 5, 1899 [NEW YORK]

REMINGTON was at the club and we talked of the trail together. He was against the man who stood in criticism of the army, lumping me with Bryan and the Injuns, all sons-a-bitches. He would assault me if he dared to do so, no doubt. That is to say, on the question of the army and the Indians. He was a little confused by drink, so I said nothing.

## WILL ROGERS

### DECEMBER 28, 1930 [LOS ANGELES]

AT Rogers' invitation I went to Fox Hills to see him as "The Yankee at the Court of King Arthur." We found him in the center of a papier-mâché courtyard, surrounded by a mob of knights, squires, men at arms, peasants, ladies in waiting and the like. A long gibbet was erected in the middle of the court and a ferocious hangman was

manipulating the drop. Rogers came to greet us in the dress of a
squire but with trousers over his tights. He explained what the
producer was doing to Twain's play. "He has brought it up to the
minute by using little Austin cars." He talked for some time about
the play, breaking into Oklahoma vernacular now and again. His
grammar was eccentric also but his wise old head is in the right
place. It was hard to realize his world-wide fame as he stood there
in the midst of that frowsy and nondescript crowd of actors. His
face, rough-hewn and lined and bronzed, was strong and serious. He
made no attempt to be funny and assumed no airs of authority. I
wondered what his attitude toward his lack of education might be.
Did he regret it? Did he hesitate to meet scholars and gentle folk?
Has he the slightest inferiority complex? What would education
and social polish have done for him? There are no answers to these
questions. He has achieved more than almost any other man of his
time. Why should he regret a lack of grammar? He is no longer the
clowning cowboy, he is the cowboy philosopher and humorist,
earning a half-million dollars per year.

He is reported to be getting a half-million dollars for making
these pictures and fifteen thousand dollars for thirty minutes on
the radio and his syndicate telegrams appear each morning in hundreds of papers so that his income is larger than that of any other
man connected with the motion picture business.

SEPTEMBER 25, 1932 [LOS ANGELES]

*[Garland frequently saw Rogers at the Sunday afternoon polo
matches in West Los Angeles.]*

WILL ROGERS in a brown suit and slouch hat was on the side lines
watching his young son play in one of the games. He is a devoted
father. They called him to the microphone to make some an-
nouncements, but as always he bungled it. The microphone seems
to inhibit his utterances. He stammers and feels around for ideas in

a painful fashion. He nearly always snaps out a witticism which redeems his bungling but I wince when he is called upon. Mrs. Rogers was also on hand, looking less distinguished than I had remembered her. Will is one of the chief Democratic propaganders this year but I can see that he has passed his prime as a wit. Things come slowly off now. For all his vast reputation he carries himself like a rancher and finds himself most at ease with horsemen and polo players.

AUGUST 16, 1935 [LOS ANGELES]

[*Rogers and Wiley Post were killed on August 15, 1935, while attempting to fly to the Orient.*]

NEWS came this morning of the death of Will Rogers in Alaska and the whole world is paying tribute to him as our beloved American. He has been a part of our daily life so long that I cannot believe in his passing. His paragraph has been my first reading in the papers each morning for ten years. His humorous comment on men and affairs has been so shrewd and so kindly even in its opposition that I have been guided by it in many of the decisions I have been called upon to make. I have seen almost all his pictures, especially the speaking ones, so delightfully droll and witty did he contrive to make them. His fun was always clean. He had no need to be obscene to be amusing. I have read his printed works with this feeling: "If he could construct a book, if he could follow out a continuous line of thought, he would rank with Mark Twain." Now he is gone and he has left only these multitudinous paragraphs, each complete in itself but lacking unity except that which his character supplies. Many volumes of these daily notes and addresses can be made and will be made but they are so topical, so of the moment, that much of their humor and keen common sense will not be sensed by those who have forgotten the man or the political event which gave rise to his witticisms and jocund judgment. His fame is that of political jester and actor. He will become a tradition like Artemus Ward and

Josh Billings—much greater in fact but with far less of a record bearing his name. I miss him as something out of my daily life. I am sorrowful when I think of the many, many words and pictures of which his death at fifty-five has deprived us. When we say, "We shall miss Will Rogers," we mean just that, so much of our daily life he had become. However, he went away as I think he wished to go, at the height of his fame, in the midst of an adventure in a wild, strange country. He loved to take chances, and this was his final chance. It accomplished nothing. It was foolish.

### AUGUST 18, 1935 [LOS ANGELES]

THE papers this morning are filled with news and letters concerning Rogers. No one, not even a president, could command such space by dying, for Rogers has no enemy and politics does not bar anyone from speaking well of him. He is on the way to become a mythical character but to me he was a homely character, a rancher with the mind of a wit and philosopher. I think of him sitting obscurely on the ground with the grooms while a polo game was going on. Even when playing he avoided notice as much as possible. He came usually in ranch clothing, a soft hat drawn low over his face. On a horse he was transformed. He rode lightly, gracefully, in cowboy style, and he played a superb game. He wore a red overshirt which showed his white sleeves to the elbow and my dim eyes were able to follow him. He was everywhere on the field, his voice ringing out in command. When his boys played with him, they were a host!

## ERNEST THOMPSON SETON

### AUGUST 9, 1910 [WEST SALEM]

*[Seton was an English-born naturalist and author. He was active in the scouting movement.]*

SETON was up early and at his work while I went on superintending my carpenters. At night we all went out to picnic in the open air. I cooked the steak as usual. After supper we drew round the fire and Seton gave out the calls of loons and wolves and we all took turns telling stories. Some boys who camped near were scared by the howling of a wolf—Ernest—and came up to see what it was all about. Seton was at his jolliest and made friends of everyone he met. He is nearly fifty years of age but the boy is in him yet. He seemed to enjoy being with us and we certainly enjoyed having him in our home. He is a great figure for the American boy and his books are likely to be read by many generations of boys.

## GEORGE BERNARD SHAW

### MARCH 28, 1933 [LOS ANGELES]

*[Shaw, who was on a trip around the world, was making his first visit to America.]*

BERNARD SHAW has come and gone. He gave most of his time to Hearst at his oriental palace in San Simeon and an hour or two to the movie people, then took ship at six o'clock. It is his last big flurry before going down. He has done his great reputation no good by his recent utterances, the utterances of an old man who has no intention of gaining the reverence which age customarily wins. Despite his snow-white beard, he continues to assume the wise-cracking insolence of his forties. I've no doubt the people on the boat find him a genial companion, as I did in Ayot St. Lawrence, but in public, on the land, especially here in America he will scoff and orate for the benefit of the press. He will specify all our short-comings and laugh at our panic Congress as a collection of "boobs," which many of them are, and he will go home to tell the world about our failure as a republic. However, he will do us no harm by his plain speaking.

## UPTON SINCLAIR

### MARCH 13, 1911 [CHICAGO]

[*The book was the novel* Love's Pilgrimage.]

ZULIME went to hear *Macbeth* at night. I stayed at home and read Upton Sinclair's new book, an appallingly frank book, reflecting all the storms of his private—his most private—life. It is the frank-est book ever written in America, franker than any German or French book I have any knowledge of. I don't quite see the use of such an exposition of sex history. Apparently he is willing to make literature—or what he calls literature—out of anything which comes into his life.

## PAUL JORDAN SMITH

### AUGUST 16, 1933 [LOS ANGELES]

BEAMAN arranged a lunch with Paul Jordan Smith, the literary edi-tor of the *Times*, and as I was sitting in the hall of the University Club, a tall, smooth-faced blond man of fifty came up to me. He was alert, humorous and genial. He told me that he was Jordan Smith and that he had followed my work for many years. I spoke of his painter's hoax which was so much talked about some years ago. It was quite as funny as I had remembered it. He painted pictures as raw and awful and amateurish as he could and it was accepted as an example of "the new untrammeled school." In our luncheon I got at his history. He studied at Chicago, came to California to teach in the university—17th century literature—was an ambitious novelist of no success when Chandler called him to work on the *Times*. He joked about his one novel. He is a rather superior type of newspaper reviewer but manifests, as he must, that sympathy with experiment which constitutes literary news. I think I shall find him congenial on some lines.

## EDMUND C. STEDMAN

### JANUARY 24, 1900 [NEW YORK]

*[Stedman was a poet, anthologizer, and stockbroker.]*

IN the evening we took the train for Bronxville to dine at the Stedmans'. Stedman himself was not home. He was in town struggling to earn the money necessary to keep his home going. Mrs. Stedman, complaining of his absence, seemed not to comprehend that he was killing himself at his desk for her. It was not a happy household for the old poet. One son is reported a reprobate, and the older is deaf and rather ineffectual. And his wife is busily complaining in the midst of the comfort of her lovely home. I came away with a sense of discouragement and disillusion. Is this all that literary fame and financial success can bring? It made clear to me his melancholy as we meet at the club.

### [1920-1925]

### [MEETINGS WITH AUTHORS. LECTURE NOTES]

STEDMAN, broker-poet, man of books and letters, was a slight man with a large nose, fine gray eyes and a bushy beard parted in the middle and brushed smartly. He walked alertly, carrying his head with a bird-like air. He was genial, humorous—though not as Howells was humorous—and greatly given to quotations of verse. I never heard Howells quote but Stedman was always reminding himself and his auditor of somebody else's poems. He was an editor of anthologies and read incessantly.

He wrote little and most of what he wrote is forgotten already but he was a charming talker. He was—unlike Howells—a ladies' man, a gallant. His air with women was distinctly Gallic though refined in tone. He flattered women as a habit, something which Howells never did.

He was not a great poet and he knew it. He once said to me, "We got our reputations easy in those days. When I began to write, there were not ten poets in America who could write good verse."

## JAMES STEPHENS

### NOVEMBER 16, 1935 [LOS ANGELES]

JAMES STEPHENS, strange, ugly little man, came in to have coffee with me, and Dr. Greever and John Bradley also came. Stephens looked older and smaller and frailer than when I saw him last but his wit and his Irish mysticism were as delightful as ever. It is said that he was born a waif, that no one knows who his parents are and that as a boy he wandered the roads and streets of Ireland. Where did he get his philosophy, his poetry? His knowledge of men and books? I got him talking of the land of the Shee and this interested all the other guests as deeply as it did me. He was a sad, unhealthy small man but his sardonic humor came to the surface now and again.

## BOOTH TARKINGTON

### SEPTEMBER 8, 1903 [NEW YORK]

BOOTH TARKINGTON was at the club surrounded by a lot of other drinkers. He looked heavy and prosperous, a totally different man from the author of *The Gentleman from Indiana* who came to

New York with boyish delight some three years ago. Success has done a lot of bad things to him. Unless he pulls up soon his work will suffer. I never see him now except in this company, and it seems a pity. He had in him something fine—too fine for this roistering life.

## AUGUSTUS THOMAS

### NOVEMBER 5, 1925 [NEW YORK]

AT the club Augustus Thomas and I had a visit of an hour or two on all sorts of matters, psychical, dramatic, and the like. He was as nearly despondent as I have ever known him to be."My play is not coming on as well as I had hoped and my son is getting a divorce from his wife!" I fear this son is not a comfort to him in his old age. He admitted also that he had not saved as much of his income as he should have done. He has had a great career and I hate to see him go into his later life harassed by the question of a living income.

He is one of the easiest men to talk with I have ever known. First because his own speech is so ready and so musical but more because of his wit, his keen perception and his humor.

### MAY 28, 1930 [NEW YORK]

IT was raining when I reached the house at the end of a short street or place, and I tried two doors before I found that the entrance was at the back. Augustus met me and gave me his hand, but he had aged shockingly since I saw him. He speaks very well but he can not walk much and is aware of his decay. He laughs and jokes, however. "My only fear is that I may have a sorry time getting out, the way Brander Matthews went." We talked of old friends and especially of Ingersoll and Mark Twain. He spoke of his winter in Florida. "I didn't do a thing but sit," he said. "I couldn't walk much and I didn't feel in the mood to model or write." He outlined an article on the law of gravity, designed to show how all life and all art is affected by it—"but I shall probably never write it." He spoke of having had his first play produced fifty years ago. As I came away, it was raining hard, and he was alone in the big gloomy house.

### AUGUST 12, 1934 [LOS ANGELES]

As I was listening to the radio this evening, the announcer read a dispatch saying "Augustus Thomas died today at a country club near New York." So ends a most successful, busy, and happy life. He was enormously popular at one time, shepherd of the Lambs, most sought after as speaker at dinners and elsewhere. His plays were picturesque, crisply written, and theatrically effective, but they were not lasting literature. Personally he was delightfully witty and clear-thoughted. His mind was nimble in the use of the material which his experience had stored up. He lived extravagantly and died almost destitute. I fear his last year was a sad one, although I found him cheerful when I last saw him. His death brings the final shadow very close to me, almost as close as when Fuller died. I had few friends who were more delightful as a companion.

## LEO TOLSTOY

### OCTOBER 30, 1898 [CHICAGO]

[*Aylmer Maude later translated and edited Tolstoy's complete works. Tolstoy's* What Is Art? *was much discussed in 1898.*]

CALLED on Mrs. Zeisler, the Kohlsaats, the Monroes, and later at Hull House where I heard a certain Mr. Maude from England speak on the teachings of Tolstoy. Tolstoy's thought goes deep. It rips up rooted prejudice like a breaking plow. His questions are not to be settled offhand. He sets human happiness above all else. Not beauty, not truth but happiness is his aim. I find myself in sympathy with many of the things he has uttered but I do not believe that I shall ever agree to this tremendous indictment which he brings against the art of our day. That art is about to take some new and important deflection from present lines, I believe.

## MARK TWAIN

### DECEMBER 9, 1904 [NEW YORK]

[*The occasion was a dinner in honor of Henry James. Twain's beloved daughter Susy had died in the 1890's and his wife in 1904. His daughter Clara had suffered a nervous breakdown and was in a sanitarium.*]

MARK TWAIN was present, looking old and sad. His work is nearly done. He and James are antithetic, antipodal. I doubt if Twain cares for James. When Mark Twain's humor vanishes he is tragic. His wife is dead, one daughter is dead, another is in a sanitarium. "I am living alone with Jean," he told me. "We are mother and daughter and sister and father to each other," and the gray old man took the somber mask of tragic grief.

### MARCH 13, 1906 [NEW YORK]

AT noon I lunched with Colonel Harvey, Mark Twain, and others of the Harper group. They were all very hot over the recent "battle" with the Moros. The report of the killing of women and children incensed them all. "The President has made a mistake in applauding the army for this thing. It may turn out a boomerang."

Harvey was quite vehement, predicting a big revulsion in a few months. Twain looked old and sluggish and congested, his purplish face and bushy yellow-white hair making him a picturesque figure. He drank more than he should and ate more than he should. He is old and his work is nearly done. He was very bitter against the

"Christian soldiers." He and Harvey both seemed extreme to me and I was saddened by their vehemence.

[1920-1925]
[MEETINGS WITH AUTHORS. LECTURE NOTES]

*[Twain and Garland met in London in 1899. Garland had pub-lished* Ulysses S. Grant: His Life and Character *in 1898.]*

ONE winter when I was about seventeen or possibly eighteen my teacher in the Cedar Valley Seminary gave me as the theme for an essay, "Mark Twain." I wrote upon *Roughing It* gladly but I recall the criticism which Professor Call wrote on the paper. "Too lauda-tory," he penciled in the margin as I praised Twain's description of Lake Tahoe. I was greatly hurt by those remarks, for I found Twain's descriptions very vivid and fine.

I saw Twain first in Music Hall, Boston, when he gave a reading. I recall one Negro story which he told in a very dramatic fashion. He read and spoke with a slow drawl which added to the charm of his talk. He imitated the Negro's tone and manner admirably. After I came to know Howells I heard much of Mark's peculiarities and I was eager to know him but I did not get the opportunity till 1899, although I saw him on the platform now and again.

I was in London and hearing Mark was at a West End hotel I went to call. I wanted to get his story of the way in which he helped General Grant publish his memoirs. I found him in a small, select hotel. He was cordial and responded to my questions freely, told of saving the General from signing away his rights for a small royalty. "I'll draw a check for $50,000." Ended by saying, "I had the satis-faction of bending over the old commander when he could no longer speak and saying, 'General, there is in the bank subject to Mrs. Grant's order six hundred thousand dollars.' "

*         *         *

One of the finest things in Mark's life was his friendship for

Howells. They were exact opposites. Howells never swore, never used vulgar phrases or committed solecisms. His tact, his grace, his humor were unfailing. But Mark blundered into many a corner. He was educated on the river. His fund of coarse anecdote, his vocabulary of cuss words were amazing.

His profanity was oriental in its richness and power.

He was an elemental character, a kind of natural outgrowth. Howells was self-educated, refined, wise, witty. Mark had no education in books but a profound education in life and men.

As he rose he brought some of the river-muck with him. His wide levels carried trees and roses and cities as well as soil.

He loved to talk. Howells was content to listen. Their friendship a singular one, but it was genuine. His life went out in tragic loneliness.

## HENDRIK van LOON

### JANUARY 19, 1931 [LOS ANGELES]

[*Van Loon's* The Story of Mankind *(1921) had been a great popular success.*]

I HEARD Hendrik van Loon lecture at the Ebell club to a house filled with women. I had never heard him before and I am not greatly in need of hearing him again. He is a big man with a dark, fat face. His voice was good but he had a habit of letting his sentences die away into a rapid mumble, usually for humorous effect. I had placed him among those who make a living by "jazzing up" history, and his address did not change my estimate. For half an hour he rattled on saying nothing of importance. I found the latter part of his talk only moderately interesting. His idea of an economic League of Nations is only a more inclusive form of the present idea of an economic federation of Europe against America.

As I listened to him I took the attitude of the auditor and wondered that anyone should care to listen to him or to me for an hour.

It is not an easy thing to hold the interest of an audience. The funny man is the most successful of us all. I came away with a feeling that I had bored the most of my hearers in the past.

## H. G. WELLS

[1920-1925]

[MEETINGS WITH AUTHORS. LECTURE NOTES]

*[The dinner occurred in London on July 4, 1922. St. John Ervine was a popular English playwright.]*

AT the P.E.N. Club dinner Wells sat opposite me but I could not hear what he said. His voice is an absurd little pipe, ludicrous in a man of his size and character. It scarcely reached across the table.

If he were introduced to a big American audience laughter would break forth the moment he started to speak, so ludicrous is the opposition of his body and his small voice.

It was a singular situation to have him and . . . seated at the same table. She is reported to have been his mistress for several years. She has a child of twelve or fourteen years old of which Wells was the father. It is a singular attitude to take, a bit disgusting to an old plainsman like myself. Wells has another illegitimate child, some say two, these by another woman. His "socialism" includes free love, apparently. I had very little talk with him across the table. Mainly he was advising me about what to see by way of ancient British monuments.

Ervine, who knows Wells, told me many things about him. "I like him but he is a 'gamin'—a gamin grown up. He spoke of himself as 'a bit of a rotter' but claimed he couldn't help being that." He asked Ervine's advice concerning the education of his sons. "I don't want them to go the way I have gone."

Ervine was astonished and in a way pained by this revelation of

Wells's weakness. "To have him ask my advice was a little like having Jove come down from his throne to ask the way to Olympus."

The best thing about Wells is the fact that Barrie likes him and speaks well of him.

## WILLIAM ALLEN WHITE

### MAY 13, 1910 [CHICAGO]

WE had William Allen White at the Cliff-Dwellers today and his coming brought out some sixty men. I introduced him to them in a few minutes' talk to which he replied briefly. He seemed deeply impressed with the club and its members. He was very fat, though less fat than when I saw him last, and I could not quite find the author of *A Certain Rich Man* in his round blond face. I was profoundly pleased with this book which seemed to me big with the humanities, a rambling, loose-jointed book but a big book in its content after all. White himself is so plump and awkward, so like a fat boy, that it was only after talk with him that his fine spirit was discernible in his mask of flesh.

### NOVEMBER 19, 1930 [EMPORIA, KANSAS]

AFTER a warm rather uncomfortable day we left Chicago for Emporia to visit William Allen White. Zulime stopped at Kansas City but I went on, arriving in time for luncheon. White met me at the train and took me at once to his house—a spacious home with a very large sitting room, a handsome dining room panelled in native walnut. He was not as fat as he used to be and was less sad than he seemed when we saw him in New York some years ago. As he talked I found him deeply imbedded in his town, which is a pleasant college town of fifteen thousand people. He was a singular mixture of the small town and the cosmopolitan. His home was of the same mixture. It was handsome in some of its features but almost pathetic in others. His little garden with its pool and its pagoda was so restricted, so commonplace in its surroundings that it gave me a sense of wonderment that he should be willing to draw attention to it. Similarly when I saw his small printing plant I was puzzled to find expression suitable. His desk, heaped with books, papers, and manuscripts, was as typical of the country editor as were the bare walls of the room where a boy was inking type to "pull" a proof. The town, flat, bounded by the limitless prairie, had wide, elm-shaded streets, comfortable homes and two small colleges. He showed it all to me with a gesture of pride. It was an astonishment to me, this enthusiasm for a small commonplace town. It was like Zona Gale's interest and pride in Portage. I could not but feel something self-protective in this. White is here and is making the best of it. He has been here over thirty-five years.

## WALT WHITMAN

### JANUARY 3, 1926 [NEW YORK]

[*Horace Traubel had published* With Walt Whitman in Camden *in three volumes (1906-1914). Garland had been a fervent defender of Whitman during the 1880's and 1890's.*]

IN going over one of Whitman's books, or rather Traubel's books about Whitman, I acknowledge a twinge of nausea. That he is a large figure, a very large figure in American Literature, I still believe but I have nothing of the proselytizing zeal of those days. I am wearied with all this apology, argument, explanation. He was a far finer person than his earlier poems express. His brother testifies to his sanity and decorum in life and so I found him, but he has become the high priest of all the sexual perverts since that time. The proportion which he tried to maintain in sex and life becomes in the minds of these modern, small rebels a license to self-indulgence and an attack upon the home and family which to him were the cornerstones of our republic. He had pity for the prostitute but his reverence and admiration were for the mother and homekeeper. Promiscuity, state nurseries and all the rest of the socialistic "freedom" he abhorred. Everywhere he celebrated the wifely virtues, the noble, manly traits. His plain speaking is a part of his plan. He is vital to me yet but not in the way in which he once was.

## FRANK LLOYD WRIGHT

### NOVEMBER 17, 1910 [CHICAGO]

[*Wright had left his wife the year before in order to live with Mrs. Mamah Cheney.*]

FRANK LLOYD WRIGHT was a striking figure at the club. I met him as ever, for I really know nothing of what the basic facts are. He seemed quite the same frank, intense, and poetic soul.

### DECEMBER 23, 1926 [NEW YORK]

[*Mamah Cheney was killed at Taliesin in 1914. Shortly afterward Wright began to live with Miriam Noel, whom he married in 1923. When this marriage collapsed, Wright lived with Olga Hinzenberg, by whom he had a child. He was arrested on a Mann Act charge in late October 1926, but the charge was later dismissed. Wright and Olga were married in 1929.*]

A TELEPHONE call today disclosed a man's deep and pleasant voice. He said, "I am Frank Lloyd Wright. I haven't seen you for one hundred and fifty years." "At least that long," I interrupted. "I want to see you," he went on. I agreed to meet him at the Town Hall Club. I found him not very much changed, but he told me his tragic story. He was—and is—one of the greatest living architects but he is under indictment today for carrying a woman, his common-law wife, from one state to another for "immoral purposes." When I knew him first he was a happy father of a family in Oak Park near Chicago. He left his wife and children for a woman who was his "affinity." She was burned to death in his house by a crazed Negro janitor, and within a year Wright became associated with another woman and lived with her for seven years without marriage, his first wife refusing a divorce. Then at last he married this third woman, who proceeded to make life a hell for him. He succeeded in buying her off and she went away. He then became interested in another young woman, had a child or two by her, wanted to marry her but refused to fight for the divorce. The second wife came back and started a fight for the house and more money. He fled. At Minneapolis he was arrested and is now out at bail. A tragic figure. "I have lived like a hermit for twelve years. My art has gone by the board. I have been unable to earn anything and all my property is out of my hands." It is about as complete a ruin as a man ever brought upon himself. What he expects me to do I cannot quite make out. As I hate all such ways of life, it would not be very consistent for me to champion him, and yet I feel sorry for him as a great artist.

## WILLIAM BUTLER YEATS

### FEBRUARY 23, 1914 [CHICAGO]

WE did some shopping and at night went to hear Yeats lecture on Irish poetry and the drama. He pleased his audience and was gracious though a little remote. Like so many English lecturers he was a bit too informal and lounged across his reading desk.

## ISRAEL ZANGWILL

### NOVEMBER 1, 1898 [CHICAGO]

AFTER my call at Mrs. Palmer's I dined with Zangwill at Mrs. Cowen's. I found him a gentle, weary, wise and deep-thinking Jew. Quite simple, genuine and profound. On Tuesday morning I went to ride with him. Spent the whole day with him. A queer, stumbling, rapt, swift-thoughted creature with immense powers of absorption. We rode till 1. Then he came to my room where I loaned him a shirt and collar (his trunk had gone astray). Then we went to the Zeislers' where we had lunch and a good time lasting till 5. I then put him on his car and came home to rest. In the evening I went to hear him speak before a big Jewish audience and wound up by taking a midnight lunch at the Lakeside (Jewish) Club. All this brought me very deep in Jewry and I was profoundly interested in them. There were many handsome men and fine looking women in the audience, the women very beautiful in front view, less so side view. All full [of] life and keen humor.

### JANUARY 27, 1899 [NEW YORK]

SPENT a good part of the day reading *The Master* by Zangwill. The first part of the book is a wonderful tour de force, for he never saw Canada but it makes unsatisfactory reading. I felt much relieved when he struck the ground he knew in London. It is full of thought and is broadening as I go on.

9 p.m. I finished Zangwill's book. A big book in every way. I do not understand why this has not made him one of the really great writers of his day. It puts him above every one of his fellows except Kipling and in many ways he is bigger than Kipling. He is so great in two fields, as the delineator of the Jew and also as a novelist of English art life. I have done nothing today but read and ponder this book and now I shall sleep with its tremendous problems in my mind.

FEBRUARY 16, 1899 [NEW YORK]

[*Herne's play was* Griffith Davenport.]

DINED with Zangwill and together with the Guggenheims went to see Herne's play again. It cannot succeed and I feel sorry for the man. Zangwill was a study as he shuffled about the room dressing. He showed me his coat with the buttons off and his lack of collars and cuffs and explained that his trunk was in Philadelphia and that he did not know where his dress suit was. He rang all the bells there were and started the search for his evening dress, then began piling crumpled heaps of bills on the table preparatory to changing his trousers, talking with much delicious candor about his own lack of order and system. His great head seemed to float about like a globe dangling on a string. His legs were quite aimless and unimportant as means of locomotion. He amuses me by his quaint and witty remarks.

## POLITICAL FIGURES AND EVENTS

GARLAND's involvement in American political affairs spans the more than forty years from the Populist revolt of the 1890's to the New Deal, a period during which he shifted from radicalism to conservatism. Always a firm believer in Herbert Spencer's doctrine of absolute individual freedom, he defended his changing position on the grounds that the Populists and single taxers of the 1890's were seeking to guarantee this freedom while the Democrats of the 1920's and 1930's were seeking to guarantee the authority of the state. But Garland was also shrewd and honest enough to recognize the connection between his shifting allegiances on the one hand and his advancing years and acquired property on the other.

Garland's most important political relationship was with Theodore Roosevelt. Whereas Garland and W. D. Howells had had a common interest in economic and social injustices during the 1880's and 1890's, Garland and Roosevelt were both active conservationists during the years of their friendship, from 1898 to Roosevelt's death in 1919. During the 1920's and 1930's Garland came to know and admire Herbert Hoover, but never with the same hero worship which characterized his response to Roosevelt.

\*    \*    \*

## WILLIAM JENNINGS BRYAN

### OCTOBER 26, 1900 [NEW YORK]

["The Sitting Bull," one of Garland's best Indian stories, did not appear until 1923, when it was published as "The Silent Eaters" in The Book of the American Indian. Although a friend of Roosevelt's, Garland favored Bryan and the Democrats in this election.]

CLOSED the contract for *Her Mountain Lover* with Century Company and worked a little on the revise[d] "The Sitting Bull." In the evening Z. and I went out to see the Roosevelt demonstration. A superb display of fireworks, made me think of the old Roman shows to appease the discontent of the people. The crowd was singularly lethargic and gave the impression of being onlookers merely. Many Bryan men in the crowd. I came home with a feeling that McKinley needs all the votes he can get. It would be making of history, a great turning point in our career if Bryan should win. The bigness of it all comes over me now and again. To reelect McKinley is merely to do the expected thing. To reject his policy and elect Bryan means a mighty stirring of stagnant waters.

### MAY 28, 1904 [OKLAHOMA]

WE took a short trip to the little town of Coweta and young Mr. Bowman drove me into the country for a couple of hours to look at farms. It was very beautiful away from the town which was ugly and new and merciless. Father was too feeble to drive and remained in the little hotel. Returning to Muskogee, we waited for the train and got away at last at 10 p.m.

Colonel W. J. Bryan was in our car and I introduced myself to him for a few moment's chat. He seemed very frank and boyish as he stood talking to me but afterward I caught his face at an angle which was unpleasant. He is not a great man but I think him an honorable one.

### FEBRUARY 4, 1908

[*Roosevelt had just sent to Congress a message calling for trust and labor reform. Charles R. Crane, heir to a large fortune and a famous traveler, was at this time a Roosevelt supporter. Bryan won the Democratic nomination for president for the third time but lost the election to William Howard Taft.*]

I FIND the air of New York filled with fury against the President. This rage is very illogical as well as irritating. There is hardly a man who does not assault Roosevelt at the first moment of meeting. I called on Charles Crane, finding him calm.

At night I went to hear Bryan. He was very bald, large, portly, and middle-aged. The old-time fire had gone out of him. He made a good, easy, dignified speech but was so unlike the Bryan of twelve years ago. I doubt if the men who heard him then could have realized the change.

I sat away in the top gallery where the real Bryanites should have been but it was a far cry down to where he stood. Only once did he stir us and his speech though good was without distinction of phrase. Its moral tone was high. His voice is still rich and powerful.

## THEODORE ROOSEVELT

### JANUARY 18, 1898 [NEW YORK]

DINED with Theodore Roosevelt, now Assistant Secretary of the Navy—a man who is likely to be much in the public eye during his life. A man of great energy, of good impulses and of undoubted ability. A fervent lover of the wild country and of ranch life, he is strong physically and full of talk—always interesting talk. Sometimes extremely vivid and vigorous. He is not a man of prepossessing manner at first. He is not unlike Kipling in some ways, square-headed, deep-chested and abrupt of movement. His preferences are strong, his dislikes intense but he is manly and wholesome in his impulses.

### APRIL 3, 1902 [WASHINGTON]

[*Dr. C. Hart Merriam was Chief of the United States Biological Survey. William D. Foulke, a close friend of Roosevelt's, was an Indiana author and reformer.*]

AT the request of the President, Dr. Merriam and I had a long and important talk with him on the Indian question. The President expressed himself vigorously on the subject of bad agents and inefficient field service. I told him of my plan to establish a system of family names among the red people. I asked for a card to the Secretary of Interior. He gave me his visiting card and I called on both the Secretary and Commissioner. They looked like worried and tired men and were very slow to act till I showed my card!

We dined with Mr. Foulke and afterward went to the White House to a musicale where we met Mrs. Roosevelt, the President, and a host of our friends. Paderewski played as if inspired and afterward we were introduced to him. As he took my hand he exclaimed over its strength and I told him it was broadened by the plow. Zulime enjoyed this evening most keenly. The President was quite frank and cordial with his guests. All this was a long way from Hanover, Kansas, where Zulime and I were married. It was a source of satisfaction to me to watch my wife's complete self-control in difficult moments. She charmed everyone by her manner and was as well dressed as any of the women—so far as I could see— and much handsomer.

### FEBRUARY 3, 1903 [NEW YORK]

[*Charles A. Eastman was a Sioux Indian who had received a medical degree. He was at this time a government physician at Crow Creek, South Dakota.*]

DR. EASTMAN called and made a report of his interview with McClure, and I wrote the President in his behalf. We lunched at Macy's and at night I gave a reading in Brooklyn before the Kosmos Club, which was very successful. My subject was "Western Song and Prairie Story."

This is the only request I have made of Roosevelt and as this is for an Indian and entirely disassociated from any of my concerns perhaps it will not be laid up against me. It is a source of pride with me that I have never made use in any way of my friendship with Roosevelt.

SEPTEMBER 6, 1910 [ST. PAUL]

[*Roosevelt and Taft were speaking at a conservationist meeting. Charles Crane had been appointed Minister to China by Taft in 1909. He had released some information about his mission to a Chicago newspaper and had resigned when publicly rebuked by the Secretary of State.*]

AFTER a bad breakfast at the Aberdeen, I went down to the St. Paul to meet my friends. Saw Charles R. Crane there and at the Roosevelt lunch I had a long talk concerning his affair with Taft. He confirmed what I had been told about the affair. Taft never so much as sent him a word of condolence or explanation and yet he had spoken on Taft's urging.

The Roosevelt meeting was a great one and I thrilled with new admiration and love for the man. To listen to Henry George's doctrine from the mouth of such a preacher was gratifying. His greeting by the audience was as intense and fervid as Taft's had been tepid and perfunctory. He is an idol of millions.

JUNE 22, 1912 [CHICAGO]

[*Taft and Roosevelt had broken bitterly, but Taft controlled the Republican convention and received the nomination. The Progressive insurgents met informally immediately afterward and named Roosevelt as their candidate, though he was not formally nominated until August 7.*]

TODAY really offered some excitement. The Roosevelt men decided to act as progressive Republicans and this decision rather stumped the standpatters. At the club I met Bancroft and Albert Shaw. Bancroft gave me a ticket and I galloped down just in time to be in at the death of the Grand Old Party. It was a singular and rather sorrowful spectacle. There was no enthusiasm for Taft, none whatever, and as the Roosevelt men, delegation after delegation, rose and announced themselves as "present and not voting" there was consternation on Senator Root's face. The bosses had run the convention into the ground. At the close the Taft victors cheered feebly. There was a listless, contemptuous counter-cheer from the crowd and then we filed out.

Up on the avenue was a different story. The street was lined with automobiles for a half-mile, their occupants waiting patiently for a sight of Roosevelt as he passed. Thousands of men and women moved up and down on the sidewalks. The Orchestra Hall was jammed. I got in at last by means of the janitor and so was in at the birth of the new party. It was a vivid, powerful and young convention. No old fogies here. No bosses. No cut and dried program. Roosevelt was cheered mightily when he came and listened to with deep attention although it was twelve o'clock. As soon as he had accepted the nomination which came by roaring acclamation, he left for the East with a splendid cheering throng outside. All were young, most noticeably so. I got home this morning at about 1:30.

### AUGUST 6-7, 1912 [CHICAGO]

AT the convention Roosevelt made his declaration of faith and was received with vast acclaim. Lasted an hour. He seemed very well and quite happy and secure in the admiration of his followers. His statement gave them a chance to let him out but no one wanted to do so. He will be a candidate.

*     *     *

AT the convention, which had all the fire of a moral revolution, Roosevelt was nominated without a dissenting voice. It was really very fine and thrilling. It was evidence of a swift movement in American politics.

SEPTEMBER 11-13, 1912 [WISCONSIN]

*[Garland campaigned for Roosevelt in Wisconsin (his home state), accompanying Governor Hiram W. Johnson of California (the vice-presidential candidate on the Progressive ticket) and Senator Miles Poindexter of Washington. Senator Robert M. La Follette of Wisconsin had opposed Taft for many years and was at one time favored by reform Republicans for the nomination. When Roosevelt reentered the field, La Follette was pushed aside, with the result that he supported neither Roosevelt nor Taft in the election.]*

IN accordance with my promise to accompany Governor Johnson I got to the depot at 7 a.m. only to find that his special car was not on that train. I took the 10 a.m. train and connected with the party at the Pfister Hotel in Milwaukee. A luncheon was to be given to Governor Johnson and a place was reserved for me. Mr. Morehouse, chairman of the City Club, was in the chair. Senator Poindexter was the principal speaker, a nice fellow but by no means a moving orator. I was called upon last and spoke briefly in defense of Roosevelt. They listened respectfully and a portion of them applauded. I went to the convention and heard Governor Johnson whose fierce seriousness and fluent oratory moved the audience to enthusiasm. I went to his car.

*        *        *

THE car left at 6 a.m. and reached Madison at about nine. We were met at the station and taken to the Assembly Hall. A pitiful little audience awaited us. The home of La Follette and therefore without managers for the new party. The place was half empty. From here we went to Baraboo where two fine men, the McFettridge brothers, met us and took us to the courthouse. A pretty good meeting. Thence to small points—Leroy, Reedsburg, and Sparta. At Sparta I introduced the Governor, and again at La Crosse I introduced him —badly, of course, for I can not think and yell at the same time.

There was a fairly good crowd but it is plain that Wisconsin is poisoned against Roosevelt by La Follette's friends. I dined with the Eastons and home at 9:30.

*    ★    *

GOT up with a bad taste in my mouth over my venture into the political field. It is very disagreeable to me, and yet it seems my duty to do something in the fight.

## DECEMBER 21, 1917 [NEW YORK]

*[Joseph B. Bishop later published a biography of Roosevelt. Roosevelt's son Quentin, a pilot, was killed in France in July 1918.]*

ROOSEVELT's secretary called up and asked if I could dine with Mrs. Roosevelt and a friend at the Langham. I was free and gladly went down. I met Mrs. Roosevelt first. She was very complimentary about the *Middle Border*, told me that it had been great comfort to her. She added that it seemed an important book. A Mr. Bishop came in, an old friend, and we went into the dining room. The Colonel came in a little later, looking extremely well but decidedly gray. He was very kindly, human, and companionable. He, too, spoke of my work in most flattering terms and said to Bishop, "Garland's stories have given me more information about the Middle West than all other books." He thus made it evident that he had studied them. He wanted me as a "wise radical" to take a hand in the discussion of our problems. He feels that we have a Bolshevik movement here and that we must head it off by real reform. He was very bitter against the delays of the administration and alluded to a high official as "that Pearl Gray Skunk." He was not specific in his plan and I did not get the notion that he contemplated a league. We have so many leagues. But I did get his notion of the urgency of the need. He spoke of his sons in the Army and said with a little tremor in his voice, "I don't know just how I am going to break the news of their death to Mrs. Roosevelt, for I know some of them are almost sure to be killed. Wilson is counting on making peace before we get into the war but I have no such hope. We will get into it and will get into it without adequate equipment."

I could see that this was a source of his bitterness. He felt his sons, our soldiers, were in danger of being without proper support. Brett feels the same way. Our cannon, gas masks, and aeroplanes are all supplied by France.

## WILLIAM HOWARD TAFT

### FEBRUARY 22, 1906 [CHICAGO]

CHARLES [Francis Browne] and I went to hear Judge William H. Taft, Secretary of War, speak on "Our Army." It was able, clear, and convincing to others, but to me out of place. It sounded too much like an apology for war and yet I suppose it is true that ample preparation for war is the best way to prevent war. Taft has a good clear voice and a fine simple manner. He might have made a great speech by dropping part of the details.

### SEPTEMBER 17, 1909 [LA CROSSE, WISCONSIN]

LOTTRIDGE came by at three and took us all down to see President Taft go through La Crosse. We had good positions and heard every word he said but the words were not inspiring. It was only a pleasant commonplace speech. His mind is essentially unimaginative and his manner in this case was too casual. The boys in the trees mocked him and no one rebuked them. This treatment of our chief magistrate is characteristic of us.

He should have been dressed as commander of the nation not as a plump citizen. I no longer hold with this "democratic simplicity" idea. The man who is chosen our ruler should look and act the part.

## ENGLAND AND WORLD WAR I

### OCTOBER 1, 1915 [NEW YORK]

AT the club Francis Neilson, the author and single tax M.P., sat
with Graham and myself and told us of England and her mighty
struggle. Others joined us and Neilson was quite outspoken against
the way in which the nation had been sent into a war they abhorred. He was quite pessimistic on the outcome. He saw only an
inconclusive peace with an enormous debt saddling the working
men of England. He was opposed to the whole plan of armament
and said the great bulk of English people were not in favor of the
war at all. It was most interesting to get this inside information
regarding the way in which Kitchener had failed.

## HERBERT HOOVER

### MARCH 20, 1920 [NEW YORK]

[*Charles R. Crane continued to be prominent in Republican
politics despite his falling out with Taft.*]

DINNER at Crane's where I met a certain Frederick White, an Englishman, a superb specimen. One of the most attractive men I have
met in years. A man of power, tact and fairness. He has spent seven
months studying America, lecturing at colleges. One of the editors
of *Europe*. A man to count upon.

Herbert Hoover was also there in a bitter and perturbed condition. He cursed Lodge and the president both—"two stubborn old
Presbyterians." He seemed at times a good deal like a sulky unhappy boy. Brought us home in his car, alternately joking and gird-
ing. He seems too literary, too moody to be president. I do not see
him getting anywhere near the chance. He is not judicial. He said,
"I don't think the call for me is very loud now. It's pretty weak; in
fact, hardly more than a whisper. When it gets a little weaker I'll
kill it."

### SEPTEMBER 28, 1920 [NEW YORK]

[*The setting is the Century Club.*]

As we were in the midst of the discussion Herbert Hoover came in and took a seat at the center table almost entirely unobserved. I would not believe that he could come into any public room and be so little regarded. He looked young, plump, a little sour of temper but capable. He spoke to no one. No one spoke to him for half an hour. He was almost painfully alone at the big table.

### MARCH 21, 1928 [NEW YORK]

AT three I met a representative of Herbert Hoover's campaign committee and agreed to send out some letters to my friends in the hope of enlisting them in the campaign. I am not disposed to go very deep into the political pot, but I admire Hoover and think him admirably fitted for the presidency.

### MAY 3, 1931 [WASHINGTON]

AT two I was dropped at Mark Sullivan's house and had an hour's talk with him. He looks white and old but assured me that he was going on with his syndicated letters. He told me that he went each morning to the White House and often breakfasted with President Hoover. He did not say that he was unofficial advisor to the President but this is what I consider him to be, for I have seen how the President relies upon him. He talked of the President rather freely, for we at once regained our confidential relationship. He admitted that Hoover had his moods of depression and that the situation was still very bad. He saw no immediate way out but his confidence in Hoover's ability to meet the crisis was unshaken.

### MAY 6, 1931 [WASHINGTON]

[*William Hard was a Washington correspondent and radio commentator.*]

OUR dinner at the White House was rather dull and unimportant. "Bill" Hard and his wife, a man from Texas, two young girls and ourselves made up the party. The man from Texas or Kansas said nothing and I was equally helpless. After we reached the library Hard did all the talking. He kept the President busy answering questions which were like those of a reporter. Hoover has no sparkle, no humor, no small talk of any kind and the hour was spent in talking national debts, taxes and the like. The President's mind is capacious in many directions but the aesthetic or the literary has had small place in his life. He is a business man, an engineer, a political economist. He thinks slowly and cautiously, never on impulse or in flashes of intuition. He made me think back over our line of presidents and aside from Jefferson and Roosevelt I could not name any of them who were capable of general conversation on aesthetic subjects. Jefferson was a man of some pretensions to art and literary knowledge but it was not as wide-ranging nor as definite as Roosevelt's. Lincoln had a liking for literature but could not be called a literary man. Cleveland was out of the literary world, so were Hayes, Arthur and Garfield, although Garfield was a college professor. Harrison was a country lawyer, Grant the plain soldier who wrote with amazing clarity and good taste by some instinct for good writing. I came back to Roosevelt as our one president who could talk art with artists, literature with writers and politics with politicians.

Hoover reads and has the air of a thoughtful man of books but the books he reads are not of aesthetic content. His mind moves slowly and like the Quaker that he is he speaks quietly with rather monotonous tones. He smiles only occasionally and I have never heard him laugh. It will not do to call him "stodgy" or "commonplace" but his utterances are uninteresting. He is a poor companion to one who like myself is not much concerned with national or international finances.

Mrs. Hoover, beside whom I sat, was much more alive and humorous. We got on very well. She told me that she was born on the Cedar River in Iowa, not far from my boyhood home. She is not pretty but is handsome and pleasing in expression. She spoke with a slight lisp.

JANUARY 23, 1934 [PALO ALTO, CALIFORNIA]

*[Garland was visiting Stewart Edward White in Burlingame.]*

WE drove down to ex-president Hoover's home in time for luncheon. No one else was at the table. Mrs. Hoover was most gracious and understanding, but Hoover was silent, said almost nothing till he and Stewart and I went into his smoking room. Then he talked, ably, sadly, and somewhat bitterly of the course of events in Washington. To him it is all experimental and most of it wrong, as Stewart and I, for the most part, agreed.

He surprised me by speaking well of Vice-President Garner and this was an assurance. He feels that Garner, though a rude sort of demagogue, is after all a patriot and an American. Hoover himself impressed me not merely as a beaten man but as a man crushed by the overwhelming mass of votes against him. He is done. He knows he will never come back in any degree.

He is, in a sense, a shy man. At night when the professors and their wives came in to greet me, he sat apart and said nothing, hardly a word, a sad, brooding figure, which is an astonishing action to me. He acted the host perfunctorily with no light word, hardly a smile. He sat apart as if filled with other thoughts while we discussed art and authors. He was kindly, hospitable but remote, absorbed, gloomy. I think this troubled Mrs. Hoover, who did her best to keep things going. She made much of me and so did the company, a singular situation when an old novelist is centered and an ex-president of the United States sits silently on one side.

The home is spacious, original and tasteful. Mrs. Hoover, a fine character, quite as I remembered her. I think he feels himself al-

ready a forgotten man. His position is singularly without honor. It
is hard for any man, no matter how philosophic, to go from a seat
of high power to one of comparative obscurity. He feels it so deeply
that it is an obsession. He cannot be humorous about it. He talked
of it almost exclusively in the hour which I spent with him just
before taking the plane.

### OCTOBER 26, 1934 [PALO ALTO, CALIFORNIA]

[*Upton Sinclair, a socialist, had won the Democratic nomination for governor of California.*]

AT five Stewart and I drove down to call on ex-president Hoover.
Sinclair and the administration came in for a discussion. Hoover,
very naturally, could see no great virtue in a "new deal" which gave
the Executive the power to regiment our citizens in the way of
Russia and which encouraged repudiation by its own refusal to
keep its gold payments. He looked like a man who seldom sees the
sun, a man who does not play golf or take daily walks. His mind is
narrowed down to politics.

## THE COMING OF FRANKLIN DELANO ROOSEVELT

### JULY 1, 1932 [LOS ANGELES]

WE heard the hurrahs of the delegates at the convention welcoming
their nominee who flew from New York to address the convention.
The excitement at the landing was tremendous and we were able
to hear it more distinctly than as if we were there. We heard the
speeches marking time in the hall and the preparations to greet the
governor. We heard the roar of the greeting and the speech. It was a
good speech.

For the first time in a convention the delegates could all be heard
by the chairman, for they were served by pages who wore little

microphones on their lapels and these were connected with the loud speakers so that anyone as well as the chairman could hear every word—no matter how empty or silly the word.

The most of the speakers had clear, strident voices but local peculiarities were slight. They were tiresome and empty, insincere, but they were not markedly southern or western or eastern.

## NOVEMBER 8, 1932 [LOS ANGELES]

ELECTION day! I have been writing letters all the morning.

7 p.m. The coming in of the Democrats is profoundly disturbing to me. It means a period of experimenting on the part of Congress and an increase in the plea for liquor in every state. I am too old to adapt myself to these changes and my small holdings will lose in value. I must now cut down on all expenditures. No more building. No more furnishing. I see no way now to earn money but to save it and with legislation directed toward the burdening of major industries, I shall have little to save. Thirty years ago I could have met this change with a fair degree of cheer but today I have a feeling of weakness and dismay which is not, perhaps, justified. I am wholly "let down" after a restless night during which I saw myself losing this house and going back upon a farm somewhere.

## MARCH 4, 1933 [LOS ANGELES]

WITH supreme self-confidence "Roosevelt the second" was sworn in to serve the nation as Chief Executive today, with all the banks closed in an indefinite holiday and with all business in terror of the future. He proclaimed his "leadership" as though no such guidance had been known before, and he openly declared that he would accept the power of a dictator if need arises. In plain terms he served notice on his Congress that he will not tolerate the kind of bickering and feuding which made Hoover's efforts of no avail. A smaller man than Hoover, he has the enormous advantage of the spirit of desperation among his people, which will support him in any of his projects—for a time. Sooner or later dissension and insubordination will arise. What he does, he should do quickly while he has the undivided cooperation of all good citizens.

## ADOLPH HITLER

### SEPTEMBER 26, 1938 [LOS ANGELES]

WE listened for over an hour to the raging voice of Adolph Hitler defying the world. Nothing like this harangue was ever before heard. He seemed to be speaking with the voices of three men, so variant, so dramatic was his utterance. At times he screamed like a boy, then suddenly dropped to a guttural tone. At times he exploded on a word, then emphasized a phrase with a yelling high-keyed note of imprecation. He was wrought upon by his roaring, snarling, shouting auditors. He knew he was being listened to by countless millions all over the globe. No man in all history ever climbed to such a height. Alexander, Caesar, Napoleon had but limited stages in comparison. He opened his mind without reserve to the citizens of both hemispheres. He had the heroic and unbounded confidence of the megalomaniac. He told the world what he would not do and menaced Europe with what he would send his armies into the field to do. It was an appalling exhibition to us all.

# THE NATIONAL INSTITUTE AND
# THE AMERICAN ACADEMY

GARLAND played a major role in the organization and in the early history of both the National Institute of Arts and Letters and the American Academy of Arts and Letters. The Institute, organized in 1898, eventually consisted of a self-perpetuating membership of 250. Its first president was Charles Dudley Warner, followed by Howells in 1900. In 1904 Garland and Robert Underwood Johnson took the lead in calling for an Academy of limited size to be drawn from the most distinguished members of the Institute. This group initially numbered thirty but was increased to fifty in 1908. One of the original members of the Institute, Garland was elected to the Academy in 1918 after the great success of *A Son of the Middle Border*.

The Academy was governed by a president, a chancellor, and a board of directors. Howells was the first president, succeeded by the historian William M. Sloane, who was himself followed by Nicholas Murray Butler, president of Columbia University. Soon after entering the Academy, Garland was elected to its board and thereafter served as its secretary. Garland's active years in the Academy, from 1918 to 1930, brought him into close contact with two of its principal figures, Robert Underwood Johnson and Archer Huntington. At the inception of the Institute, Johnson had been appointed its permanent secretary, and he later assumed the same office in the Academy. Huntington, who had been elected to the Institute in 1911 and the Academy in 1918, was the major financial supporter of the Academy.

Garland's participation in the Institute and Academy had its obvious ironies. First, the author of *Crumbling Idols* became himself a pillar of the temple. Second, despite his own advanced years,

Garland was troubled by the dominance of age and passivity in an organization which he believed should play an active, youthful role in American cultural life. A final irony is that although Garland's position as an Academician contributed to his reputation as a conservative during the 1920's, he viewed himself as a radical force within the Academy because he advocated an active role for the organization.

★   ★   ★

### JANUARY 30, 1899 [NEW YORK]

[*The American Social Science Association included for some years a Department of Arts and Letters. In August 1898 this department was permitted to become a separate organization (or annex), the National Institute. During the winter of 1898-1899 various preliminary meetings were held in New York, and Garland and Augustus Thomas were instructed to prepare bylaws for the new group. Although Garland continued to be active in the Institute, his participation was limited to some extent by his Chicago residence.*]

IN the evening went to see Mr. Howells and we discussed the "Academy of Literature" which is now a supposed annex to the Social Science Organization of America.

### FEBRUARY 20, 1908 [NEW YORK]

THE annual dinner of the Institute came at seven with only twenty men present, a discouragingly small number indeed but we had a profitable time. All were gray, myself among the rest, and with four obituary notices—Stedman, Aldrich, MacDowell, and Saint Gaudens—the scene was not gay. I spoke on MacDowell. Notwithstanding the insistence upon the passing of the Death Angel, we maintained a cheerful tone. It is typically American—this struggle to get a recognition for literature and the arts.

[*Not fully named by Garland are William Crary Brownell, Henry Mills Alden, Lorado Taft, Henry Van Dyke, William Lyon Phelps, Augustus Thomas, George W. Chadwick, and Bliss Perry.*]

THE Institute assembled at the New Theatre at 10, a fine body of men. Mr. Howells presided. The audience was depressingly small. Old John Bigelow read a reminiscence, a wonderful old man, ninety-two! Brownell's paper was too long, so was Alden's. Lorado came in to the meeting. We took lunch together and then returned to the theater. Another small audience assembled. The young men took an inning. Walter Damrosch had a fine paper. So did Percy MacKaye and Lorado spoke nobly.

The dinner at night was notable. A fine spirit was over it all. Van Dyke presided with singular grace and charm. Phelps, Thomas, Chadwick and Perry spoke.

[*George Washington Cable was born in 1844. In 1920 More was fifty-four, Childe Hassam sixty-one, and Edward Channing sixty-four.*]

AT the meeting of the Academy this morning I saw Cable wandering about, half-blind, feeble and senile. He gave me a shock. He is old, I know, but he should not appear like this, a ghost of himself. He cannot last long.

There were ten members present, among them [Elihu] Root who begins to show age also. He is slow of speech. Matthews seemed a little better but I could not keep from thinking how it would all seem to a vigorous young man like Lindsay or Tarkington, although Tarkington is not so young. It is not a growing but a dying band of craftsmen; that is its defect and must continue to be.

They asked me to serve as secretary, which I did. The youngest man in the group was Paul Elmer More. All the men they spoke of electing are old—Hassam, Channing. "No one is eligible till after fifty." This means in most cases that creative work is done. Can the Academy renew itself along these conservative lines? Howells and Cable and Burroughs must go soon. Who will take their chairs? Journalists?

### NOVEMBER 18, 1920 [NEW YORK]

[*Howells had died in May 1920.*]

THE work of the Academy will fall very largely upon President Sloane and me, which is right and proper, but it will make a great deal of difference with my own leisure. It took nearly two hours to get the minutes in order. The Howells meeting will also call for much care and thought on the part of the committee. At the club I met some of the members who spoke of the failure to award a medal in poetry. They felt as I did that our poets were all "minor poets"—that they did not work in large forms or with sustained effort.

### MARCH 16, 1921 [NEW YORK]

WE have the money for our Academy building but I am not as hopeful as I was, for the reason that I do not see writers coming in who will adorn the building. We old men are dying off. The men coming in are either journalists like Lewis or critics like Sherman and Van Doren. We have no really large size poets or novelists or dramatists because they are all playing up or down to editors and managers. Only a few like Frost or White are content to live in quiet places and say the best that is in them.

As for the Academy itself, it is dependent for its administration on five or six men, among whom I happen just now to be, although I do not believe in a close corporation of this kind. I feel disposed to widen the responsibility and yet it is not easy to do this. So few writers and artists are able or willing to act as committeemen and our distances are so vast that they could not serve if elected.

## AUGUST 9, 1921 [NEW YORK]

AT the office of the Academy I met President Sloane who is much perturbed over the question of what to do with our present building after the new one is ready for use. He does not seem well and the query "who is to follow him" came into my mind. Matthews is hardly any stronger physically. Whitlock would make an admirable president, but it is probable that Matthews will succeed Sloane and Butler become chancellor. To maintain an organization of men past sixty is like keeping the top of a fountain in permanent form.

## SEPTEMBER 26, 1921 [NEW YORK]

THE meeting of the Directors took place at 11 a.m. and seven of us came together. Dr. Butler was there looking very handsome and vigorous. Sloane is plainly ill and Matthews is a cripple. Hastings and Thomas are fairly well but as a lot we are elderly—a group of men whose creative work is mainly done. To writers like Tarkington we would have seemed a poor lot. Some of us know it and some of us don't.

"We can't afford to neglect youth," I said as I came away. These Directors come in once in two or three months, sit about the table for an hour and go away. They never write and never come near the place until they are summoned again. Indeed, they take great credit to themselves for coming.

This Academy could be and ought to be an active force for better literature and finer art, but the Directors do not feel that way about it. I lie awake nights trying to think out some plan for its service.

## OCTOBER 17-18, 1921 [NEW YORK]

[*Archer Huntington had donated the land and the money for*

*an Academy building on West 155th Street. The cornerstone*
*of the building was laid in November 1921 and the building*
*was officially opened in February 1923.*]

THE news from Sloane and Butler was bad. The entire program for
our "Gala Week" is off. Sloane will not use the money to make the
cornerstone a notable ceremony. It makes us merely janitors of the
building. I came home dejected and inclined to give up all notion
of doing anything for the Academy.

Sloane, old and timid and living in Princeton, is not only not a
force in the forward movement, he is subservient to Butler and
would not oppose him in any way. Matthews—dead to the knees
and nearing the end of things—doesn't care what happens. Hastings
does not initiate anything. Huntington, who could do much to influence Sloane, is inclined to keep his hands off—refuses to inter-
fere, in fact—and Gilbert and Thomas, the men of power and influence, have not been very close to the situation. They are all I can
depend upon to make the Academy a living force, for Butler is concerned primarily—and naturally—with Columbia whose fortunes
must be regarded first of all.

Altogether I give so much troubled thought to the problem that
I must hereafter keep out of the office. The whole thing will go back
to Johnson. Nevertheless we have made swift progress this year,
mainly due to Huntington, who has the historian's outlook and is
not so much concerned for this year or next. He is building for a
century ahead. No doubt they are all nearer right than I, for we
must lay foundations slowly. It has taken nearly twenty years to get
beyond the zone of the pornographic and flippant comment. With
a palatial home we are entitled to a measure of respect.

### DECEMBER 16, 1921 [NEW YORK]

FOR the first time since I took on the office of Secretary of the Academy I was absent from a meeting of the Board. This was premedi-

tated on my part. I wished to leave the Board free to discuss my special report and to dispose of the question of authority between Secretary Johnson and President Sloane. Johnson's attitude irritates so that I can not sit through his prosy harangues. He holds to the idea that he is chief executive officer of the Academy, and the rest of us and the Constitution hold that the President is chief in authority. As Johnson plumply said, "I object to taking orders from Sloane," it becomes necessary for the Board to put itself on record either for or against this claim. I hope it will be settled today. I will accept the majority vote of the Board whatever it may be, but I hope it will put Johnson in his place. He is not and can not be made the chief executive of the Academy. He has done good work but it is not well to have any one man known as "the Academy."

NOVEMBER 10, 1922 [NEW YORK]

THE Academy meeting was not very satisfactory. No one agreed with anyone else. It was hard for them to listen to the President. Butler and Matthews were frankly contemptuous of Johnson who looked a bit dazed and out of it. Huntington, big, vital, good-humored, let us know that he had ordered the furniture for the new building. This means he will pay for it. Sloane looked sick. He is suffering from auto-intoxication and in danger of a stroke. Matthews, old and white, was very censorious and difficult. Cass Gilbert, big, impassive and able, made some good points. It all comes down to Butler, Huntington, Sloane, and Mrs. Vanamee, the President's secretary. Huntington is going to see the thing through. No question about that.

JANUARY 12, 1923 [NEW YORK]

[*Mrs. Schuyler Van Rensselaer won the Gold Medal of the American Academy in 1923.*]

SLOANE tried hard once again to get the Directors to put through the business of the Academy, and succeeded in spite of Matthews with his jokes and Johnson with his long-winded explanations.

Butler and Huntington are a source of satisfaction to us all. They know what they want and how to get it. The voting for the medal was too "sudden" to please me. I agreed with Brander that Edith Wharton was the logical recipient, but Sloane, Butler and Johnson were for Mrs. Schuyler [Van Rensselaer] whose work I do not know except in magazine articles.

I was for a referendum to the whole Academy but the others claimed the award was in the power of the Directors. This may be true, but as only six of us were present, it seems to me the approval of all the Directors should be sought. I wrote Sloane to this effect. The award will mean more in coming from the entire Academy. More and more it appears certain that the Academy will exist by reason of the interest of Archer Huntington. We cannot carry on the work without his aid. For a time at least he is our stay.

### FEBRUARY 2, 1923 [NEW YORK]

IT is increasingly difficult for me to write and so today I left off and went up to the new Academy building where I found our employees moving in. It is a wonderful advance over our former office at Fifth Avenue and 44th Street. This building has much more space than appears from the outside but it is not as I expected it to be. It is less a temple of the arts and more in the nature of a museum than I expected, but as Huntington has made it all possible his ideas have naturally prevailed. His is a museum mind. He likes to collect things. He is a natural conserver of records and has less regard for our other activities. However, the essentials are here. We have a home and a force of employees to carry on the work. So much is gain—immense gain.

### OCTOBER 5, 1923 [NEW YORK]

WE met today in the members' room. Eight of us sitting in the front row of chairs, one of which was draped in memory of Thayer. It was a fairly brisk meeting, although the Chancellor was looking very ill and Augustus Thomas and Gilbert both looked worn and in poor condition. We are a group of dying men holding in our hands a legacy for the nation which can be of great value. Johnson, Sloane, Matthews are old and Thomas shows signs of premature decay. Only Butler and Huntington are vigorous and confident. I fear I am no better in appearance than Gilbert. How can we old fellows carry on the work which this superb plant now makes possible? How can we fill our thinning ranks?

This building is due to Archer Huntington alone. Without him we could not go on except in a small office and with an occasional dinner. His wishes for the present should be carried out. After he and the rest of us have fallen away, the purposes may change leading to a more active career.

The action of the Directors today was for "passive action," to sit tight and do nothing. I suspect that this is a reflection of Huntington's mind. He is disposed to make the building a literary museum rather than an educational center of influence. To this I have no objection. On the contrary it is a most valuable part of our program as I see it, but I do not agree that it should be all of our program.

However, as Huntington is paying most of our bills and has provided this wonderful home for us, we cannot do a handsomer deed than to fall in with his general notion, for I suspect that he intends to do wonderful things for us. Later we can act in other directions than that of collecting literary treasures, if we have the spirit for it.

### MARCH 18, 1924 [NEW YORK]

A VISIT to the Academy was like entering a private house closed for the summer. The Librarian alone was on hand. Mrs. Vanamee being ill, the machinery goes on with less direction. The place looks less regal than it used to do. The superintendent tells me the work had to be done over—much of it. The contractors cheated on the finishing. Huntington's wishes are that not much be done while he is away and so the place stands empty and not forlorn. It is a beautiful, cheery place but a kind of blight is over it. As Huntington has made it possible for us, there is nothing to do for the present but wait. When he sees fit to fully endow it, we can then function in some such way as we originally intended to do.

### NOVEMBER 14, 1924 [NEW YORK]

[*Royal Cortissoz was elected in 1924, Irving Babbitt in 1928.*]

THE meeting was barely a quorum and the ballots for new members coming in, we discussed them informally. The best men had few ballots whilst others whose work makes it possible for their fellow craftsmen to vote intelligently were elected, although they seemed to me less worthy of the honor. Cortissoz, a good man but on the edge of journalism, was known to all the artists and to enough others to get a pretty good vote. Babbitt was a poor second.

### APRIL 10, 1925 [NEW YORK]

PRESIDENT SLOANE was at the Academy this morning and seven Directors were present. Huntington seems pleased with the way things are going and indicated in his indirect way that he wanted to do more. We lunched together as usual and discussed candidates. It is not easy to find men who fill all the requirements. Sloane presented Edwin A. Alderman's name, on the basis of his being a great orator and educator, but the other Directors were dubious. Fraser, the sculptor, and Paul Dougherty, the painter, were presented. The question of being able to elect them was discussed. I argued again that they could not be elected unless they were known to our members in other fields.

### OCTOBER 9, 1925 [NEW YORK]

OUR Academy meeting today brought out only four of the Directors. Sloane's illness threw a cloud over our proceedings, for it is obvious that he can never meet with us again. We rode home with Huntington who was deeply affected by the news of Sloane's plight. The question of a new president inevitably came into his mind as into ours. It looks like Butler. Brander Matthews and I rode down with Huntington. On the way he spoke of his inheritance of pictures and said, "I don't want them. I have more than I can house now. I don't know what to do with all these Rembrandts, Corots and Millets." Brander suggested dryly, "You might give some of them to Garland and me," but Huntington only smiled. He was not quite as eager to get rid of his old masters as all that would indicate.

### AUGUST 11, 1926 [ONTEORA]

*[Not fully named by Garland are Joseph Pennell, James Earle Fraser, Hermon A. MacNeil, and Frederic Bartlett.]*

JOHN VAN DYKE and I had a conference today looking toward starting the machinery for nominating three candidates for the vacant seats in the Academy. His opinion on painters is as good as anyone's and I wanted to get his judgment on several whom I was willing to endorse. I made statement to him (as I have so many times stated to the Chancellor) of the three important requirements of a candidate: first, qualifications; second, availability for meetings; third, administrative ability. I said, "It is of no use to attempt to elect a man who is known only to his group and a man on the Coast is of no use to the Academy. Geography should not [sic] count in these elections. Then, too, we must be sure every nominee is willing to make the race. We can't be put in the position of offering a membership to a man who will put it by with the back of his hand. Let those who are 'wild' flock by themselves. Those who are progressive we want. I should like to see Robert Henri and Ralph Adams Cram come in, if they are willing to associate with those of us who build on the past. I think they both could be elected but I am not so certain that Paul Manship could win a majority vote. A man like John Finley while not a great author is a noble citizen, a polished orator, and an educator and editor. I should like to have him join us. He would be helpful to us. Cram and Henri both write and speak very well and they are fine artists."

To all this Van Dyke agreed and we are to feel out [others] in these directions. We both agreed that it was impossible to fill John Sargent's seat but that Cram would follow Pennell very satisfactorily. Fraser or MacNeil would either one follow Bartlett without loss in some ways, though he had more old-world culture than MacNeil and a finer technique, perhaps, than Fraser.

We agreed also that the men of today are less urbane, less cultured, less fine men than the generation before them, although Pennell and Bartlett were not gracious personalities. And yet it may be that this is a misimpression. We may be idealizing the older men and misjudging the men about us. It may be that Robert Frost, Ridgely Torrence, and Edwin Robinson are as fine as Longfellow, Whittier, and Lowell. They seem of smaller stature and of coarser clay because they are nearer to us. I did not propose Frost to Van Dyke but I thought of doing so. Frost has done distinctive work but not enough of it to make his election possible. A man to be elected must be known not only to his fellow craftsmen but to the workers in other crafts. A writer has a better chance than a sculptor or architect, but a man can be the author [of] several noble books of verse or prose and still be unable to win a majority vote. All these make our problem a difficult one.

### OCTOBER 14, 1927 [NEW YORK]

OUR meeting at the Academy today was small and sad. Brander Matthews sent through his nurse his resignation and Chancellor Butler reported that our President Sloane would never act with us again. Johnson is old and hesitant. Hastings is ill and Augustus is not yet fully himself. Only Butler and I presented a vigorous front to the world. Huntington and Cass Gilbert could not be present. They are vigorous still but too busy to attend. The question of a quorum of younger men was discussed. We *must* for the sake of administrative efficiency bring in young and vigorous men. The problem is to elect men who will serve and who know what we are standing for.

OCTOBER 9, 1928 [NEW YORK]

AT our meeting, which was almost a full Board, we elected Butler to the presidency of the Academy and transacted considerable business—but the luncheon was given up entirely to a discussion of politics which bored me. We should talk Academy affairs at these meetings and not discuss the tariff and prohibition. Butler is fine on most occasions but in this matter of prohibition he is almost rabid. Most of those who were present agreed with him but I did not, and said nothing. We need an administrator at this time and so Butler is the safe man. Anyhow, he could not be overlooked in the progress of the reorganization.

NOVEMBER 30, 1928 [NEW YORK]

*[Garland was chairman of the Academy committee which awarded a medal for good diction over the radio. Cass Gilbert was an architect.]*

THE committee meeting and lunch at the Academy was pretty nearly a failure. Cross and Johnson were old and slow and we got nowhere. Cross shocked me by his slowness and mental feebleness. We are all too old to be on so important a committee. The weakness of the Academy was shown as never before. If Butler should die or be disabled, we would flounder, for Huntington, being our chief donor, would not feel like taking active direction. Cass Gilbert, our most active man, is after all not literary and the directing force of the Academy should be literary. Then, too, our men are wanderers.

They are often abroad and for long periods. More and Wister and MacNeil are of this type. Most of us have reached the age of leisure or, as artists and men of letters, we wish to study conditions in the old world. All of these facts militate against a vigorous and influential organization. However, Huntington goes ahead confidently.

APRIL 23, 1929 [NEW YORK]

*[The "great day" included the Academy's twenty-fifth anniversary exercises, part of which were broadcast. Garland, as chairman of the good diction committee, made the award to Milton J. Cross.]*

THIS was the Academy's great day and in some ways it was its greatest day. The one cloud in the sky was the illness and absence of Dr. Butler who would have done so much to make our proceedings orderly as well as illustrious. Although lame in my ankle and with a stiff neck, I got up out of my bed at ten and went to the Academy where I made my report to the official session and an hour later read my address into the microphone to some millions of listeners, so I was assured the largest audience I have ever had or shall have. I then called the winner of the medal, Mr. Milton J. Cross, to the microphone. He made an admirable impression, self-contained, quietly authoritative in tone and smoothly flowing in speech. He quite justified all we had been saying. He gave a highly satisfactory finish to the whole campaign and the members were delighted and voted to go on for another year. Cross and I were quite overwhelmed with compliments and congratulations. No sooner did I reach home than I received a wire from my daughters saying I was "superb." They had heard the whole program clearly in far-off Hollywood.

JUNE 3, 1929 [NEW YORK]

AFTER a bad night caused by pain in the muscles of my neck, I perked up and did considerable work during the day. Mrs. Vanamee and Colonel Crasto came to dinner and we had a great deal of talk about the Academy and Huntington's method of helping to build and keep it going. Mrs. Vanamee is in his confidence, and she told us that he was highly pleased with all that we have done this year. He reported himself well pleased with our work on the radio. His added gift of one hundred thousand dollars insures the new building, but we have no tangible endowment to carry it on. Dr. Butler is certain that we will have the money but that is only a promise and dependent on Huntington. No doubt he has included the Academy in his will but that does not provide for now. Current expenses must come partly from his cash at the annual settlement. In all this we must be content, for without him we would have no home. Through him we can build for the future. We have advanced the position of the Academy.

### JUNE 4, 1930 [NEW YORK]

WE had our first Director's meeting in many months and succeeded in getting a good deal of work done. I made my radio report and it was approved as read and the announcement authorized. We lunched together and talked of the finances of the Academy, and afterwards Gilbert took us through the new building. I confess to a disappointment in it, all but the auditorium. That was really beautiful. The exhibition room was not attractive to me, and I believe the other men felt the same disappointment. It was too high and too square to be beautiful. Then, too, a great many of the rooms were under ground with no ventilation. I don't know who changed the designs but I suspect Huntington had his way in many changes. It should have been an exquisite little building. As it is, it is just fair.

### NOVEMBER 12, 1930 [NEW YORK]

[*Edna Ferber and Cecilia Beaux were elected to the National Institute in 1930.*]

THIS was the night of the Institute dinner. Some thirty-four men gathered at the Academy and a fairly live meeting took place. It was better than last year or the year before but not as numerous or as vigorous as it used to be. It elected two women—one a Jewess— and it gave me a feeling of distrust of its future. I do not believe it can be as vigorous, as independent, if one third of its membership is women, no matter how eminent they may be. It is not a question of the ability of these candidates but the probability that their election will lead to others less able and tactful. It is impossible at present to keep the sex element subordinate the moment a woman comes into a room. Several feel as I do. I fought for the women till I saw that it would weaken and divide the organization.

### MAY 9, 1931 [NEW YORK]

*[Garland was planning his permanent move to Los Angeles.]*

MRS. VANAMEE and I held a two-hour conference on the situation in which the Academy now rests. President Butler is disinclined to spend any money on any active campaign and hence our noble plant is lying substantially idle. Huntington, I think, would like to see it wholly given over to museum uses, art exhibitions and the like, but Butler and Cross are disposed to curtail even that expenditure. To me the outlook is not encouraging for the reason that Butler is making it too much like an annex to Columbia. It is governed, in effect, by a one-man directorate. Huntington's wishes no longer count with Butler and the remainder of the Board have little to say concerning any measure brought before them.

Mrs. Vanamee urged me to remain on the Board, saying, "You are the only one who takes a vital interest in our work." She was so earnest in this that I promised to withhold my resignation. I see no possibility of change in the chairmanship, for Butler is admittedly the best administrator we have on the Board and while he is not a great writer or a profound thinker, he is able, widely known as orator and educator, and presides with great skill.

NOVEMBER II, 1931 [NEW YORK]

*[Not fully named by Garland are William Lyon Phelps, Burton J. Hendrick, Harrison S. Morris, Lorado Taft, Irving Bacheller, Charles Loeffler, Frederick Law Olmsted, Gamaliel Bradford, and Adolph Weinman.]*

THE Institute dinner was a lifeless affair. Phelps presided and Hendrick and Morris rambled some reports. There was no vigor or sincerity in any of the proceedings and the talk dragged on till Lorado and I and Irving got tired out and came away. Unless something is done to liven up these dinners no one will come. No real discussion took place and no issue was defined. It all seems rather hopeless at this time. I think I detected disappointment in several of the men who had hoped to be elected to the Academy. From my point of view several were more deserving than two of those selected. I would have elected Deems Taylor in place of Loeffler, and Olmsted in place of Bradford. It was not a highly distinguished group, so far as the outside world can judge of the men. Loeffler's work is done. Bradford is an old man. Weinman is not widely known outside his art and Phelps is most illustrious as a lecturer. His books are not important so far.

SEPTEMBER 6, 1937 [LOS ANGELES]

*[Not fully named are Van Wyck Brooks and Donald C. Peattie.]*

NEWS of Henry Hadley's death came over the radio today. This creates another vacancy in the Academy, the eleventh or twelfth. The filling of these vacancies is likely to change the character of the institution. The pornographic novelists and dramatists are certain to be nominated. There are four or five of the old fellows like Johnson and Markham who are certain to go soon and my chair is equally certain to be vacant before long. The Academy, if it survives all these changes, will be a different institution. If we could put men like Brooks and Peattie into these vacant chairs, the traditions would be carried out. However, I find most of this "democratic" art repellent to me and am more and more resigned to the thought of slipping over into the Fourth Dimension.

NOVEMBER 10, 1938 [NEW YORK]

*[Garland delivered the principal address at the annual meeting of the Academy, an address in which he attacked the salaciousness of modern literature.]*

WHILE I counted for little at the eleven o'clock meeting and was not able to do much at luncheon, the meeting in the auditorium at three was a most brilliant ending of my career in the East. The beautiful auditorium was filled to the last seat in the balcony, a most distinguished and sympathetic audience. They applauded so long and cordially that I was compelled to rise and acknowledge their enthusiasm, which I suspect had an element of gratitude in it, for the proceedings preceding me were lifeless and almost inaudible. All my friends who were able to reach me cheered me by their praise of what I said as well as of my way of saying it. I rode down the riverside in a bus while the purple dusk was falling on the river. If I should never see it again, I shall feel that I saw it at its best. Altogether, it was a triumphant close to my visit. The chances of my return are small.

# AMERICAN LIFE AND ITS PROBLEMS

GARLAND's response to the principal historical and social events of his time confirms Richard Hofstadter's hypothesis about midwestern reform movements of the 1880's and 1890's. According to Hofstadter, the Populists were descendants of Jeffersonianism both in their humanitarian sympathies and in their distrust of the East and the city. Garland's progress from a single-tax, Populist reformer to an embittered commentator on the sexual immorality and ethnic degeneration of American life is thus less an example of hopeful youth turning into crabbed old age than of the uncovering of deep roots of midwestern belief. Drawn to the city yet repelled by it, antagonistic toward alien cultures yet chagrined by his prejudices, Garland's social attitudes of the 1920's and 1930's dramatize a major paradox within the midwestern mind.

\*    \*    \*

## THE SPANISH-AMERICAN WAR

### APRIL 19, 1898 [WEST SALEM]

AT 7:30 p.m. five trainloads of soldiers passed through here en route for Atlanta to rendezvous in readiness for Spain's attack. The village was much excited and assembled en masse to see the warriors go by. They were from Fort Snelling and included five hundred cavalry and a regiment of infantry. This is a historical moment if Spain enters into a war with us. If not, not.

### APRIL 21, 1898 [ST. PAUL]

[Garland was preparing for a pack trip from British Columbia to the Klondike.]

235

THE first half of a very rainy day I spent in Minneapolis. After buying the rest of my clothing I took car for St. Paul where I fell into the hands of my good friends the Severances. I dined with them in my blue drill shirt and spent the evening discussing the war with Spain. Our ships are reported sailing from Key West to reduce Havana before the fleet of Spain can reach there. Everybody but myself seems to be thirsting for blood. It is a startling return to the primeval man and woman. Severance expressed a desire to go. It seemed so much more worthwhile. It was a chance!

### FEBRUARY 10, 1899 [NEW YORK]

[*Most American writers were opposed to American imperialism in the Pacific. William Vaughn Moody voiced this attitude in his "Ode in Time of Hesitation," written in early 1900.*]

IN the evening called on the Moodys and we inveighed against the government for its haste in wiping out the poor Filipinos. Nearly every one of my acquaintance feels disgraced but the press is all on McKinley's side.

## WORLD WAR I

### JUNE 26, 1916 [NEW YORK]

ROOSEVELT having endorsed Hughes there remains but one thing to do, to defeat Wilson. At the club there were but few men but they were all full of patriotic fire and ready to go to war if need be. The Mexican situation gets worse. The poor fellows are going to attack us in force. Several thousand troops left here today and the President is about to call for volunteers. I would be willing to help defend our border but I don't believe in subjugating these small brown men.

Everywhere I went downtown I saw women of wealth buying supplies for sons, brothers, and husbands. Limousines drew up to the door of the Army and Navy store. The War Spirit is aflame and I fear we are entering upon a long period of militarism.

## OCTOBER 14, 1917 [NEW YORK]

THE day was lovely and I got out for a walk in the park. I felt like one who had been walking for a week in a tunnel. The city's power and swarming life reasserted its charm and I rejoiced to think we were all here in the midst of it. There is no sign of war except in the alert brown figures of our soldiers who come and go buoyantly. The spirit of the city is young, confident and critical. There is a huge socialistic peace party on the East Side but we see little of it. It meets and speaks and the papers report it but it is not much regarded except as it may influence the reelection of Mayor Mitchel.

## JULY 25-26, 1918 [ONTEORA]

[*The Battle of the Marne was taking place.*]

AT seven o'clock word came over the wires that Foch had captured the Crown Prince and all his armies. Our first knowledge of it came in sounds of horns, hurrahing and whistling at the village. These sounds kept up until at last we all went down to the little street. A mob of mingled Jews and Gentiles filled the walks, and automobiles crowded with people waving flags confirmed our news. An ambitious local politician was making empty speeches merely to put himself in the spotlight but no amplification of the news was obtainable from him or anyone else. The children were wildly excited. They wanted to join the procession and yell. Of course, I told them to do so. I would have marched myself but for my foundered feet. I yelled, however.

If this news is true it is the end of the war. The German morale is already weakened. This will destroy it. To have the Crown Prince is a death blow to the Kaiser.

*     *     *

Alas, it was all a false report! Nothing of the sort happened. The Allied armies are advancing slowly but as for capturing armies, they are merely bagging companies. The Germans are holding their line but suffering sharply. They will sooner or later be obliged to evacuate their "salient," but there will be no sensational capture.

DECEMBER 14, 1919 [NEW YORK]

*[Eleanor was the daughter of Solomon Guggenheim; Edith, of Isaac Guggenheim.]*

FOR dinner at night we had Eleanor and Edith, and Curtis Wheeler to meet them. Eleanor told of her farmerette experiences and it was an astonishing tale. Such folly, such brave endurance, such childish ignorance of how to do the work. She told a highly comic story. The thought of this small, delicate girl going from the grandeur of the Plaza Hotel to a job of digging rocks out of a potato field and cutting briars with a rusty scythe makes fiction a dull thing. They worked bare-headed in the sun. They went in two garments to endure the heat. They cultivated corn on a stony hillside for five weeks and then suddenly they went back to the Guggenheim yacht, the automobiles and marble palaces of her friends! It is an incredible tale. She told it well, with keen humor, not sparing herself, and we shouted with laughter. The fact that at a specially exasperating moment she "damned" the horse and surprised herself. "I didn't know I had such words in me," she said. Edith sat quietly by to confirm or remind.

## RADICALISM AND WEALTH

SEPTEMBER 17, 1920 [NEW YORK]

*[The Wall Street Explosion had occurred on September 16. A bomb exploded near the offices of J. P. Morgan, and thirty people were killed. The incident was attributed to Bolsheviks or*

anarchists, though its perpetrators were never found. Frederick
C. Howe had been Commissioner of Immigration of the Port of
New York, and Louis F. Post was Assistant Secretary of Labor.]

CARL AKELY, Frank Chapman, Fred Walcott, also Bert Taylor, were
at the club and much talk of the explosion in Wall Street took place.
Red labor does not advance its cause in that way.

Fred Howe came in looking small and pinched and worried. He
has been far too lenient with these red agitators and he knows it.
Post has also done a good deal to foster it by his easygoing policy of
releasing the violent leaders. These men have counted me one of
their number but as an evolutionist I have never believed for an
instant in disorderly change. In this country we can advance without violence. These revolutionists are all foreign-born or foreign-
bred.

### JUNE 10, 1921 [NEW YORK]

DR. AND MRS. BRIDGE dined with us and had a neighborly time. He
told us of his great good fortune in oil wells in Mexico. His income
is enormous and likely to be more and he is seventy-six years of
age. All this wealth is coming out of Mexico. It ought not to come
here. It is all wrong that it should not go to relieve Mexico rather
than to enrich a few Americans—even if some of them are my
friends.

### AUGUST 17, 1922 [LONDON]

AT seven, Nevinson, Miss Sharp, a Dr. Hertsel and I dined at "The
Revolutionary Club" which was formed in 1917 in honor of the
Russian Revolution. It is a small and very plain clubhouse in Soho
Street. The people at the table looked like Greenwich Village types
—short-haired girls confronted intensely serious men. One of the
guests was Ben Turner, the labor leader, a short, fair, broad-faced
genial man with a big beard. His companion looked like a Pole and
several of those seated near were Polish or Russian Jews. The first I
have seen here. Miss Sharp is of this "Soviet" persuasion—made so

by her relief work. She has been twice in prison for violence in the
suffragette cause before the war. She is of that intense sort. We fell
into a wide difference discussing Russia and Bolshevism, with
which I am not sympathetic.

## PUBLIC MORALITY AND TASTE

### MARCH 31, 1898 [NEW YORK]

*[Mary Shaw was a well-known actress and Ibsenite. Garland
had met her in Boston in the 1880's.]*

MARY SHAW and I had a long talk on dramatic matters. She is a very
remarkable woman. She was all kinds of a woman during our talk.
She imitated Modjeska, Mrs. Fiske and Joe Jefferson. Her powers of
mimicry are marvelous. In the midst of it all, her really fine serious
self came out. She shocked me at times—not because of the words
she spoke but because I was sorry to have her speak them. She
smoked a cigarette, which I detest in a man and all the more in a
woman. The whole scene was very significant. She has gone beyond
maidenly modesty but she is wholesome and good for all that. I
wish she had not been quite so plain-spoken. And her imitations of
some of the player folks were not nice. All the same she was the
same big fine woman I first knew.

### OCTOBER 9, 1898 [MADISON, WISCONSIN]

MADISON seems to me almost squalid in some of its phases but
the fine oaks and maples redeem it. Youth glorified infinitely worse
surroundings in my time. It is impressive to me now to see two
thousand young people meeting in this intimate relation—working
out the sex problem for themselves. To them there is no problem.
Naturally man and woman were made to mate like ducks or eagles
and these youngsters are not yet far enough out in the world to feel
any problem.

FEBRUARY 8, 1909 [NEW YORK]

AT night I went to see Mary Garden in *Salome* and was bored and disgusted. The music at times was splendid and the costumes rich and (I suppose) accurate but the whole thing was of that unnatural and decaying brilliancy which is poisonous. Surely we do not need the vile soul of Wilde so decked and ornamented and suffused with music. I feel as if I had been contaminated.

FEBRUARY 20, 1910 [NEW YORK]

[*Charles Evans Hughes was at this time governor of New York. Riis and Richard Watson Gilder had worked together in various reform movements. Sir Johnston Forbes-Robertson was an English actor. Mitchell is apparently S. Weir Mitchell, the Philadelphia novelist.*]

AT 3:30 the Gilder memorial meeting took place, a beautiful ceremony arranged by Lamb. I sat on the platform beside John Burroughs. Hamilton Mabie introduced the Governor, a good-looking man of rather commonplace mind. Then Jacob Riis spoke very feelingly and to the point. Talcott Williams rather rambled but was emotionally sincere. Dr. Butler spoke moderately well and Forbes-Robertson and Robert U. Johnson read from Gilder's verses.

Altogether it was a remarkable outpouring of men and women of distinction, a nobly planned tribute to the many-sided poet.

It was appalling to think how soon Burroughs, Howells, Alden, and Mitchell must go. I got a sudden sense of the great change about to fall upon American letters. Distinction and scholarship seem to be passing.

OCTOBER 27, 1913 [PHILADELPHIA]

REACHED the Boks's in time for dinner and Edward and I talked all the evening on the momentous change in motion just now—the woman's movement, which grows each day more pronounced. No doubt in the breakup many women are to take up the vices of men, to claim the same sex freedom, and I cannot deny the justice of their plea. If men have a "right" to have "fun" whenever they please, women have the same right. The only curse is the women must bear the weight of the pain.

### FEBRUARY 7, 1921 [NEW YORK]

[*The Nineteenth Amendment, on woman's suffrage, had been ratified in August 1920.*]

KATHERINE HERNE came to dinner and during the evening we fell to discussing the further extension of Woman's Rights and Katherine was ready to affirm that women would not much longer bear the whole burden of that kind of immorality which had been a pleasure for man and a torture and social ostracism for women. As she talked I realized that my daughters were growing into a world where many of the age-old standards would no longer apply—and perhaps ought not to apply. Religious restraint has weakened, is almost gone, and social custom is much more tolerant than ever before.

### AUGUST 21, 1922 [LONDON]

[*William T. Stead had edited the* London Times *until his death in 1912. Murry's book was probably* The Things We Are, *a novel published in 1922.*]

BY reflecting on what would probably interest a man like Stead of the *Times*, I was able to write some recollections of Roosevelt as a man of letters, but now that I have written two or three thousand words of it, I am in doubt of its value. Nothing seems worthwhile to me just now—nothing but the past. I have no sympathy with this selfish and pleasure-seeking age. The lists of books sicken me. I got two from the library today, Hutchinson's new book, which is most irritating, and Middleton Murry's book, which is well-written but does not interest me. Most of the men who interest me are forty or more. The others seem only seekers after sensation and success. This is, I know, an old man's view, the disgust of a man who has had his cakes and ale, but why pretend to an interest which I do not feel? Why not acknowledge a distaste which is very definite? Hutchinson's book, *This Freedom*, is a very irritating preachment. A poor book in its expression. Repetitious and vexatious with its silly ejaculations. It is well-meaning but hasty and bad in technique.

### APRIL 1, 1928 [NEW YORK]

[*Helen Arthur was a lawyer who also wrote on the drama.*]

AT 4:30 we sat in at a discussion of censorship at Alice Foote Mac-Dougall's coffee house. It did not interest me much. Helen Arthur ran on for an hour in a personal way, and most of the speakers were for abolishing censorship, apparently for the reason that they wished to be free to put "truthful" sex plays on the boards—by which they meant plays which show their breadth of sympathy with prostitutes and pimps. Strange that freedom means only this to some people!

### FEBRUARY 1, 1929 [LOS ANGELES]

LOS ANGELES has, apparently, no distinguished workers in the arts, and Hollywood is filled with purveyors of moronic art. Its writers when eminent are giving their worst to the public, for their public is one which does not think but is content to see men pawing half-naked women. It is appalling to think that such sex excitations have come to be a necessity.

### SEPTEMBER 27, 1930 [NEW YORK]

[*The book was* Roadside Meetings.]

REVIEWS of my book continue to be on the whole favorable but the young newspaper critics are disposed to be patronizing in their comment. Many of them are of Russian or German derivation—directly or indirectly—and have been schooled in the Freudian theory that all drama springs from sex impulses and hence any writer who refrains from dealing with the illicit is "weak." These reviewers are following in the European school and are not national in spirit. One young man—representing this school—regretted that I had not carried my iconoclastic writing into the present. He forgot that thirty-five years is a long while to carry a mood or a literary fashion. None of them seem to realize that their fashion will also change, that literary Bolshevism will be followed by something other. Just now all is for animalism, for sexual license—for nakedness and shamelessness—but that has happened at other times in the past to give way to other times and other manners. However, there is nothing for me to do but travel my own road.

### NOVEMBER 8, 1933 [LOS ANGELES]

At the request of Dr. Greever I went over to his house to meet some of the professors of English. Paul Jordan Smith made the opening talk mentioning things he did not like and deploring tendencies which he regarded as un-American. This set me off! After some of the other men had talked about "humanism" and "collectivism" and other vague subjects, I brought out the significance of Smith's allusion to the sex-obsession of all these novelists and essayists who claim to be "advanced." I argued that they were mainly interested in the fame and money which came from shocking their readers and that what was being advocated was promiscuity, not "free love" but "free lust." I called attention to the fact that there was no originality in novels of incest, seduction, bigamy. These themes are centuries old and have been made the stock in trade of France for two hundred years. As usual I went too far and said too much and as a result came home feeling *empty!*

There is no use kicking against the stone wall. The millions are interested in lewd women and vicious men. They prefer the language of the bawdy house, so what is the use of my attacking play producers and book publishers who are merely meeting an overwhelming demand for smutty stories. In private they argue that the use of any sexual material is legitimate. It does not seem so to me but of what value is an old man's protest?

### JULY 21, 1934 [LOS ANGELES]

WE have a lovely home but almost no recreation. Zulime feels this more than I do. She is hungry for some sort of diversion but I hate the moving pictures with such bitterness that to go to them with her is to destroy all her pleasure in them. They all seem bent on showing the sexual organs of women. Somehow in every picture there is a disrobing scene or a dance which displays not merely legs and thighs but the female crotch. Seemingly no other object can be depended upon to interest our public. I come away from such exhibitions disgusted and sad. Only at long intervals do I see a play that has genuine interest.

### AUGUST 12, 1936 [LOS ANGELES]

As I look back over the fifty years of my literary life, I see myself and my fellows in a light which reveals all my own crudities as well as theirs. America has continued to be provincial in style as well as in literary material. I began early to urge that we should be local in our subjects but cosmopolitan in our technique, but only a few attained this. Howells had it. James was born with it. Fuller acquired it with early travel, but, for the most part, our novelists and playwrights were "American" in the cheaper sense. They were newspaper reporters becoming fictionists. They appealed to a newspaper-reading public. With the rise of New York as a publishing center, this moronic public came into its dominion. The magazines became advertising bulletins. Some of them like *McClure's* became monthly news journals. As editors sought wider circulation, they pandered to the less discriminating public. This led to yellow journalism, to the radio, and to moving pictures.

### AUGUST 17, 1936 [LOS ANGELES]

I HAVE almost stopped reading the papers. They are so given over to nude women, divorce suits, savage war news and political buncombe. Hollywood irritates me more and more with its stories of promiscuous sexual commerce and its glorification of female libertines. They are not prostitutes in the legal sense. They give their bodies to those they call their "lovers," and women . . . find their fame increased by the number of their lustful partnerships. And yet where can one go to escape these newspaper exploitations of oversexed men and women? Every paper in every city is filled with the same stinking mess. The same obscene movies, the same debasing songs are corrupting youth in every village as well as town. Hollywood is the capital of the "free lovers" and their doings reach every man and woman in America. The radio is cheap but not yet obscene.

### FEBRUARY 14, 1937 [LOS ANGELES]

[*Van Wyck Brooks's* The Life of Emerson *had been published in 1932.*]

IN reading Brooks's *Emerson*, I felt once again and more keenly than ever "the village littleness" of most American towns and cities. Brooks has the cosmopolitan tone in his vital pages. He is not a journalist. He is a critic and a man of thought. He is not pedantic or dryly academic. He stimulates my thought more profoundly than any other literary critic of America. He is an American writer who is neither subservient or bumptious. As I read him today, I felt the scrappiness of our poetry, the cheapness of our fiction and the commercialism of our drama. All our writers are playing down to the democratic masses. Drinking, lechery, and ribaldry are employed to win success. The radio and the motion pictures are given over to the moronic millions. I am disgusted and saddened by these phases and forms of popular art.

### APRIL 16, 1939 [LOS ANGELES]

THE *Times* this morning had a full page given up to women sporting on the beach with nothing but loincloths to cover their so-called private parts. To such a social condition have we come. Shameless women of this sort fill our plays, our newsreels, and crowd our magazines. We seem on the way to a removal of all inhibition between men and women. Nude women are employed at the San Francisco Fair—as they were at Dallas—to draw the public. It is an enlargement of the "peep show" of the city forty years ago which drew the nickels from the country boys as they came in for the day. To me all this is a sign of decay. Rome was less shameless in its decline. We are outdoing Paris in the business of exciting fornication. It may be only a phase, as some argue, but it is not a wholesome phase.

## MODERN INVENTIONS

### AUGUST 1, 1902 [WESTERN WISCONSIN]

[*The automobile trip, in a machine owned by Easton, was from Trempealeau, on the Mississippi, to Winona, a distance of sixteen miles one way. The four hours included the round trip and a stay of a half hour in Winona. Garland's article on the journey appeared in* Harper's Weekly, *September 6, 1902.*]

THIS day we passed as before in keen enjoyment of the glorious scenery as seen from this exquisite little floating bungalow. About four o'clock we started for Winona in the auto, Easton, Miss Losey, Z. and I. We had one of the wildest, most exciting rides I have ever taken. The day was very beautiful and the roads fairly good. We made the trip in about four hours including all stops, which seemed wonderful to me.

This was my first long motor ride and I decided to celebrate it by writing an article descriptive of it. It is predicted that this is the coming mode of travel but at present the farmers resent it for it scares their teams into fits of rearing and plunging.

### AUGUST 14, 1911 [CHICAGO]

*[The Cliff-Dwellers Club faced on the lake front, from which the barnstorming group of airplanes was taking off.]*

I WENT down to the club where I found everything in confusion but working toward order. Luncheons begin again on Tuesday—tomorrow. At 3:30 as I stood "on the ledge" at the club I heard a puffing clattering below and then for the first time I saw a heavier than air flying machine rise from the ground so illogically, so unexpectedly that I did not realize it for a moment. Half an hour later seven were in the air together and before the end of the day two had mounted to the clouds and nine more were playing about. *The air is conquered!* I realize it now as never before. And yet, before an hour had passed it all seemed a part of my daily life, as little surprising as kiteflying. I wrote at once for father to come down. I want him to see the miracle.

### OCTOBER 4, 1914 [CHICAGO]

ANGUS came at noon and we got the Darrows and went away down to La Porte for a "pleasure trip." It is not much pleasure for me to be whizzed through a landscape at twenty-five miles an hour. If we could have gone slowly on some cross street and eaten our lunch under some of the beautiful trees we saw, I should have enjoyed it. As it was I got home in a used-up state, eyes aching, weary with 140 miles of dangerous going, and Angus was in worse case, for he had been driving. Darrow was interesting and we had some good talk, only the rush and roar of our speed made speech difficult.

### SEPTEMBER 28, 1915 [NEW YORK]

IT is announced that wireless telephone conversation passed between Washington, D.C., and Mare Island, California—2500 miles. This is another of the big events of the world's history, and the barbarism of war goes on!

### JANUARY 2, 1926 [NEW YORK]

THERE is something rather terrifying in the fact that by pulling a knob one can open the sluiceway for all the cheap music, droning speeches, commonplace singing and dreary wit of the radio stations of the world. I dread to think what the results will be to men who are engaged, as I am, in work which requires solitude and silence. It is not merely the actual voices, tones, and words of this frightful horn but the sense of being open to invasion. The fact that it is always there!

### FEBRUARY 8, 1927 [NEW YORK]

[*Garland's son-in-law, Hardesty Johnson, was appearing as a tenor in this early attempt at a sound film.*]

ZULIME and I felt well enough to go down to Warner's theater and hear the vitaphone reproduction of Hardy and his orchestra. It was all quite as marvelous as we had anticipated but it did not give us pleasure. Some of it was almost lifelike but the knowledge that it was not substantial kept us from being really moved. This may be only a necessary first stage of the process. We came later to take them as real bodies rather than as shadows. We are stuffed full of marvels in these later days. Beginning in a quiet age without telephones, automobiles, mechanical pianos, radio and all the rest of it, I am even now at sixty-six overwhelmed with all these devices. If I live ten years more I shall be completely alien to my neighbors who will find all these things necessities.

OCTOBER 13, 1928 [NEW YORK]

[*The* Graf Zeppelin *was making its first trip across the Atlantic.*]

THE approach of the Zeppelin airship was announced from time to
time by wireless all day. Wonders are now commonplace with this
age. Nothing really thrills us. We say, "Well, well! I never expected
to see this in our time," and straightway forget it or cry out against
any further allusion to it. We get bored by radio, airships from Europe, or television within a week and clamor against the news of
them. Everything gets to be an "old story" with us even while it is
only a few days old. But there is [no] use arguing for or against this
tendency. It is inevitable. What its effect is to be, what it will do to
our life and literature, is too vast a problem for any man's attempt at
solution. All we can do is drift with the immeasurable current of
what most thinkers call "progress." It is no doubt an old man's
weariness but I am tired of the incessant clamor concerning inven-
tions to spread intelligence when there is so little that is worth dis-
tribution.

JANUARY 30, 1932 [LOS ANGELES]

TODAY, at noon, I tuned the radio in on the Metropolitan Opera
House broadcast of *Die Valkyrie* and for an hour and a half Mary
Isabel and I sat entranced by the glorious voices which uttered Wag-
ner's elemental music. These voices had a dignity and fervor almost
unequalled by any I had ever heard on the stage. The orchestral
harmonies came to us with finer effect than we could have obtained
while sitting in the orchestra of the opera house. We could hear the
faint echoes of the vast building and the rap of the conductor's
baton and every lightest note of the violins. All this we heard seated
in easy chairs in our own reception room three thousand miles
away.

Adjectives are of no value when such a marvel comes into one's
life. The music moved me more strongly than at any other hearing.
With no rustling, coughing, whispering to distract me and with no

bobbing heads between me and the actors, I was free to lave in the billows of harmony which came rolling with elemental power from the amplifier. We could not have heard it with the same fullness of power in the hall, for here the instruments were subordinated to the voices.

### APRIL 27, 1939 [LOS ANGELES]

ONE of the growing institutions of the city are the circular "drive-in" restaurants, and tonight we took our dinner at one of these, sitting in our car with trays hung in the windows. They are springing up all over the western part of the city. As we sat at our fried chicken, I remarked, "This is about a million miles from Osage, Iowa." Below us the city gleamed with lights and endless streams of cars swished by. I have lived into another world already.


## JEWS AND FOREIGNERS

### FEBRUARY 8, 1910 [PITTSBURGH]

ARRIVING in Pittsburgh I went at once to the Henry Hotel and set to work freshening up my MS.

I read "Joys of the Trail" at night to several hundred Jews of the temple. They were not very responsive and yet I think they liked the talk. I met and threshed out the Jew question with Charles Joseph, the editor of *The Jewish Criterion*, who admitted all the slights and irritations which the Jew feels, and said rather hopelessly, "I don't see the way out."

He is young, able, and sees both sides of the problem. He is American but not as I am an American. Much depends upon men like this young Jew. His leadership is vital. Can they assimilate? *Or* will they assimilate us?

### JUNE 24, 1917 [NEW YORK]

WE all enjoyed an outing in Van Cortlandt Park. Our picnic supper was pleasant but we didn't entirely like the crowd that we encountered. They are so vulgar and so slovenly. They litter the walks with papers, and they "spoon" in shameless fashion under the trees. I don't like these squat little greasy types. I oughtn't to feel so about them, but they nauseate me. They are such silly little animals, the women all with high white shoes with tall wobbly heels, the men with short tight trousers and pointed toes. All their fool vanities come out in these walks in the parks. Howells would be patient with them; so would Roosevelt, I suppose, but they get on my epigonistic nerve. I don't like them. They are like insects or worms.

AUGUST 12, 1917 [NEW YORK]

*[Garland was on his way from Onteora to New York.]*

I LEFT at 3 p.m. for the city in the midst of the most amazing collection of New York City Hebrews. Pink, brown, hook-nosed, straight-nosed, young, old—all chattering or bawling. They mobbed the train. They shoved, elbowed, pulled and pushed for seats, clamoring, shouting, all in perfect good humor. They were not poor, nor illiterate, but they were without a particle of reserve or politeness. Their nasal voices silenced all other outcry. The few "Americans" on the train were lost in this flood of alien faces, forms and voices. The women [were] mostly all short, many with handsome features but no grace of body. From a humanitarian point of view I should have been glad of their number for they were returning from a happy outing but as I was lame, their jostling greediness made me angry and their lack of the ordinary civilities of life disgusted me. I was glad when I got to the flat and to bed.

NOVEMBER 17, 1921 [NEW YORK]

LILY MORRIS sent her car and on tickets given by Mrs. Haggin we all rode to the Metropolitan Opera House to see *Lucia* and to hear

Galli-Curci. It was a delightful experience for the girls, especially as they sat next to Ann Seton and in a front row. They all looked very lovely and girlish. Zulime looked to be about thirty and was radiant with maternal pride. In walking about the foyer with Constance we noted that nearly half of all the people we saw were Jews. The boxes were filled with Jews. The city of New York is to become a Jewish city unless they are headed off from coming here. It is a depressing thought to me. An aristocracy of newly rich Jews will have the effect of a calamity to many people and in this feeling I am beginning to share. A minority could be endured but what will we do when they are a majority in every department of life?

### JANUARY 15, 1923 [NEW YORK]

THE *Times* this morning contained an interview with President Lowell of Harvard which will arouse a storm of comment. He told of the efforts being made to keep the Jews from overrunning eastern colleges and was outspoken in his belief that to have a large percent of Jews would be a detriment to Harvard or any other university.

The Jew who reported this talk did not minimize Lowell's antagonism—quite the contrary—and no doubt he intended to bring on a discussion of the exclusion of Jews.

Here again is an indication of the rising tide of Americanism. The Jew is in most cases alien to our traditions in fact as well as in appearance. Unless we rigidly exclude Jewish immigration the hatred of them will increase. It is quite within the bounds of possibility that violent measures will be taken to keep them in what the other races regard as their place. Rightly or wrongly this antagonism will grow. After all this nation is Anglo-Saxon. Not even two million German, Polish and Russian Jews can alter that fact. But with millions in Poland, Russia, and Germany eager to come to us, New York is in danger of being swamped with them. Already we are "Jew York" to the Midwest.

*[Garland had met the Ehrich family in Colorado in the 1890's.
Louis Ehrich had been a prosperous art dealer.]*

IN dining today with the Walter Ehrichs we came into the atmosphere of the Jewish problem, for though no direct word was spoken,
we could read in the tones of Walter's voice a hint of the position he
occupies. He is almost as fine as his father was and yet he finds the
lines drawn against him. Even in my own case, though I have
known him for thirty years, I was conscious of being on my guard
against saying something derogatory to the Jews. He cannot separate himself from his race and yet he would like to associate wholly
with the Americans. He was brought up as an American boy. His
father ranged clear of the Jewish church. He has no real connections with the Jews but they claim him, presume upon his blood
relation.

SEPTEMBER 26, 1924 [ONTEORA]

A YOUNG man by the name of Savage came to ask me why I am
about to vote for Coolidge. I told him some of my reasons, which
may not seem very cogent, but he professed to find them of value
and went away to write them up in order to submit them to me later.
My general feeling is one of weariness and disgust with the whole
situation. We are so near to being dominated by our latest comers,
the half-educated peasants fresh from the dirt floors of European
cabins. Our politicians are afraid of this vote which, while still a
minority, is (when deftly manipulated) a governing body. The Russian and Polish Jews of New York City can at any time tip the balance either way—so the German-American "bloc" finds itself in a
place of power. It is this fear of foreign domination which lies at the
bottom of the Ku Klux movement. A resurgence of the Anglo-
Saxon sentiment of the nation. However badly the movement is
directed, I feel in it something more than fanaticism.

MARCH 29, 1926 [NEW YORK]

[*It was the Passover season.*]

AFTER waiting till half past eleven for the judge, we served for an hour on a foolish case and then, as more than half the jury were Jews, the judge adjourned court till Thursday morning. I came away heartsick over the whole situation. Nearly one half of the citizens here are Jews or Mediterranean people. I am sick of their brutal faces, their speech, their manners. The only way to get away from them is to abandon the great city which holds also the best as well as the worst of our citizens. I cannot bring myself to do that yet. I may come to it in time. The Jews are gaining possession of courts, the law business, publishing, theater, moving pictures and by the weight of their numbers and wealth they will soon control the expression of opinion here. And as the whole nation gets a large part of its information from here, that information is un-American at its very source.

MAY 14, 1927 [NEW YORK]

[*Henry Ford had founded the* Dearborn Independent *in order to express his conservative views.*]

IN an attempt to do an article for the *Independent* I got out an old MS. on psychic matters and rewrote it and mailed it. I take comfort in the thought of those young editors in the small town of Henry Ford's making, for they are so far away that the foreign influence of New York does not reach them. They are fighting a rear guard action for the New Englanders. The Jews are in control here. Each year will make New York more of a "Jew York." They dominate our theaters, our moving pictures, our newspapers—they will soon dominate our book publishing. They color all our music, all our criticism, all our humorous paragraphs which are so potent in educating—or corrupting—our people. Against all this the *Independent* stands opposed. On its positive side it says these things but on its negative side it is helpful in that it ignores the books and criticism which are counted so highly here. Feeling myself a survivor of a vanishing race, I am grateful for the stand the *Independent* is taking.

IN lunching today with two very admirable citizens of Jewish origin, I strove all through the meal to analyze the slightly unpleasant effect they both had upon me. First of all I detected in their attitude an unspoken acknowledgment that there *is* a difference between them and me, an American for six generations. Then they boasted a little too much of their money and their culture, which was perhaps another form of humility. They were not proud at heart. Successful as the man was, he felt that something was lacking to make him entirely acceptable.

He spoke of his Belgian father and mother as if to let me know that he was neither a German, Polish or Russian Jew—just as another of my acquaintances makes much of the fact that he is a Swiss. They know, of course, that all these tailors they despise are "Kykes," and do not wish to be included among them. This I can understand. I would make the same distinction if I were in their position. They were kindly, intelligent and cultured—and yet.

## AMERICAN DEMOCRACY

### MAY 30, 1923 [LONDON]

[*Garland had "cried down" English influence on American taste and literature in his* Crumbling Idols *(1894).*]

MY growing love for England is a natural result from the alien invasion of America, the war, the Bolsheviks of Russia, and increasing years. I am of this race. There are more points of contact than with any other people. There are things I don't like in England but there are more things which stir me to my ancestral deeps. Then, too, I no longer feel obliged to cry England down in order to exalt America. America is not in need of that kind of backhanded compliment.

### MAY 25, 1930 [NEW YORK]

As I read the *Times* this morning, I had a most vivid realization of the morning when I should have no smallest part in the world it chronicles, of the hour when I would be silent while the ever-widening, multiplying mass of human desires and activities will sweep on without my knowledge or care. It is an appalling thought. How can this ever-increasing complex web of human life here in America flow on peacefully? Already our millions, or our wealth, have raised up against us an angry party in England and France. We may be rushing to calamity. Who knows? And I am nearing seventy. Whatever happens will not concern me—only my children. I have not the faith I once had in the future of the Republic. The far future is now a stormy shadow!

### MARCH 22, 1932 [LOS ANGELES]

LATE at night as I was watering my lawn, a young boy looking like a college boy came by and asked for the privilege of cutting the grass. He said he was without a cent and that he must pay his room rent for the night. This is an example of the dire straits into which labor has fallen. A few years ago, two in fact, there were more jobs than men. Now a fine lad like this is in danger of actual need.

### MAY 5, 1932 [LOS ANGELES]

THE papers are disquieting reading these days. Nothing but fear, doubt, suspicion, gloom. When I read I am scared. I lose confidence in everything but as I ride out into the sunshine and see the streets flashing with new cars and watch the well-dressed people coming and going in the shops, I cannot believe in the collapse of this great republic. Congress is futile. How can a crowd of small merchants, country lawyers, farmers, mechanics, and professional politicians manage this colossal country? The big men are helpless in this jostling mob.

NOVEMBER 1, 1933 [LOS ANGELES]

EVERY day now increases my distrust of the future. The theoretic meddling of the administration with the laws of supply and demand is disturbing to those who, like myself, have brought together a small capital to provide against old age. The man who has nothing welcomes change. He has nothing to lose, but the man who is past earning power resents having his earnings taken away from him either by tax or by deflating the currency.

MAY 9, 1934 [WASHINGTON]

AT noon we drove down to the Capitol and sat in for a few minutes at the deliberations of the Senate. It was not an impressive proceeding. One man was droning away. Young La Follette was in the chair and the place was nearly empty. Senator Ashurst of Arizona saw me and came up to greet me and ended by inviting us all to luncheon. He was very complimentary, had read my books and thought them worthy of long life, etc. We lunched in the noisy Senate café, which was about as undignified as a dairy lunch counter. We liked Ashurst and enjoyed our hour with him. We then passed to the Folger Library, a very beautiful building, the expression of a cultivated and aspiring individual man. Congress seems more and more a useless appendage. I can understand the old world dictators' contempt of such bodies. The theory of a democratic assembly is fine. In practice, it is a failure. It is a debating society, not a high-minded deliberative body. It made me doubtful today, as it has always done.

FEBRUARY 28, 1938 [LOS ANGELES]

As I read the papers these days, I am filled with foreboding which is akin to despair. The reckless spending of money by our Congress, dictated by the President, the war threat in the old world and the lowering of standards in human conduct appall me. Part of this feeling may be due to age but more of it arises from a sense of the growing weight and complexity of national responsibilities. It does not seem humanly possible for orderly and just human government to go on for another generation.

That I shall soon be out of it does not comfort me, for my children and my grandchildren must continue to live under these increasingly complex and hazardous conditions. They may be regimented by a dictator and his aides. They may be rationed by heads of bureaus. They may cease to be free agents.

# AMERICAN PLACES

GARLAND was one of the great literary travelers of his day. He ranged over the entire country from the 1890's to the late 1920's, both as a lecturer and as a gatherer of literary material. He brought to his descriptions of the American scene the novelist's eye for significant detail and the traveler's weariness with local pride and pretension.

★ ★ ★

## ABERDEEN, SOUTH DAKOTA

### JULY 4, 1911

*[Garland and his father had homesteaded near Aberdeen and the James River in the early 1880's.]*

IT was hot and wet in Aberdeen, a rain having fallen the night before, but it came too late. The crops were already burnt up. The county had developed much since my last visit, in 1891, but it was not inspiring to me even yet. The flat expanse was depressing. The town was ugly and the little park along the muddy "Jim" pathetic, with its tiny unkempt grove of water elms and box alders filled with flimsy cabins and huts. The performances in the hall were all of the same pathos. There was so little to see or do! I was busy all the morning visiting with old friends of father's. I spoke at 2:30 and left at six, glad to get away. I shall probably never see it again. It makes me wonder at human patience.

## AMARILLO, TEXAS

### APRIL 7, 1923

THIS is hell! All day we ran through a land in which there had been no rain for months, a land of lonely, barren little houses, tin cans, barbed-wire fences, desolate, drab, dusty towns. The sky was gray with dust and rivers of dust ran along the roads. The grass was short as a dog's hair and tawny in color. The men in broadbrim high-crowned hats rode along on horseback or in buggies. What brought these people here? What keeps them here?

Amarillo is a newly built town with a few clean attractive stores and one hotel which is the show place of the county. It is all pitiful, pitiful! At 3 I started down the line toward New Mexico—glad to get away from the heat and dust of Amarillo.

## ASHCROFT, BRITISH COLUMBIA

### APRIL 27, 1898

*[Garland and his boyhood friend Burton Babcock were about to undertake an overland trip to the Klondike.]*

ANOTHER bright clear day. The town is full of big freight wagons, green or blue with canvas covers. All about is a big land of mines and ranches with no railway connections. The freight must all be moved by wagons or horses. We are still waiting for all things to come together for our start. Some of the citizens consider our trip a hard one. Others think it worth a great deal of trouble and expense. At times I have my misgivings because of flies and mosquitoes but we must be prepared for such pests.

During the afternoon a band of cowboys happened into the town. "Whale me out," said one. Each horse bucked. They went out whizzing, well satisfied with themselves. They had liquored. They had caught glimpses of women and they had touched "civilization" again.

### MAY 3, 1898

ANOTHER warm day and another attempt to get away. More wrestling with horses. We are determined not to be "done" by these horse-jockey elements. They are eager to crow over us. The sun

blazes down here hard, hot, vivid, pulsating. The town swarms
with men unkempt, bibulous, profane, libidinous. How far they all
are from civilization! They make horses and their care a test of
character. All else is of no account. All talk horse, drink, cattle.


## BISMARCK, NORTH DAKOTA

### JUNE 28, 1900

*[Garland was on his way to Standing Rock Reservation in order
to gather information for a novel about Sitting Bull.]*

ARRIVING  in Bismarck, North Dakota, at noon I tried hard to get
away to Standing Rock but failed to find a team. At last I managed
to go by stage. The day was gloriously cool and bright, the plain
very beautiful but the earth was dry and the crops short. Bismarck
was sadder and poorer than ever, a busted boom town without one
line of grace or touch of charming color. Drab, flimsy, sun-smit,
wind-warped and dusty, it expressed the worst phase of western
pioneer life. It was worse than when I saw it last. It had gone down
instead of up. I marvel at the courage of its citizens who stay on and
work on under such a sky and exposed to such winds.


## BUTTE, MONTANA

### AUGUST 1, 1900

LEFT on the early train for Butte. Arrived at about noon and
walked  up to the city. The sky was brilliant and clouds beautiful
but the city was the most desolate I have ever seen. In sooth it was
a mining town. It had no grass, not one green thing, nothing but
scarred naked hills, dusty streets, wind-swept great heaps of stock
from the deep mines. The hills terraced with mud. Big mills in the
midst of squalid little homes. The gardens pathetic, a few feeble

trees, a trickly spring. All else smoke, dust, hot glare of sun—desolation. We escaped on the 9 p.m. train for the coast.

## CLEVELAND, OHIO

### OCTOBER 15, 1920

CLEVELAND as horrible as Pittsburgh was depressing. Sharp-angled, dirty, hopeless—a destructive place in which to live. A feeling of horror comes over me now as I contemplate these monstrous towns —so heartless and so hideous. As they are, so they will be after I am gone. My most optimistic mood must admit this.

It may be a sign of age but these raw, unkempt, graceless towns oppress me. They are such hopelessly sprawling abominations. There is so much to be done! Somebody else must do it.

## GREELEY, COLORADO

### JULY 23, 1911

GREELEY, a clean progressive little town on the plains, filled with people from the low country. Clear, dry, sweet air, cool and brisk. The mountains afar, blue streaked with white. The clean, bright rooms filled with cheap and tawdry rugs and furniture. The nice yards. The big old cottonwood trees. The turbid water in the ditches wherein vines lave. The bluffness, heartiness of the West. All essentially commonplace and drab. With a week of lectures before me I shall manage to survive the tedium of my life at a rude hotel in a small town on the flat lands of the arid slope.

## IOWA CITY, IOWA

### APRIL 25, 1927

*[Garland was lecturing at the University of Iowa with the aid of his daughter and son-in-law.]*

AT three I spoke to about one hundred students in a small amphitheater in the science building, talking informally of Howells, Clemens, Riley, Eggleston and Burroughs. At four my young people came and took a little turn about the place. At eight we faced an audience of nearly two thousand people in the auditorium and pleased them mightily with our "show." It was a fine audience with many young people in it. They liked Mary Isabel and Hardesty and applauded them heartily.

The general effect of Iowa City is heartening. It is American, although it is evident that the literary "radicalism" of Mencken and his crowd is largely followed. There are certain of the professors who worship at the Mencken-Wellsian shrine and instill in their pupils a cynical disregard of "the nineties." To all I said they listened respectfully but no doubt held to all their radical notions. They all want to write. They all hear of fortunes being made in authorship and so they are for it.

## KANSAS CITY, MISSOURI

### MARCH 7, 1928

AWAKE at six, I caught the early train for Kansas City and with Zulime visited some of her friends. The town was appalling to me by reason of its dusty, smoky air and its sprawling ugliness. It has grown tremendously but it has not grown less ugly, at least in my estimation. I did not see its finest part, perhaps, but I did perceive the all-pervading noise of its trolley cars, its ragged and dusty streets and its air of rusticity. I did not see a Jew; in fact, I have hardly detected a Jewish profile in Kansas and Colorado. There are many southern types here, and the voices are mostly unpleasant and the expressions southern. I am eager to get away. The thought of living here is horrifying and yet many fine people do and are content in the life. It is narrow and base in me, perhaps, but the rawness and self-assertion of such towns irritates and depresses me. I have no desire to attack these people. I marvel at their courage, but I want to flee.

## ONTEORA, NEW YORK

### MAY 15, 1925

OUR drive down the Hudson was so glorious that again we congratulated ourselves on having our summer home in the Catskills. As I thought of the plains, the monotonous level land of the Midwest, of the pitiful little hills, the barbed-wire lanes running at right angles, the foul rivers and stagnant ponds which make up the landscape of so much of the Midwest, I shuddered at the thought of being condemned to a lifetime of such surroundings.

I have no desire to exult over or make game of such people who make the most of their drab outlook. I realize that their brag, their loud complacence are defensive. They can't all live in lovely valleys. They must scorch in the sun and wither in the winds of their farms or villages. It is incredible, it is heroic that they are able to keep moderately cheerful under their burden while here am I speeding through the most beautiful and most humanized valley in America, rich in friends and secure of my future—moderately secure.

## RALEIGH, NORTH CAROLINA

### MARCH 3, 1920

*[Charles E. Brewer was president of Meredith College in Raleigh.]*

LEAVING Spartanburg I rode all day in a day coach changing at Greensboro, thus seeing much of the Carolinas. Signs of prosperity were everywhere noticeable. Many new buildings gleamed in the midst of the dun landscape. In the high land about Greensboro and on the way to Raleigh some good farmhouses. The Negro shacks were the same but wheat fields and corn fields showed differing industry.

Dr. Brewer met me at the train and took me to the Yarborough Hotel where I was soon at home. I like to be among these people. They are real Americans. No Jews, Germans, or Italians among them. The old tobacco-spitting Southerner is getting scarce. The young fellows smoke but do not chew. The Confederate vets are almost gone. "The War" now means the World War and not the Civil War. This is a gain. These young fellows do not care to discuss "the lost cause." It is a dead issue with them—a kind of melancholy legend.

## THE SOUTH

### FEBRUARY 8, 1928

ALL day through the rugged, bleak, unkempt Southland. Hardly a trace of beauty all day. Garbage, shanties, factories, gashed and rusty fields, unpainted homes and muddy rivers. It is improving but very slowly. To an Englishman or an Italian, even to a German or Frenchman, this landscape would be distressing. It is distressing to me. It will take fifty years for the South to come to a state of tidiness and broad-minded thought.

## TULSA, OKLAHOMA

### MAY 19, 1904

BARTLESVILLE, our first stop, turned out to be a small town surrounded by oil derricks and permeated by the smell of gas. The land was still held by the Indians and was not for sale at all. We left at noon for Tulsa which pleased us very much. It is a larger town than Bartlesville and built on handsome hills near the Arkansas River, a tawny shining flood. The town is rather slipshod at present but its site is noble and some day will be a beautiful place to live. It would be decidedly tolerable now. The weather was delicious. Roses and other shrubs in bloom made the air sweet and the distant hills and green prairies even alluring.

The psychology of the place is confident and happy. For a short stay the boom talk is exhilarating but to live in it all the year round might come to be intolerable. It is the spirit which has built the West for a hundred years, however. Father felt it and grew animated in it.

## WEST SALEM, WISCONSIN

### MARCH 11, 1901

IN the evening we attended a supper party at Mrs. Ball's house, a curious experience, some twenty guests "in our honor." Little tables such as seamstresses use were brought in and set about—on these we ate—and later we played dominoes on the same cloth. It was a mad riot of fun! Nine widows present, all the most singular, angular and timidly assertive of mortals. One or two fairly up-to-date persons. All the others good, wholesome village souls. Z. seemed to enjoy them all hugely. This preponderance of widows is comic or tragic, as you look at it. It means that the husbands are usually older and go first.

## MAY 26, 1903

I AM feeling very much like work these days and the novel grows under my hands. The rains continue distressingly and though I punch the bag and play tennis between showers I feel the confinement of the mud. The old people of the town depress me. In an unexpected phase of western life the small town has become in a certain sense the hospital home into which the farmers and their wives, old and gray, drift to wear out a few short years of decrepitude. Looked at in this way this is a pleasant ending. To think that they are removed from the drudgery of the farm and that they have found it possible to enjoy a few simple comforts is consoling. But as constant reminders of a generation's decay they are sadly depressing. In my life in the city I do not come into such close contact with loveless old age. I am concerned only with well and happy people of my own set. Here we see the old on the walks, in the gardens, on the porches, waiting, waiting!

## SEPTEMBER 22, 1905

WE went for a drive in the afternoon admiring for the hundredth time this lovely valley and speculating on what people of refinement and taste would find to do [with] it. What noble homesteads could be here built. As it is these houses of the Germans are given over to airtight stoves. No one thinks of a fireplace. The rooms are small and "smelly" and in winter cold, only the kitchen being habitable.

## APRIL 24, 1908

RAIN set in early and I spent the day at work in the house rearranging things. I called on Aunt Maria and Aunt Deb, finding them a little soured and markedly avid for tales of sickness and suffering. The surface of the town is bright and fragrant but deep down lies sickness and decay. I left on the night train for the city, glad to return to my wife and children.

## WYOMING

### AUGUST 26, 1907

I SUFFERED today a long and tedious ride made almost intolerable by the barren and obscene talk of two stage drivers whose vocabulary included only five or six words beyond the "cuss words" of their world.

They were so petty, so filthy that I felt like thrusting them from the seat. At noon we took the worst lunch I have met yet at a wretched ranch filled with wretched little women, the rancher a still more shiftless "critter" than Rathburn or Maginnis.

The ride from here to Pinedale grew more interesting but the talk of the drivers made its beauty of no avail. I landed in Pinedale at sunset disgusted with the whole country and its people. The "hotel" was incredibly flimsy and ramshackle, but the air fine.

### AUGUST 5, 1908

I DID not go out of town except for a short ride back into the hills. In talk with the young lawyer Fort and his pretty and intelligent typist I gathered much material of the sort that gives "atmosphere." I was impressed with the attitude of the young girl who in the midst of the savage men of the region walked in a defensive armor of indifference or disdain. As she passed down the street (like the Greek maiden of story), she caused the old men as well as the young men to stare and cackle. There are so few like her here. She seems out of place.

# INDEX

Abbott, Lawrence F., 37
*Abraham Lincoln*, 126
Adams, Suzanne, 28
Addams, Jane, 15
Ade, George, 148
Adler, Felix, 108
Adler, Mrs. Felix, 108
Akely, Carl, 239
Alberti, Mrs. William M., 40
Alden, Henry Mills, 31, 219, 241
Alderman, Edwin A., 226
Aldrich, Thomas Bailey, 218
Alexander the Great, 216
Allen, Mr., 40
Allen, Grant, 21, 22
Allen, Mrs. Grant, 22
Altgelt, John P., 148
American Academy of Arts and Letters,
 2, 39, 54, 59, 63, 117, 147, 159, 160,
 161, 168, 176, 217-234
American Council of Learned Societies, 37
American Social Science Association, 218
Amherst College, 130, 132
Anderson, Margaret, 19
Antoine, André, 24
*Arena*, 10
Armory Show, 18
Arthur, Chester A., 212
Arthur, Helen, 243
Art Institute of Chicago, 14, 15, 79
Ashurst, Henry F., 258
Aubert, M., 123
Aus der Ohe, Adele, 29
Authors' Club (London), 143
Authors' Club (New York), 125
Authors' Society, 143

Babbitt, Irving, 226
Babcock, Burton, 261

Bacheller, Irving, 6, 31, 54, 61, 62, 107,
 109, 123, 154, 174, 233; *The Scudders*, 6
Bacheller, Mrs. Irving, 109
Baker, Ray Stannard, 174
Ball, Mrs., 267
Bancroft, Edgar A., 205
Barbour, Mr., 39
Barnard, George Grey, 109-110
Barnum, P. T., 7
Barr, Mark, 120, 121
Barrie, Sir James M., 94, 110-111, 180, 195
Barrus, Clara, 116, 117
Barry, Richard, 43
Barrymore, John, 111-113
Barrymore, Mrs. John, 111, 112
Bartlett, Frederic C., 227, 228
Baxter, Sylvester, 127
Beach, Rex, 113
Beach, Mrs. Rex, 113
Beaman, Gaylord, 45, 46, 74, 186
Beaman, Mrs. Gaylord, 74
Beaux, Cecilia, 231
Bell, Lilian, 177
Bellamy, Edward, 151
Benét, Stephen Vincent, 132
Bible, 7, 78
Bigelow, John, 219
Bigelow, Poultney, 113-114
Billings, Josh, 184
Bishop, Joseph B., 208
Bixby, Sara, 144
Blashfield, Edwin H., 176
Bodenheim, Maxwell, 34, 35
Bok, Edward, 50, 51, 163, 241
Bok, Mrs. Edward, 241
Booth, Edwin, 32, 108, 112
Borden, Mr., 58
*Boston Evening Transcript*, 10, 11,
 127, 151

271